THE NEW AND LIVING WAY

THE NEW AND LIVING WAY

Invitation to Biblical Worship

Ron Man

Foreword by Bob Kauflin

CASCADE *Books* · Eugene, Oregon

THE NEW AND LIVING WAY
Invitation to Biblical Worship

Copyright © 2025 Ron Man. All rights reserved. Except for brief quotations in critical publications or reviews, no part of this book may be reproduced in any manner without prior written permission from the publisher. Write: Permissions, Wipf and Stock Publishers, 199 W. 8th Ave., Suite 3, Eugene, OR 97401.

Cascade Books
An Imprint of Wipf and Stock Publishers
199 W. 8th Ave., Suite 3
Eugene, OR 97401

www.wipfandstock.com

PAPERBACK ISBN: 979-8-3852-3084-6
HARDCOVER ISBN: 979-8-3852-3085-3
EBOOK ISBN: 979-8-3852-3086-0

Cataloguing-in-Publication data:

Names: Man, Ron, author. | Kauflin, Bob, foreword.

Title: The new and living way : invitation to biblical worship / Ron Man; foreword by Bob Kauflin.

Description: Eugene, OR: Cascade Books, 2025 | Includes bibliographical references and index.

Identifiers: ISBN 979-8-3852-3084-6 (paperback) | ISBN 979-8-3852-3085-3 (hardcover) | ISBN 979-8-3852-3086-0 (ebook)

Subjects: LCSH: Public worship—Christianity. | Worship in the Bible. | Worship—Biblical teaching.

Classification: BV10.3 M36 2025 (paperback) | BV10.3 (ebook)

VERSION NUMBER 11/11/25

Emphases have been added to Scripture quotations.

Unless otherwise noted, Scripture quotations are from the ESV® Bible (The Holy Bible, English Standard Version®), copyright © 2001 by Crossway Bibles, a publishing ministry of Good News Publishers. Used by permission. All rights reserved.

PowerPoint slides by Tom Avery, "Worship Wars and Ethnomusicology," are used by permission of Kristy Avery.

Artwork by Kirsten Malcolm Berry is used by permission. www.kirstenmalcolmberry.com.

Lyrics of "How Great Thou Art," by Stuart K. Hine, © 1949, 1953 The Stuart Hine Trust CIO. All rights in the USA its territories and possessions, except print rights, administered by Capitol CMG Publishing. USA, North and Central American print rights and all Canadian and South American rights administered by Hope Publishing Company. All other North and Central American rights administered by The Stuart Hine Trust CIO. Rest of the world rights administered by Integrity Music Europe. All rights reserved. Used by permission.

There is *one mediator* between God and men, *the man Christ Jesus*.
(1 TIM 2:5)[1]

Therefore, brethren, since we have confidence
to enter the holy places by the blood of Jesus,
by *the new and living way*
that he opened for us through the curtain, that is, through his flesh,
and since we have a great priest over the house of God,
let us draw near
with a true heart in full assurance of faith,
with our hearts sprinkled clean from an evil conscience
and our bodies washed with pure water.

(HEB 10:19–22)

---

1. Artwork by Kirsten Malcom Berry.

CONTENTS

Foreword by Bob Kauflin | ix
Preface | xiii

Part 1: Introduction | 1

1. The Privilege of Drawing Near through the New and Living Way | 3
2. Studying Biblical Worship | 5

Part 2: Foundations | 9

3. Revelation and Response: The Paradigm of True Worship | 11
4. The God We Worship | 28

Part 3: The Centrality of Worship in God's Program | 37

5. Everyone Worships | 39
6. The Centrality of Worship in Creation and the Fall | 41
7. The Centrality of Worship in Redemption and the Gospel | 47
8. The Centrality of Worship in Missions | 52
9. The Centrality of Worship in All of Life | 59
10. The Centrality of Worship in Heaven | 65
11. Worship Is Central | 68

Part 4: Worship in the Old Testament | 71

12. Important Themes in Old Testament Worship | 73
13. Worship in Old Testament History: Pentateuch | 79
14. Worship in Old Testament History: Pre-Exilic Israel (Joshua–2 Chronicles) | 92

15 Worship in Old Testament History: Exilic and Post-Exilic Israel | 100

16 The Psalms: Israel's Worship Book . . . and Ours | 105

Part 5: Worship in the New Testament | 111

17 Similarities and Differences Between Old and New Testament Worship | 113

18 Important Themes in New Testament Worship | 115

19 Significant New Testament Worship Passages: Gospels and Acts | 120

20 Significant New Testament Worship Passages: Epistles | 127

21 Eternal Praise: The Great Scenes of Worship in the Book of Revelation | 140

22 Worship in the Book of Hebrews | 147

23 The Holy Spirit and Worship | 155

24 Jesus Christ and Worship | 161

Part 6: Worship in the Church | 175

25 The Nature and Priority of Worship in the Church | 177

26 The Importance of Worship in the Church | 183

27 The Content of Worship in the Church | 187

28 Worship and Culture | 196

Part 7: Conclusion | 213

29 Biblical Principles of Worship | 215

   Biblical Principles of Worship (short summary) | 239

30 Summary and Benediction | 242

Bibliography | 245
Subject Index | 251
Scripture Index | 259

FOREWORD

I was about three years into my new role as the director of Sovereign Grace Music and doing all I could to find out what I was supposed to be doing. Being thrust into a position of influential leadership, it wasn't long before I realized how unprepared I was for that role. So I gave myself to voracious reading and was delighted when I received a quarterly church leadership journal on the topic of worship. God had heard my prayers!

That particular issue contained numerous articles that explored the theology and practice of congregational worship. I was challenged and inspired by all of them. But two articles stood out. The first was entitled "Jesus Our Worship Leader." The second was "Worship and the Glory of God." Both were written by Ron Man.[1]

In the first article, Ron made a compelling scriptural case for seeing Jesus not only as the object of our worship, but as the one who worships *for* us. "It is not the excellence of our worship, but the excellence of Christ which makes our sacrifices of praise worthy and acceptable offerings!" Jesus is not only *present* in our worship, but actually *leads* our worship. He is at the same time the temple, the high priest, the sacrifice, and the receiver of our worship. Ron later developed those thoughts in his book, *Proclamation and Praise: Hebrew 2:12 and the Christology of Worship* (Wipf and Stock, 2007).

In the second article he explored the implications of John Piper's classic and oft-repeated statement, "Missions exists because worship doesn't." I remember my thoughts about worship being sharpened and deepened as I read statements like, "Our primary responsibility is not service or even obedience. We are to be first and foremost lovers of

---

1. Both articles can be found at https://worship-resources.org/articles-by-rm/.

God—people who glorify him and enjoy him forever, and express that love through a life and lifestyle of worship."

I had the opportunity to meet Ron a few years later and thank him for his labors. Around that time, I learned about his twelve "Biblical Principles of Worship," which shaped much of the way I approached my own teaching. I subscribed to his monthly *Worship Notes* emails. They were brimming with insightful quotes he had mined from a wide variety of sources on different topics related to worship. Ron was passionate about pulling together the best resources from the best minds about the best topic we could explore—the glory of God in Jesus Christ.

Ron has remained a good friend through the years. We've corresponded regularly and hung out at conferences. The man he chose as his replacement at his church in Memphis turned out to be one of my former interns. That transition took place so Ron could devote more time to teaching the course on biblical worship he had been developing. His commitment to that task has both inspired and exhausted me, as it has now taken him to forty-one countries. I haven't met anyone more qualified than Ron to bear the name of "ethnodoxologist"![2]

So when I heard Ron was writing a book that contained the components of his course, I was thrilled. As I wrote in my endorsement for *Let Us Draw Near: Biblical Foundations of Worship* (Cascade, 2023), "Ron's book will serve pastors, music leaders, musicians, and church members as a resource on worship for decades to come." To have such a thorough and expansive compilation of resources on worship is a unique gift to the body of Christ worldwide. It helps us set whatever secondary issues regarding worship we might explore in the context of a clear and comprehensive biblical theology.

But when Ron emailed me to say he was writing a pared-down version of his first book, I was even happier than I was the first time! I knew the length of *Let Us Draw Near* was going to intimidate some of the people who needed it most. Pastors pressed for time. Musicians who want something more emotional or practical. Church members who, apart from the Bible, shy away from long books.

But in *The New and Living Way: Invitation to Biblical Worship*, Ron has taken all that makes *Let Us Draw Near* so helpful and packaged it in a more concise and accessible format, including questions to spur

2. Ethnodoxology is "the interdisciplinary study of how Christians in every culture engage with God and the world through their own artistic expressions." See www.worldofworship.org.

reflection and stories of teaching this material in other countries. This is a book that will benefit anyone who reads it. Pastors and musicians, of course. But songwriters, ministry leaders, and media teams as well. Homemakers, accountants, cashiers, students, nurses, truck drivers, office workers, journalists—any Christians who want to better understand why they were created and redeemed.

That's because in this book Ron shows us clearly, precisely, and biblically what God wants our worship to be. Even better, he shows us how God himself has provided all he desires for our worship through the perfect life, substitutionary death, and victorious resurrection of Jesus Christ in the power of his Spirit. Ron's disregard for the breathless pursuit of creativity and innovation enables him to pursue simply being faithful to Scripture. And the result turns out to be original, insightful, thrilling, and most of all, Christ-exalting.

And I have no doubt you'll feel the same as you read this book.

Bob Kauflin
Director, Sovereign Grace Music

PREFACE

Worship is very much at the forefront of congregational thought in our day: that's the good news. The bad news is that worship has become a primary source of conflict, strife, even division among our churches (the so-called worship wars). It is a travesty that the worship of Almighty God should have become a source of division and conflict in the church of Jesus Christ! As a result of this situation, I became convinced that pastors, worship leaders, and churchgoers need more grounding in a biblical understanding of worship (see chapter 2) to inform their thinking and discussions about worship.

This volume is a condensation of my 600-page encyclopedic study entitled *Let Us Draw Near: Biblical Foundations of Worship* (Cascade, 2023). The basic structure is the same, but the book has been shortened to make it accessible and manageable for more readers.

There are a number of fine studies dealing with the biblical material on worship (referenced elsewhere in this book), to which this author and many others are indebted. Some of the distinctives of my previous book and of this version include:

1. The consistent emphasis throughout the work on the pervasive Revelation and Response paradigm of Scripture and its foundational significance for worship.

2. A more extensive treatment of the New Testament material than in some other works of the sort.

3. The development in depth of the crucial theme of Jesus Christ as the true leader of our worship (the topic of a previous book of mine, *Proclamation and Praise: Hebrews 2:12 and the Christology of Worship* [Wipf and Stock, 2007]).

4. The concluding synthesis of twelve "Biblical Principles of Worship" distilled from the inductive study, and the emphasis on their application to personal and corporate worship.

5. The perspective brought from being a church worship leader for more than forty years, as well as a student and teacher of worship on the academic level.

In addition, a couple of new additions to this volume are:

1. A number of footnotes designated *"From the Field."* These are human-interest anecdotes drawn from my experiences in teaching this material overseas in forty-one countries over the past thirty years.

2. Questions at the end of each chapter entitled *"For Reflection and/or Discussion."* These, along with the summary chapter "Biblical Principles of Worship" (chapter 29), will help to make this book suitable for individual or group study.

It should be added that the book does not deal a lot with specific practices, because its focus is on identifying unifying principles that transcend cultures and ecclesiastical traditions. I pray that this work, building on the work of others, through its systematic, thorough, and distinctive treatment of biblical worship, will be a help, blessing, and inspiration to many students of worship, leaders of worship, pastors, and Christian worshipers of all kinds.[1]

---

1. For further study, the reader is directed to the website of *Worship Resources International*, worship-resources.org. There you will find a wide variety of articles by this author and others, as well as links to other worship ministries, websites, and resources. Also posted there are all of the issues (dating from 2006) of *Worship Notes*, a free monthly worship newsletter. *Worship Quotables* (worr.wordpress.com) is a source for daily insights from many different authors.

As with *Let Us Draw Near*, this book is released with love and appreciation for the support and encouragement I have received from the people of First Evangelical Church in Memphis over these past thirty-seven years.

From the Field: At the end of a two-week course at Jordan Evangelical Theological Seminary, a student asked, "Why do you quote John Piper so much?" Indeed I do, and do so in this book as well: that is because I have learned more about worship from him than from anyone else. So I want to express appreciation for his God-saturated and -glorifying influence in my life (as in so many others').

Part 1

Introduction

1. The Privilege of Drawing Near
2. Studying Biblical Worship

1

THE PRIVILEGE OF DRAWING NEAR THROUGH THE NEW AND LIVING WAY

The curtain of the temple was torn in two, from top to bottom.
(MATT 27:51; ALSO MARK 15:38, LUKE 23:45)

Therefore, brethren, since we have confidence
to enter the holy places by the blood of Jesus,
by *the new and living way* that he opened for us
through the curtain, that is, through his flesh,
and since we have a great priest over the house of God,
let us draw near
with a true heart in full assurance of faith,
with our hearts sprinkled clean from an evil conscience
and our bodies washed with pure water.
(HEB 10:19–22)

"Let us draw near" is the climactic pronouncement ("Therefore...") of the book of Hebrews, and in a sense of the new covenant itself. This invitation, challenge, and command goes to the very heart of what God has accomplished for us through the work of Christ: extending to us sinners the inestimable privilege of entering into the very presence of God in worship through, in, and with our Lord Jesus Christ, who has opened *the new and living way* through his atoning death and even *takes us with him* to the Father's throne of grace (Heb 4:16). This free and open access means that we can come with "confidence" and "full assurance of faith." This mind-boggling reality sets us on our course in this book, as we delve into God's word to see more of his heart and to relish his mercy and grace in allowing the likes of us to "draw near" through "*the new and living way*" opened for us by our Lord Jesus.

For Reflection and/or Discussion

How could a deeper understanding of the privilege of drawing near to God through Christ impact your life?

2

STUDYING BIBLICAL WORSHIP

Our task in this book is to explore and mine the depths of Scripture in order to learn what the Bible teaches about worship.

Why Is a Biblical Understanding of Worship[1] Important?

There are at least six reasons:

> 1. A biblical understanding of worship is important because God's word tells us *who God is*.

God, after all, is the *subject* of our worship; worship is *about him*. We must worship him *as he really is*; and we learn who he really is primarily through the pages of Scripture.

> 2. A biblical understanding of worship is important because God's word tells us *what God wants*.

God is not just the *subject* of worship; he's also the *object* of worship: it's *for him*. It is for his pleasure, and he has every right to tell us how he wants us to worship him. And we learn that from God's word.

---

1. A "biblical understanding of worship" is the essence of what in academic circles is sometimes called a "theology of worship."

> 3. A biblical understanding of worship is important
> because God's word is *our guide*.

> "Your word is a lamp to my feet
> and a light to my path."
> (Ps 119:105)

God's word is to be our guide in *every* area of life; and so, certainly, in this crucial area of worship we need biblical guidance.

> 4. A biblical understanding of worship is important because
> God's word tells us that *all of life is to be worship*.

> I appeal to you therefore, brethren, by the mercies of God,
> to present your bodies as a living sacrifice,
> holy and acceptable to God, which is your spiritual worship.
> (Rom 12:1)

This key New Testament verse on worship, which we will return to again and again, teaches us that worship involves a total commitment of one's life in every area to the worship of God, and is an appropriate response to God for all that he's done for us in Jesus Christ. Because God's word tells us that all life is to be worship, a biblical understanding of worship will have implications *for our entire lives*.

> 5. A biblical understanding of worship is important because
> God's word is *our only unchanging standard*.

> "Forever, O Lord,
> your word is settled in heaven."
> (Ps 119:89)

People change, cultures change, traditions and preferences change; only God's word does *not* change. We need a standard for our worship that does not shift and change with adjustments in culture or times, but rather remains true and steadfast and unchanging—and we find that in God's word.

6. A biblical understanding of worship is important because it's only God's word that can give us *a unified understanding of worship.*

Around the world there are multitudes of denominations, and a huge variety of practices and styles of worship. The God who created a world of such beautiful diversity delights in manifold creativity.

But underneath it all, it is important that we have a basic, unchanging, unified understanding of the foundations of worship. That will be the focus of this book: What are the essentials of worship? What does *not* change from place to place?

What This Book Is Not

This book does not undertake a detailed history of worship or of liturgical practice. There are many fine volumes on those subjects, many of which will be referenced in the text.

Neither does this book attempt a prescription for detailed forms or styles of worship. It seeks to be decidedly nonsectarian as it mines the text of Scripture for underlying and overarching principles of worship.[2]

What This Book Is

1. An exploration of the biblical and theological foundations of worship.

2. An examination of the centrality of worship to all of life and ministry (not just Sunday morning).

3. An attempt to highlight unifying truths and foundational understandings of worship: those things that should remain true in every culture and church setting.

4. An affirmation of the considerable freedom that the New Testament apparently gives a local church to apply the foundational truths to

---

2. *From the Field:* When I teach on worship overseas, my regular disclaimer is that "I have not come to tell you exactly how to do worship in your culture, for I am not from your culture. What I *can* share with you are biblical principles of worship that, precisely because they are *biblical*, by definition transcend culture." My students' responsibility has been, then, to take those principles and apply them in their own contexts. Similarly, this book does not deal a lot with specific practices of worship—because of its deliberate nonsectarian intent.

its practice of worship, and a call to give grace to other churches that may apply the truths differently.

5. An encouragement to the reader to think about and evaluate styles of worship in the light of foundational biblical truths.

> Worship is about God and for God.

For Reflection and/or Discussion

How might the biblical study of worship enrich your own walk of worship?

Part 2

Foundations

3. Revelation and Response: The Paradigm of True Worship
4. The God We Worship

3

REVELATION AND RESPONSE
The Paradigm of True Worship

The most foundational of all principles underlying true worship is the principle of *Revelation and Response*. It is the pattern of all true worship; in fact, as we will see, it is the pattern of all of God's interactions with humanity.

We can worship God because he has *first* revealed himself to us. *Worship is always a response*, a response to God first showing us himself. We can represent the pattern visually in this way:

Revelation is of course from God to us, followed by our response to him.

A Crucial Order

Now the *order* of these arrows is *absolutely* crucial, because God always speaks *first*, or we could never know him. Hebrews 1:1–2 says:

> Long ago, at many times and in many ways, God spoke to our fathers by the prophets, but in these last days he has spoken to us by his Son.

We can know God because he has *spoken*. Because worship is always a response, until God has shown us himself we have nothing to say to him.

The order of the arrows is so important because other religions get it exactly *backwards*.

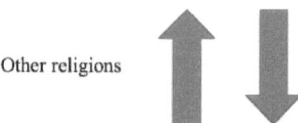

Other religions

In the absence of a direct revelation from God, people have always tried to figure out: *What do we need to do? What do I need to offer to God? What do I need to give to him so that he'll be good to me?*

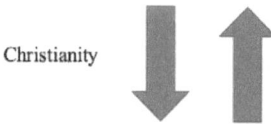

Christianity

Christianity, on the other hand, speaks of *God's initiative*. It is not what we do to reach God. It is not a guess. It is not us trying to figure out something. It is not a leap in the dark. But rather it is a *response* to God, because he has taken the initiative to *reveal* himself to us. As Robbie Castleman has written: "The basic pattern of biblical worship . . . is that it is God who initiates the encounter, not the worshiper."[1]

Or, in the words of the apostle John, "We love because he *first* loved us" (1 John 4:19).

A Biblical Pattern

We see the pattern of revelation and response throughout Scripture (and hence we will see it throughout this book), for it is in fact basic to all the ways God relates to us as human beings.

---

1. Castleman, *Story-Shaped Worship*, 37.

Time and time again in the biblical story, we see God taking the initiative to call men and women into relationship with, and service to, himself. In Genesis 3, for example, after disobeying God and eating from the tree, Adam and Eve hide themselves from God (vv. 8b, 10); but God *goes looking for them* (v. 9). Abraham is a pagan whom God calls to establish a new people for his name (Gen 12:1–3). In Exodus 3, Moses is not in the desert drawing up plans for rescuing his people from Egypt—he is just tending sheep; but God calls him and sends him to be the divine instrument in the Lord's hand. Similarly, David has no royal pretensions whatsoever as he tends his father's sheep; but God steps in and makes it clear that he has chosen David to be king over Israel (1 Sam 16:12–13). And the apostle Paul obviously has a complete and unexpected reversal of course (physically, spiritually, and vocationally) after Jesus appears to him and commissions him on the road to Damascus (Acts 9).

How many other examples can you think of from the pages of Scripture where God takes the initiative to break into people's lives? (This is also this author's story, and probably yours as well.)

The Biblical Pattern of Redemption

The primacy of God's initiative is likewise foundational to his work of redemption in both testaments.

The Biblical Pattern of Redemption Under the Old Covenant

God *reveals* himself to Abraham and makes (and reiterates throughout Abraham's life) a series of promises (Gen 12:1–3; 15:5, 7, 18–21; 17:1–8; 22:15–18). Abraham *responds*, by first of all going where God shows him. And then, significantly, we read that Abraham "*believed* the Lord, and he counted it to him as righteousness" Gen 15:6); Abraham was justified by responding in faith to God's revealed promises (as Romans 4:1–5 makes clear).

It is crucial to recognize that the Mosaic law and its sacrificial system were *not* a way of salvation for the people of Israel. The law was to be a way of life for a people whom God had *already* redeemed by his own sovereign and powerful initiative in the exodus.

In Exodus 20, where God through Moses gives the nation the Ten Commandments, he first declares:

"I am the Lord your God, who brought you out of the land of Egypt, out of the house of slavery." (Exod 20:2)

Then, and only then, does he proceed with "You shall have no other gods before me" and the other nine Commandments. In other words, God is in essence saying to the people: "I *have* redeemed you; now this is how I want you to live in *response*."

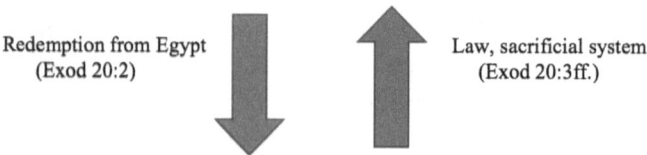

Redemption from Egypt (Exod 20:2) Law, sacrificial system (Exod 20:3ff.)

The Biblical Pattern of Redemption Under the New Covenant

God's initiative in his redeeming work through Christ is clearly articulated by Paul in Ephesians 2:8–9:

> For by grace you have been saved through faith. And this is not your own doing; it is the gift of God, not a result of works, so that no one may boast.

This is immediately followed in verse 10 by:

> For we are his workmanship, created in Christ Jesus for good works, which God prepared beforehand, that we should walk in them.

Salvation by grace through faith (Eph 2:8–9) Response of works (Eph 2:10; 1 Cor 6:20)

Once again we see what God *has done* (indicative), followed by what God *commands* in response (imperative). Similarly we read in 1 Corinthians 6:20: "you *have been* bought with a price; therefore *glorify* God in your body."

Or, as the old hymn puts it, "Jesus paid it all, all to him I owe."

The Biblical Pattern of Worship

As mentioned above, worship is always a *response* to God's prior activity in revealing himself and showing himself gracious to us. We find this pattern of worship through the Scriptures, as a few examples will demonstrate.

The Fall

It has often been observed that Romans 1 is Paul's *theological commentary on Genesis 3*. Genesis 3 tells us what *happened*, and Romans 1 tells us what it *meant*. In this light, we can see that in the fall Adam and Eve refused to respond faithfully to the revelation they had been given by God:

For his invisible attributes, his eternal power and divine nature, have been *clearly seen*, being *understood* through what has been made. (Rom 1:20)

For even though they knew God, they *did not honor him as God or give thanks*. (Rom 1:21)

They . . . worshiped and served the creature rather than the Creator. (Rom 1:25)

REVELATION   RESPONSE

Adam and Eve's fall into sin was *not* a result of ignorance or insufficient information: "they *knew God*." Rather it was a refusal to give God the honor, thanks, and worship that he alone was due. (More on this in chapter 6.) So at the very beginning of the biblical story there is a breakdown of the proper response to God's gracious revelation of himself.

Altars in Genesis

One vivid example has been observed by Robbie Castleman. She points out that at the time of the Old Testament patriarchs, all the surrounding peoples were building altars and offering sacrifices on them. What they were hoping to do with these altars and these sacrifices was to invoke their gods, to appease them, to placate them, in hopes that the gods would be merciful to them, would make their crops bountiful, would give them victory in battle, etc. In the absence of direct revelation, they were left to guess at what they should do to gain favor with their gods. That is the pattern of other religions, as we have already seen: getting the order backwards.

Castleman points out that in the book of Genesis, we find *exactly the opposite* situation: in every case that Noah, Abraham, Isaac, and Jacob build altars, it is only *after* God has appeared and spoken to them, and is always in *response* to his self-initiated communication with them.[2]

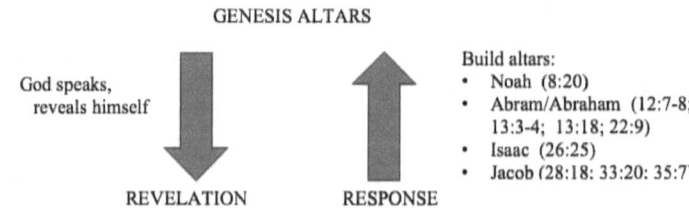

Abraham's worship

As we have seen, God took the initiative to reveal himself to Abraham, calling him and making promises to him (Gen 12:1–3). God spoke to Abraham, showing him various aspects of his nature through names such as *El Shaddai* (God Almighty) and *Jehovah Jireh* (the Lord who sees/provides), and revealed himself through theophanies. And in response, we see Abraham's walk of worship: believing God (and that being counted towards him as righteousness [Gen 15:6]), building altars, calling on the name of the Lord. God revealed his "name" (his nature), and Abraham

---

2. Castleman, *Story-Shaped Worship*, 37.

responded in worship by calling on that name, that nature, those attributes, which God had revealed to him.

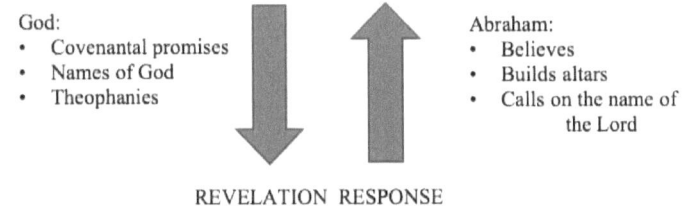

God:
- Covenantal promises
- Names of God
- Theophanies

Abraham:
- Believes
- Builds altars
- Calls on the name of the Lord

REVELATION RESPONSE

Psalms

A few examples from the Psalms:

48:10 As is your Name, O God, ⬇ ⬆ *so is your praise to the ends of the earth.*
(Praise to God is lifted up in response to his self-revelation.)

96:4 Great is the LORD ⬇ ⬆ and [therefore] greatly to be praised.
(Great praise is the commensurate response to God's greatness on display.)

⬆ 150:2 Praise him . . . *according to* his excellent greatness. ⬇
(We praise him precisely for all the ways in which he has shown himself to be excellently great.)

Romans 12:1

This is one of the most important New Testament worship passages. After 11 chapters of expounding on God's wondrous works in the world in Christ, Paul turns in Romans 12 to *application*:

> I appeal to you therefore, by the mercies of God, to present your bodies as a living sacrifice, holy and acceptable to God, which is your spiritual worship.

An appropriate *response* to all those mercies that God has revealed, and that Paul himself has just dealt with in chapters 1–11, is to present one's body (i.e., that is one's entire self) to God as a living sacrifice and as an offering of worship.

Worship is the appropriate response to God's gracious initiative in showing his mercy to us in Jesus Christ.

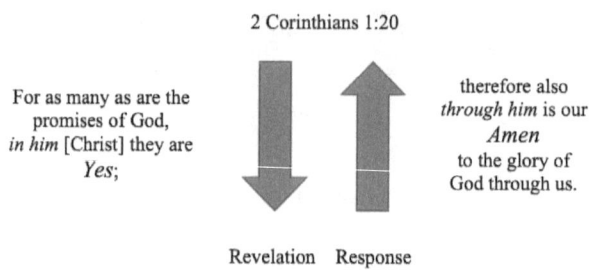

Summary

So we see through these biblical examples (and indeed we will see many more in this book) that revelation and response is *the biblical pattern of worship*. It always begins with God's initiative, showing us himself and showing himself gracious to us.

We do *not* offer up our services, our sets, and our songs in hopes that by saying or singing or doing the right thing, God will be obligated to "show up" and bless us. Rather, we gather under God's grace in grateful recognition of all the blessings he has conferred upon us in Christ. We lift our praises, not out of fear that we're going to miss something or lose out or not gain status with God. Instead, we rest in and bask in the status we enjoy with him as his beloved children, because we are in Christ by his mercy.

Practical Implications for Our Worship

The Word in Worship

Because God's revelation is primary, we must recognize "the indispensable place of Scripture in both public and private devotion. It is the Word of God [revelation] which calls forth the worship of God [response]."[3] Edmund Clowney adds:

> In every task of the church, the Word of God is central. It is the Word that calls us to worship, addresses us in worship, teaches

---

3. Stott, *Romans*, 311.

us how to worship and enables us to praise God and to encourage one another.[4]

The problem

But the word of God is not central in many of our services.

We who are Protestants love to proudly claim that we are "people of the Book," yet too often (in this author's own experience) the worship service is predominantly sets of songs with little or no Scripture read—at least until the preacher gets up for the sermon. A liturgical service (Catholic, Orthodox, or Anglican) will include perhaps ten times as much Scripture as the average free church Protestant service—because in these traditions the Bible passages are built right into the liturgy. Free churches have to be more intentional to make sure the Scriptures have a prominent place.

What's at stake

There may be devastating unintended consequences to neglecting the reading of Scripture in our services. We may be unwittingly suggesting that the Bible is not really all that important to living the Christian life—we just need to love Jesus, and praise Jesus, and all will be fine. (We of course don't believe that, but we need to be careful not to imply it.)

The biblical mandate

Paul instructed Timothy (and thereby all pastors), "Devote yourself *to the public reading of Scripture*" (1 Tim 4:13) and "Let *the word of Christ dwell richly* in you" (Col 3:16).

The Bible is the word *of God*, and when it is read it is the God of the universe wanting to speak to his precious people. What a privilege to hear him speak to us!

---

4. Clowney, *Church*, 199.

More of the word

And so, more of the Scripture is called for, in both our private and our public worship. In our services, that may mean:

- Printing (if your church uses a bulletin) or projecting a verse or verses (and if it is a thematic service, verses relating to the day's theme) for people to see and meditate on as they enter the service.
- Evaluating the songs we sing on the basis of Scripture.
- Choosing songs to go with Scripture, not Scripture to go with songs!
- Using the Scriptures in different and creative ways: reading, singing, reciting, praying, memorizing, dramatizing.
- Reading longer passages of Scripture, not just isolated verses.
- Using unison, responsive, antiphonal readings.
- Having someone read from the midst of congregation.
- Assembling original responsive readings.

This last point is exceedingly easy with the resources available to us today. Computer Bible concordances make it very simple to search for verses on a particular theme, and then they can be arranged into a responsive reading that powerfully demonstrates what God has to say about that theme in many different places in his word.

In other words, "devote yourself to the public reading of Scripture"—but do not always do it exactly the same way! Bring some creativity to bear on the presenting of the word of God before his people.

The Call to Worship

In fact, from our study of revelation and response it should be clear that we need to let God have the first word. We have nothing to say to him until he speaks! Far from being a remnant of "traditional" or "liturgical" worship (as some contemporary worship advocates claim), a Call to Worship is a powerful statement at the front of the service that it is God who is inviting us into his presence, and not we inviting him (he never left!).

So let us not start our services by saying, "Let's just praise the Lord!" Rather let us reflect the biblical dynamic by first hearing from God and about God.

The Dialogue of Worship

Worship involves a cycle of revelation and response. Worship is in fact *a dialogue between God and his people*. And, in any healthy dialogue, one side does not do all the talking. We need to listen to God, and not just talk (and sing) to him. Both parts are vital.

Balance is important. This is true in our private worship, where through Bible reading (revelation) and then adoration and prayer (response) we have the privilege of dialoguing with (both hearing from *and* speaking to) God. And it is likewise vital in corporate worship that we hear God speak through his word and respond back to him. We can represent the dialogue of worship with a series (rather than a single set) of alternating arrows:

Some elements of the service are more revelation in nature:

Call to worship
Scripture readings
Preaching
Scripture songs
Songs about God's character and acts

And some are more response in nature:

Songs of praise, lament, etc.
Prayer
Confession
Meditation
Lord's Supper
Commitment

Those who plan services need to give careful thought to the need for balance in this dialogue of worship.[5]

---

5. "A Christmas Festival of Lessons and Carols," which originated in the Anglican Church but is now celebrated annually in many kinds of churches, of course also displays this balanced rhythm of revelation (the "Lessons") and response (the "Carols").

Completing the Cycle

We need to be careful to *complete the cycle* of revelation and response, or as John Stott calls it, of *theology and doxology*.[6]

No theology without doxology

Stott writes:

> There should be *no theology without doxology*. There is something fundamentally flawed about a purely academic interest in God. No, the true knowledge of God will always lead us to worship, as it did Paul. Our place is on our faces before Him in adoration.[7]

We see in the book of Romans a beautiful example of how indeed "the true knowledge of God" led Paul to worship. In chapters 1–11, Paul has been laying out some of the most profound theology ever written, through the inspiration of the Holy Spirit. And then suddenly he can contain himself no longer: at the end of chapter 11, he bursts forth in praise! His *theology* leads him to *doxology*, and he exclaims:

> Oh, the depth of the riches and wisdom and knowledge of God!
> How unsearchable are his judgments and how inscrutable his ways!
>   "For who has known the mind of the Lord,
>   or who has been his counselor?
>   Or who has given a gift to him
>   that he might be repaid?"
> For from him and through him and to him are all things.
> To him be glory forever! Amen (11:33–36).

Theology (Rom 1–11)   Doxology (11:33–36)

---

6. From the Greek: *theology* is literally a "word about God," and *doxology* is "a word of praise."

7. Stott, *Romans*, 312.

We see Paul was not just a great theologian; he was a great worshiper as well![8]

"The purpose of theology is doxology; we study in order to praise."[9] That is true on all levels, not just for adults, but for children, youth, all the way up. We are not just teaching Bible stories or Bible facts or how to find references in the Bible. We teach our young people to know the Bible, *so that* they will learn to love and worship the God of the Bible.

Bible knowledge is meaningless unless we turn what we have learned back to God in praise for the things we have seen of him. We must give our response to his revelation, our doxology flowing from theology.

No doxology without theology

John Stott goes on to say:

> There can be *no doxology without theology*. It is not possible to worship an unknown god. All true worship is a response to the self-revelation of God in Christ and Scripture, and arises from our reflection on who he is and what he has done. . . . It is the Word of God which calls forth the worship of God.[10]

This goes back to the necessity of significant Scripture use in our services, as well as to the importance of worship leaders and planners receiving Bible training so they can handle the Scriptures competently in their ministries. God's people need to "praise him *according to* his excellent greatness" (Ps 150:2).

---

8. *From the Field:* One of my students from a Zoom course I taught in 2024, the pastor of a black Pentecostal church in Boston, wrote this in response to reading my article "Paul as Theologian and Worshiper" (on Rom 11:33–36):

> I confess that I was so moved by this reading assignment that it became the catalyst for a series of sermons. I have studied the doxologies of the Apostle but never connected his theological presentations with his outbursts of praise. . . . We now have a greater understanding of his humility poured out in worshipful appreciation for his Lord for whom he serves. For me, this principle has highlighted the necessity of the Word in worship and immediately facilitated change in the Sunday liturgy of the church I have been called to lead.

9. Packer, "Greatness of God," 599.

10. Stott, *Romans*, 311.

The cycle completed

Bob Kauflin writes:

> In the best worship songs, the two elements are combined: subjective lyrics express the heart's response to lyrics that state objective truth about God with clarity, precision, poeticism, and power.[11]

A vivid example of this can be found in the familiar hymn, "How Great Thou Art." In the first verse of this great hymn, the lyricist reflects on the wonders of God seen in creation:

> O Lord, my God, when I in awesome wonder
> Consider all the worlds Thy hands have made:
> I see the stars, I hear the rolling thunder,
> Thy power throughout the universe displayed:

Then the refrain praises God in response:

> Then sings my soul, my Savior God, to Thee:
> "How great Thou art, how great Thou art!"
> Then sings my soul, my Savior God, to Thee:
> "How great Thou art, how great Thou art!"

Similarly, verse 3 considers the grace of God demonstrated in the cross of Christ:

> And when I think that God, His Son not sparing,
> Sent Him to die, I scarce can take it in;
> That on the cross, my burden gladly bearing
> He bled and died to take away my sin:

And the refrain again responds with praise:

---

11. Kauflin, "Praise Choruses."

> ↑ Then sings my soul, my Savior God, to Thee:
> "How great Thou art, how great Thou art!"
> Then sings my soul, my Savior God, to Thee:
> "How great Thou art, how great Thou art!"

We can help to complete the cycle by:

1. Balancing elements of revelation and response.
   One seminary professor has his students mark a service bulletin or schedule with up and down arrows according to the nature of each part (and horizontal arrows as well, for body life/fellowship type functions in the service).

2. Using Scripture as a lead-in to singing.
   A practical example: how much more powerful, if we are going to sing a song about the holiness of God, to first read from Isaiah 6:3: "Holy, holy, holy is the LORD of hosts; the whole earth is full of his glory!" And then we sing the song in response to what God has said in his word about his holiness: our doxology is based on theology.

3. Allowing time for a significant response after preaching.

4. Regarding the entire service as worship.
   This means rejecting the duality of worship/sermon: seeing the entire service as *a ministry of the word*.[12]

Luther's understanding of these principles

The dynamic of the dialogue of worship, and the need to complete the cycle, were clearly understood by Martin Luther. On the door into the sanctuary of the Castle Church in Wittenberg, Germany (on the opposite side of the church from the famous door where he posted his Ninety-Five

---

12. This author once attended a conference at a sister church, where a well-known Bible teacher had been brought in as the featured speaker. Just before he got up, a choir made up of people from different area churches sang an anthem. When the speaker then got up, he first turned to the choir and said, "Thank you for *ministering the word* to us this evening." Here was a man who understood that the ministry of the word was broader than just his speaking slot—that in fact *the entire service* was a ministry of the word!

Theses in 1517, which touched off the Protestant Reformation), there is inscribed a quotation from Luther:

Castle Church | the restored "Wittenberg Door"

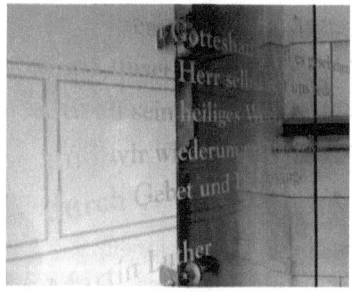

the Luther quote

Translated from the German, the quote says:

"It should always happen
in this house of God
that *the Lord speaks to us*
through his holy Word,

and that *we then speak to him*
with our prayers
and songs of praise."

The Foundation of Foundations for Worship

The most basic of all foundations for our worship is, then, *the word of God*. For the word is the record of God's special revelation, and it is that revelation that calls forth the response of worship.

True worship will always be *biblical* worship.[13]

Additional Resources (details in bibliography)

Brink and Witvliet, eds., *The Worship Sourcebook*.

Cherry, *The Worship Architect*.

Crider, *Scripture-Guided Worship: A Call to Pastors and Worship Leaders*.

Furr and Price, *The Dialogue of Worship: Creating Space for Revelation and Response*.

Man, "Worship and the Word" (audio and outline).

Witvliet, "Isaiah in Christian Liturgy."

> Revelation and Response is the pattern of all God's interactions with humanity, and of all true worship

For Reflection and/or Discussion

What are some new, creative ways you could use the Scriptures in your church's worship services?

13. *From the Field:* A professor at Singapore Bible College testified to the importance of learning and teaching the biblical foundations of worship:

> I personally have heard your messages in Windsong's *Musaic* conference in the Philippines [2008] and have learned much as you gave us the biblical theology of worship, so much so that it has prompted me to study more, which in turn ends up blessing those who I teach in seminary and in seminars elsewhere.

She added:

> We see an influx of Christians from Chinese-speaking congregations.... We want to just go one step further in ensuring they don't just know the how-to's and resources..., we feel these should know the theology and biblical foundations behind what they do.

4

THE GOD WE WORSHIP

Because worship is *about* God, and worship is *for* God (see chapter 2 above), when we study worship it makes sense that we should begin by considering the person of God—this God whom we worship. We will do that in this chapter, building on what we have already seen about the biblical pattern of worship: revelation and response/theology and doxology.

Bob Sjogren observes that when high schoolers receive their copy of their school yearbook, the first thing every one of them invariably does is to turn to one's own picture. It is a very natural and normal thing, Sjogren states, for a student to want to see how his or her photo turned out in this very public arena.

However, Sjogren laments, too many Christians take the same approach to the Bible; he calls this our "yearbook theology": we turn to the Bible and *look first for ourselves*.[1] But the Bible is not primarily about us; it is about *God*. It is God's book, God's story. We do not even turn up until the very end of Genesis 1 (vv. 26–28), as the climax of an enormous flurry of creative activity by God.

The Bible is not about me. It is important to look first for God because it is *his* book and *his* story. In fact, the Bible is *the story of God's glory.*[2]

---

1. Sjogren, *One Degree Off Theology*, 43.
2. See the insightful article by Steve Hawthorne, "Story of His Glory."

The Story of God's Glory

What do we mean when we talk about the glory of God? Some would say his holiness, some his majesty, some his absolute sovereignty. God's glory encompasses all of this, and more. It is not a single attribute of God, such as his love or his wisdom or his power. It is not *an* attribute of God, but rather it is *the sum of all his attribu*tes, all his perfections, all those things that make him God, all his "God-ness." In that sense, it is the greatest subject of all!

When we come to the Bible, we find that there are *hundreds* of references throughout its pages to the glory of God. The Bible is indeed *the story of his glory*. Let's consider that great theme.

God's Glory in Creation

God created all things for his glory.

David exclaims that "the heavens declare the glory of God" (Ps 19:1). That is why the heavens are there; that is why God put them there: to show something of his glory. But not only did God create the heavens for his glory, he created *us* for his glory as well:

> Bring my sons from afar
> and my daughters from the end of the earth,
> everyone who is called by my name,
> *whom I created for my glory,*
> whom I formed and made.
> (Isa 43:6–7).

Sometimes untaught Christians can think something like: "Maybe God made us because he was lonely, or he didn't feel complete, or he needed somebody to love." And, of course, all those things are terribly wrong. God is God. He is complete in and of himself. He does not lack anything. He does not need anything (see Acts 17:24–25). In fact, the doctrine of the Trinity tells us that before the creation of the universe, God himself existed *in community*, in an eternal fellowship of love among Father, Son, and Holy Spirit (see John 17:24).

God did not *need* to create us, but he *did* create us to show forth his glory in us, as those created in his image.

God's Glory and the Fall

The glory of God was at issue in the fall as well. Here again is that passage in Romans 1 where Paul explains the fall of Adam and Eve into sin:

> For although they knew God, they *did not glorify him as God* or give thanks to him. . . . Claiming to be wise, they became fools, and exchanged *the glory of the immortal God* for images resembling mortal man and birds and animals and creeping things. . . .
> They exchanged the truth about God for a lie
> and *worshiped and served the crea*ture rather than the Creator,
> who is blessed forever! Amen. (Rom 1:21–23, 25)

The fall was a tragically wrong decision about the glory of God. Adam and Eve were created for God's glory, but in the fall they did not give him the glory he deserved. Instead they turned to honor images and creatures (including themselves), and led the entire human race down that path.

Romans 3:23 reflects the same perspective:

> All have sinned and fall short of the glory of God.

Because of sin, we fail to show forth the glory of God as we were created to do.

God's Glory in Israel

As God's special covenant people, the nation of Israel was to reflect God's glory as well:

> "You are my servant Israel in whom *I will be glorified.*" (Isa 49:5)

God's Glory Seen in Jesus Christ

Of course, the ultimate display of God's glory is found in the person of Jesus Christ:

> And the Word became flesh and dwelt among us,
> and we have seen *his glory*, glory as of the only Son
> from the Father, full of grace and truth. (John 1:14)

> God . . . has spoken to us by his Son. . . .

He is the radiance of the *glory* of God
and the exact imprint of his nature. (Heb 1:1–3)

God's Glory Seen in Redemption

This great passage about the blessings of our redemption from Ephesians 1 mentions the glory of God *three* times:

> Blessed be the God and Father of our Lord Jesus Christ. . . .
> In love he predestined us for adoption to himself as sons through Jesus Christ, according to the purpose of his will
> *to the praise of his glorious grace.* . . .
> with which he has blessed us in the Beloved. . . .
> In him we have obtained an inheritance . . . so that we who were the first to hope in Christ might be
> *to the praise of his glory.*
> In him you also . . . were sealed with the promised Holy Spirit, who is the guarantee of our inheritance until we acquire possession of it,
> *to the praise of his glory.* (Eph 1:3–14)

"To the praise of his glorious grace," "to the praise of his glory," "to the praise of his glory." God not only *created* us for his glory, but he *redeemed* us for his glory as well.

And Christ's redeeming work enables us to do what Adam and Eve failed to do: "*glorify* God as God and give thanks" (Rom 1:21).

God's Glory and the Christian Life

God *created* us for his glory; he *redeemed* us for his glory; and he wants us to *live* for his *glory*.

> Whether you eat or drink, or whatever you do, do all to the *glory* of God. (1 Cor 10:31)

In Jesus' description of himself as the true vine in John 15, and of our need to be connected to him as branches if we are to bear fruit, he further remarks:

> "By this my Father is *glorified*, that you bear much fruit and so prove to be my disciples." (John 15:8)

Jesus is saying that when we bear fruit, the Father is *glorified* because we are showing that we are his disciples and bear fruit in our lives by being connected, and *only* by being connected, to the vine, who is Jesus Christ. So our fruit gives God *glory*, because it shows that fruit as Jesus' disciples comes only through and with the empowerment that he gives through Christ.

God's Glory in the Church

> ... to him be glory *in the church* and in Christ Jesus throughout all generations, forever and ever. Amen. (Eph 3:21)

God's Glory in the New Heavens and the New Earth

> And the city has no need of sun or moon to shine on it, for the *glory* of God gives it light, and its lamp is the Lamb. (Rev 21:23)

In the new Jerusalem the glory of God illumines and fills all. Heaven is the place where the glory of God is finally acknowledged and celebrated above all.

The Story of His Glory

We thus get a glimpse of how the Bible, from the beginning to end, is *the story of God's glory*. Paul summarizes this truth for us magnificently in the grand doxology we have looked at already:

> For *from* him
> and *through* him
> and *to* him are all things.
> To him be *glory* forever. Amen.
> (Rom 11:36)

What a powerful statement! All things have their origin in him. All things remain in existence through him. He is the goal and purpose of all things: everything is created and intended to display and vindicate his infinite *glory*.

And so, as we come to the Bible, it's important to remember that it's not about us. Primarily it is about *God and his glory*:

Not to us, O Lord, not to us, but to your name give glory. (Ps 115:1a)

The Glory of God and Worship

Defining Worship

Since worship is about God and for God, and since we have begun our study by looking at the person of God and considering his all-encompassing glory, it stands to reason that we can now define worship in terms of what we have just been considering:

> *Worship is our response to the glory of God—*
> *all that we are responding to all that God is.*

The glory of God, as we have seen, speaks of all that God is in his infinite perfections. And worship is all the ways in which we *respond* to that glory. Or, to unpack it a bit further, worship is:

- recognizing the glory of God with our *minds*,
- cherishing the glory of God with our *hearts*,
- proclaiming the glory of God with our *mouths*,
- and celebrating the glory of God in *all of life*.

Glorifying God, giving God glory, is what worship is all about. Note the parallel of "worship" and "glorify" in Psalm 89:6:

> All the nations you have made shall come
> and *worship* before you, O Lord,
> and shall *glorify* your name.

Responding to God's Glory

Worship is our appropriate *response* to all the ways in which God has demonstrated his glory throughout the scriptural *revelation*.

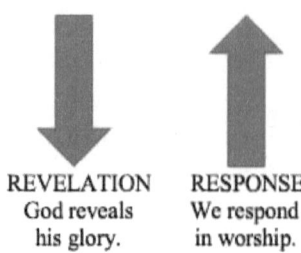

REVELATION
God reveals
his glory.

RESPONSE
We respond
in worship.

God reveals his glory, and our response is then to give God glory in worship. Because, as we have seen, worship is about God: it is about his glory. Peter writes:

> You are a chosen race, a royal priesthood, a holy nation,
> a people for God's own possession,
> that you may proclaim the excellencies of him
> who has called you out of darkness into his marvelous light.
> (1 Pet 2:9)

Worship is proclaiming the excellencies of the God who has revealed those excellencies to us.

Joining in with God's Own Purpose

Eric Alexander, a great Scottish preacher, made this statement that well summarizes what we have been talking about in this section:

> There was only one end for which God created and formed the world and made us, and that is for his own exclusive *glory* and honor. [He created us for his glory.] There is only one end for which our Lord redeemed his people, and that was to bring him a revenue of *glory*. [He redeemed us for his glory.] And when you and I find the thirst that God implants within our souls, it is only going to be satisfied when our souls are set on the same longing that God himself has for his *glory* and honor. [He wants us to live for his glory.][3]

In other words, when we seek to glorify God, we are following him in his *own* purpose of bringing glory to himself.

---

3. Alexander, "Thirsting for God" (emphasis added).

Christians sometimes struggle with the truth that God seeks his own glory above all else. After all, they may think, "Aren't we taught that it is self-centered to seek one's own glory above everything else? How then can God want that?" *How would you answer that question?*

God is different from us. He is in a category by himself. And (unlike us, when we seek to exalt ourselves) there is simply nothing greater than God for him to seek to glorify! C. S. Lewis explains that, in loving us, God wants the very best for us, and wants us to desire that for ourselves too. And the very best thing for us is *God and his glory*. Therefore, our own pleasure and satisfaction in God is central, because what is most fulfilling to us is what brings him the most glory.[4] As John Piper likes to say, "God is most glorified in us when we are most satisfied in him." That is why he created us, that is why he redeemed us—to know and enjoy and reflect and celebrate his glory.

Worshiping the God of Glory

So worship is *our response to the glory of God*, because "from him and through him and to him are all things. To him be glory forever. Amen."

That is the God we worship. We worship the God of glory forever.

> **Worship is our response to the glory of God—all that we are responding to all that he is.**

For Reflection and/or Discussion

How can you display the glory of God
in and through your daily life?

---

4. Lewis, *Problem of Pain*, 34–47.

Part 3

The Centrality of Worship in God's Program

In this part we are going to look at the big picture of worship as a central, even unifying, theme of the Bible.

> The theme of worship is far more central and significant in Scripture than many Christians imagine.[5] It is intimately linked with all the major emphases of biblical theology such as creation, sin, covenant, redemption, the people of God and the future hope. Far from being a peripheral subject, it has to do with the fundamental question of how we can be in a right relationship with God and please Him in all we do. One way or another, most of the books from Genesis to Revelation are concerned with this issue.[6]

5. Everyone Worships

6. The Centrality of Worship in Creation and the Fall

7. The Centrality of Worship in Redemption and the Gospel

8. The Centrality of Worship in Missions

9. The Centrality of Worship in All of Life

10. The Centrality of Worship in Heaven

11. Worship Is Central

---

5. *From the Field:* A few times I have heard reports that, upon hearing that I was coming to teach a two-week course on worship, a student would wonder, "How in the world is he going to talk about worship *for two weeks*?" But invariably by the end of the course that student would come to see what a huge theme in Scripture worship actually is!

6. Peterson, *Engaging with God*, 17–18.

5

EVERYONE WORSHIPS

It has often been noted that the problem in our world is not that some people do not worship. *Everybody* worships; all people worship something or someone. The problem in our world is that there are many competing worships, and so many people worship the wrong thing.

Competing Worships

In the story and film *The Wizard of Oz*, we meet Dorothy, a girl from Kansas who gets swept up by a tornado and finds herself marooned in a far-off country. She wants desperately to get home, and is told a great wizard living in the Emerald City might be able to help her. The story traces Dorothy's adventures along with her friends (a lion, a scarecrow, and a tin woodsman) as they try to get to the Emerald City so that the great wizard can solve all their problems.

But when they finally get to the city and gain entrance to the wizard, they learn that he is a fake, a fraud. He is a normal man hiding behind a curtain and using a microphone, smoke, fire, and levers to make himself seem formidable.

The writer Max Lucado compares this story to humanity's fruitless pursuit of fulfillment and happiness in all the wrong places. "You don't need what Dorothy found. . . . You don't need to carry the burden of a lesser god, a god on a shelf, a god in a box, or a god in a bottle. No, you need a god who can place 100 billion stars in our galaxy, and 100 billion galaxies in the universe."[1]

The James Webb telescope, which went online in 2022, has shown more vividly than ever before the vastness and complexity of the universe. Eric Alexander tellingly writes about "the greatest throwaway line [i.e., understatement] in all of literature: 'He also made the stars (Gen 1:16)'"![2]

The God We Need

That is the God we need: the Creator. That is a God who can meet the deepest longings of our heart because he made us and put those longings within us. That is a God who deserves our worship and our adoration.

John Piper said: "The great hindrance to worship is not that we are pleasure-seeking people, but that we are willing to settle for such pitiful pleasures."[3] The essence of sin, Piper maintains, is trying to put anything in the place of God to find meaning in our lives. "The human heart," John Calvin insisted, "is an idol factory."[4]

God wants us to seek ultimate pleasure, which can be found in him alone. In Psalm 16:11 David declares to God, "In *your* presence there is fullness of joy; at *your* right hand are pleasures forevermore."

All the competing worships, all the false claims, all the things we want to put in place of God because we think they can give us satisfaction—these are like broken, leaky cisterns (Jer 2:13) that cannot handle our expectations. Only God can.

> Everyone worships something;
> it is crucial that we worship the right thing.

For Reflection and/or Discussion

What competing worships (broken cisterns) do you see in the culture around you? In your Christian community? In your own life?

1. Lucado, *Traveling Light*, 16.
2. Alexander, *Our Great God and Saviour*, 36.
3. Piper, *Dangerous Duty of Delight*, 49.
4. Calvin, *Institutes*, I, 11, 8.

6

THE CENTRALITY OF WORSHIP IN CREATION AND THE FALL

Now let us turn to the Scriptures to see the true way of worship.

Creation

The most basic truth we can learn about God is that he is the Creator. In fact, it is, of course, the *very first* truth we learn about God in the Bible:

> In the beginning, God created the heavens and the earth (Gen 1:1).

And everything else in the biblical narrative follows from that.

Because God is the Creator, it means that everything that is not God was made by God. There are only two categories of existence: (1) there is *God*, and (2) there is *everything else*.

A Fundamental Distinction

That means that there is a fundamental, infinite distinction between God and everything else. God is utterly unique; there is no one like him.

The Old Testament writers understood this, and they constantly proclaimed that their God, the Creator, was totally unlike the false gods of the surrounding nations:

> There is no one like the LORD our God. (Exod 8:10)
>
> O God, who is like you? (Ps 71:19)
>
> O LORD, there is none like you, nor is there any God besides you. (1 Chr 17:20)

God himself makes these claims as well:

> "I am God, and there is no other; I am God, and there is no one like me." (Isa 46:9)
>
> "I am the LORD, that is my name; I will not give my glory to another." (Isa 42:8)

God is saying, "my name is mine alone, my glory is mine alone, my worship is mine alone."

This fundamental distinction between God and everything else is why idols are such terrible things—because it is taking something that God has made and giving it the worship that only God deserves. God is in his own category as the Creator.

And this distinction is *the foundation of true worship*: as Creator, he is the only one deserving of worship. As the psalmist similarly extends the invitation:

> O come, let us worship and bow down.
> Let us kneel before the LORD *our Maker*. (Ps 95:6)

Worship God!

At the other end of the Bible from Genesis 1:1, we read in Revelation 22:

> I, John, am the one who heard and saw these things. And when I heard and saw them, I fell down to worship at the feet of the angel who showed them to me, but he said to me, "You must not do that! I am a fellow servant with you and your brothers the prophets, and with those who keep the words of this book. *Worship God.*" (Rev 22:8–9)

John is so amazed at the magnificent angel who is showing him the visions that he wants to worship that angel. But the angel rejects that, and with just two words, in the very last chapter of the Bible, summarizes what one might say is the call, the invitation of the *entire* Bible: "Worship *God*."

As we have seen, everybody worships something; what is all-important is that we worship the right "thing": God the Creator.

The Fall

The fall was a challenge to that fundamental distinction between God and everything else: his unique glory that makes him the only one worthy of worship.

Satan's Prideful Fall

Many commentators hold that in Isaiah 14 the author is talking about Lucifer, a created angel who fell into sin and became who we know now as Satan. And here we see that at the root of Lucifer's rebellion against God was the attitude displayed in his words:

> I will ascend above the heights of the clouds;
> *I will make myself like the Most High.* (Isa 14:14b)

Instead of acknowledging God's unique glory, he says that he wants to be like him: "I will make myself *like the Most High.*" That is of course a revolt against the created order. *No one* can be God. Lucifer is seeking (futilely, of course) to violate that fundamental distinction between God and everything else. As a created being, his rightful place is to bow before his Creator; and that is what he refuses to do.

Humanity's Prideful Fall

We find something very interesting when we then look at the account of the fall of man in Genesis 3. When Satan in the form of the serpent tempts Eve, we see that the temptation that Satan dangles before Eve is *the same temptation to which he himself fell*:

> "For God knows that when you eat of it your eyes will be opened, and *you will be like God*, knowing good and evil." *(Gen 3:5)*

Satan wanted to make himself "like the Most High," and the same temptation (to "be like God") is what caused Adam and Eve to fall into sin as well. In their pride, they take and eat (v. 6), with the most profound implications for the entire human race.

Going again to Romans 1, we see Paul's commentary on what has transpired:

> Although they knew God, they did not honor [or glorify] him *as God* or give thanks to him. (1:21a)

Adam and Eve did not act out of ignorance. They *knew God*; they walked with him in the garden; they "clearly perceived," in the things he had created, "his invisible attributes, namely, his eternal power and divine nature." And so they were "without excuse" (1:20). They wanted to be like God; and so they didn't give God the honor and the glory that he and he alone deserves.

The paradigm of revelation and response broke down in the fall. God had revealed himself to Adam and Eve, but they did not respond appropriately.

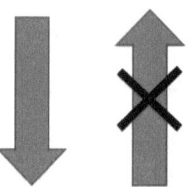

For his invisible attributes, his eternal power and divine nature, have been *clearly seen*, being *understood* through what has been made. (Rom 1:20)

For even though they knew God, they *did not honor him as God or give thanks*. (Rom 1:21)

They ... worshiped and served the creature rather than the Creator. (Rom 1:25)

REVELATION   RESPONSE

Turning to False Worship

Adam and Eve denied the foundation and presupposition of true worship, which is the uniqueness of God and his glory. And the inevitable result of denying the foundation of *true* worship is *false* worship:

> They became futile in their thinking, and their foolish hearts were darkened. Claiming to be wise, they became fools, and *exchanged the glory of the immortal God for images* resembling mortal man and birds and animals and creeping things.... They *exchanged the truth about God for a lie* and *worshiped and served the creature rather than the Creator*, who is blessed forever! Amen. (Rom 1:21b–25)

God alone is God; there is no one like him; he is the only one deserving of worship. Adam and Eve exchanged that truth for Satan's lie: that they could be like God. And because they accepted that lie, they worshiped and served the *creature*, including themselves, rather than the *Creator*.

The Central Issue

The crucial understanding that we need to draw from all this is that:

Worship was the central issue in the fall.

The issue before Adam and Eve was "*Whom* are you going to worship (and honor, and give thanks to, and obey)? Are you going to worship the God who created you, or are you going to want to be like God and try to retain some of the worship and glory for yourself?"

This is how important worship is to the biblical story. The central issue in the fall of humanity, the main conflict of the Bible, indeed the main conflict of human history, is over this issue: *Whom are you going to worship?*

That is *the pivotal issue in human existence*, the crucial question facing every generation and every man, woman, and child in the world today: *Whom are you going to worship?* Who is going to be at the center of your life? Who is going to be on the throne of your heart?

The Bible's Story: Beginning to End

So we see at the very beginning of the Bible, just three chapters in, the tragedy that falls on the human race. And the entire trajectory of the Bible is God acting in human history to restore to himself the worship and glory that he alone deserves. In the book of Revelation we see that worship and glory fully restored, in great scenes of worship around the throne of God and great views of God's glory filling all in all (see chapter 21 of this book). And we have seen the angel's climactic declaration, in the very last chapter of the Bible, that John, and we, must "worship *God*" only (Rev 22:9).

The theme of worship is central to the Bible. God created us to worship him; in the fall Adam and Eve, and in their steps we, denied him the worship that he alone deserves. The entire biblical story is God acting at infinite cost to himself, the cost of his own beloved Son, to restore people to the place of worship.

Whom are you going to worship? Worship *God*.

> The most important question in human existence is: "Whom are you going to worship?"

For Reflection and/or Discussion

What did you worship before coming to Christ?

7

THE CENTRALITY OF WORSHIP IN REDEMPTION AND THE GOSPEL

If worship was the central issue in the fall, then it stands to reason that it is also at the center of God's solution to the problem of the fall in his plan of redemption.

Redemption

The Second Adam

Through one man, Adam, sin came into the world; so through one man, Jesus Christ, salvation came to the world. (See Rom 5:17; 1 Cor 15:45.)

When we read in Matthew about Satan tempting Christ in the wilderness, the climactic temptation revolves around worship:

> Again, the devil took him to a very high mountain and showed him all the kingdoms of the world and their glory. And he said to him, "All these I will give you, if you will fall down and *worship* me." (Matt 4:8–9)

Imagine the pride of this created being saying to the one through whom the worlds were made, "I want you to worship me"!

Jesus is being confronted with what we have seen to be the question of the ages, the question that Adam and Eve tragically answered wrongly: *Whom are you going to worship?*

But Jesus, the *Second* Adam, answers the question *rightly*:

> Then Jesus said to him, "Be gone, Satan! For it is written,
> 'You shall worship the Lord your God and him *only* shall you serve.'"(4:10)

And then Jesus, through his redeeming work, enables us to become the kind of faithful followers that God wants us to be: those who worship and serve him alone.

Worshipers Out of Rebels

A. W. Tozer makes an amazingly insightful comment along these lines:

> Why did Christ come? Why was he conceived? Why was he born? Why was he crucified? Why did he rise again? Why is he now at the right hand of the Father? The answer to all these questions is in order that he might *make worshipers out of rebels*; in order that he might restore us again to the place of worship we knew when we were first created.[1]

In Tozer's view, the entire thrust of Christ's coming and of his redeeming work was to *enable us to become the worshipers we were created to be instead of the rebels we had become.*

Undoing the Fall

Going back to the downward cascade of ill effects of the fall in Rom 1:21–25, let us consider how all the things that went so horribly wrong in the fall are made right again through the redeeming work of Jesus Christ:

Romans 1:21–25	*The Reversal in Christ*
They did not honor God as God or give thanks to him	*Christ enables us to honor God as God and give thanks*
They became futile in their thinking, and their foolish hearts were darkened	*Christ enlightens our thoughts and our hearts*
Claiming to be wise, they became fools	*Christ gives us his wisdom when we acknowledge our foolishness*

---

1. Tozer, *Worship*, 19 (emphasis added).

Romans 1:21–25	*The Reversal in Christ*
And exchanged the glory of the immortal God for images resembling mortal man and birds and animals and creeping things	*Christ enables us to exchange our images and idols for the glory of God*
They exchanged the truth about God for a lie	*Christ enables us to exchange Satan's lie for the truth about God*
And worshiped and served the creature rather than the Creator	*Christ enables us to worship the Creator rather than the creature*

Seeking Worshipers

Jesus says to the Samaritan woman in John 4:23:

> "But the hour is coming, and is now here, when the true worshipers will worship the Father in spirit and truth, for *the Father is seeking such people to worship him*."

The Father is seeking *worshipers*. Jesus came to make worshipers out of rebels, to make us true worshipers—because that is what the Father is seeking. And Jesus makes that possible through his redeeming work.

The Gospel

A Call to Worship

One way of looking at the gospel, then, is as *a call to worship*: a call to turn *from* the false worships that sin has led us into, and to turn *to* the true worship that Christ makes possible.

Paul is commending the faithfulness of the Thessalonians and the reputation they have among other believers:

> For they themselves report concerning us the kind of reception we had among you, and how you *turned to God from idols* to serve the living and true God. (1 Thess 1:9)

Coming to Christ through the gospel involved turning to God and away from idols. They turned from the *false worship* of idols to the *true worship* of the living God.

Similarly, in Acts 17:22–31 Paul calls the Athenians to turn from "the objects of your worship" (v. 23) to "the God who made the world and everything in it, being Lord of heaven and earth" (v. 24).

In Acts 14, Paul and Barnabas heal a crippled man in Lystra, and the people are so amazed that they want to offer up worship to the two missionaries. But they respond in horror at the thought (14:14–15a). They proclaim that their role is as God's spokesmen to "bring you good news." (In Greek this is a single word *euangelizō*, from which we get "evangelize." The same word is translated "preach the gospel" in 14:7.) Observe how they describe this *gospel* they have come to share:

> . . . that you should *turn from these vain things to a living God, who made the heaven and the earth and the sea and all that is in them.* (14:15b)

The gospel they preached was a call to turn "from these vain things" (their false worship of Zeus and Hermes, and of Barnabas and Paul) to true worship of the living God, the Creator.

And in Revelation 14, an angel has the same message for all on earth:

> Then I saw another angel flying directly overhead, with an eternal gospel to proclaim to those who dwell on earth. . . . And he said with a loud voice, "Fear God and give him glory, because the hour of his judgment has come, and *worship him* who made heaven and earth, the sea and the springs of water." (Rev 14:6–7)

About this passage David Peterson notes: "Revelation 14:6–7 suggests that evangelism may be viewed as *a call to worship God appropriately*."[2]

Saved To, Not Just From

So the gospel is a call to turn away from false worship (of whatever form) to worship of the one true God, the Redeemer. Sometimes we are prone to think of the gospel in primarily negative terms, as simply rescuing us from sin, death, and hell (and thank God it does all those things). But the gospel does not just rescue us *from* something, but also *to* something. The goal of the gospel is to enable us to be able to draw near to God in fellowship and worship:

> Therefore, brethren, since we have confidence to enter the holy places by the blood of Jesus, by the new and living way that he

---

2. Peterson, "Worship and Evangelism."

opened for us through the curtain, that is, through his flesh, and since we have a great priest over the house of God, *let us draw near* with a true heart in full assurance of faith, with our hearts sprinkled clean from an evil conscience and our bodies washed with pure water. (Heb 10:19)

We have confidence to enter by the blood of Jesus; and so the invitation is to *draw near to God*, to come close, to enjoy that personal fellowship with him that has been made possible through the gospel and the redeeming work of Christ.

The gospel saves us *from* something, but also *to* something: a personal relationship with God. The gospel invites us to come close and give to God the worship that he and he alone deserves. The gospel is *a call to worship*, a call to turn from false worship to true worship.

In Summary

In summary, we have seen in the last two chapters:

1. God is the Creator, unique in his glory and alone worthy of worship.
2. The fall usurped God's claim to exclusive worship.
3. Christ came to undo the effects of the fall and to enable true worship.
4. The gospel then is a call to all humanity to come to the Father through Christ, a call to worship to the glory of God.

> **Christ came and died so that we might become the worshipers we were created to be, instead of the rebels we had become.**

For Reflection and/or Discussion

How might the biblical study of worship enrich your own walk of worship?

8

THE CENTRALITY OF WORSHIP IN MISSIONS

From the perspective of the previous chapter, we can regard missions as simply *taking to the whole world the gospel's call to true worship*, for the glory of God among the nations.

Missions Is for God

The Scottish preacher Eric Alexander makes a startling, perhaps even controversial, claim; yet it is one that is consistent with what we have already seen about the glory of God and the centrality of worship:

> The *ultimate missionary compulsion* is not simply that there are people who are dying without knowing Christ, nor is it that God has given us the Great Commission to go out into the world; it is that there are areas of the world . . . where *God is being robbed of His glory*.[1]

Now, Alexander is not downplaying the need of the world's peoples for Christ, nor the seriousness of the Great Commission. But he is looking beyond those things to a *God-centered* view of missions—as a call to worship for the glory of God.

Men and women rob God of his glory by refusing to "honor him as God or give thanks to him" (Rom 1:21), and by having "worshiped and served the creature rather than the Creator" (Rom 1:25). So many

---

1. Alexander, "Worship God" (emphases added).

who owe their very lives and every breath to God wake up morning after morning and live their lives in a way that in effect says to him, "I don't need you!"

In missions, we aim to go and reach people for Christ, in obedience to the Great Commission (Matt 28:18–20). But ultimately, we want to reach people for the sake of *God*. We want people to become the worshipers God created them to be, instead of the rebels they have become.

Worship as the Goal of Missions

John Piper, in his *Let the Nations Be Glad: The Supremacy of God in Missions*, spends the entire first chapter talking about worship as it relates to missions. In fact, his opening sentences make an astounding claim—one that, when I first read it, exploded in my mind and heart and caused me to reevaluate the way I saw missions, and worship, and even God. Piper writes:

> Missions is not the ultimate goal of the church. Worship is. *Missions exists because worship doesn't*. Worship is ultimate, not missions, because God is ultimate, not man.[2]

Piper is *not* saying missions is unimportant; after all, he has written here an entire book on missions. But what he *is* saying is that missions is a terribly important *means* to an even greater *end*: the end of worship. Piper adds:

> When this age is over, and the countless millions of the redeemed fall on their faces before the throne of God, missions will be no more. It is a temporary necessity. But worship abides forever.[3]

Missions is taking the call to worship to all the world, so that God will receive more glory by more people lifting his name in worship.

This is a *biblical* emphasis, not one originating with Piper. In the book of Psalms especially, we find repeatedly the call for the nations to give God their worship:

> Let the peoples praise you, O God;
> let all the peoples praise you!
> Let the nations be glad and sing for joy. (Ps 67:3–4)

2. Piper, *Let the Nations Be Glad*, 3 (emphasis added).
3. Piper, *Let the Nations Be Glad*, 3.

> May all kings fall down before him,
> all nations serve him! (Ps 72:11)

> Ascribe to the LORD, O families of the peoples,
> ascribe to the LORD glory and strength! (Ps 96:7)

The goal of missions is for the peoples to give God the glory and the praise and the worship that he deserves.

What Piper's book did was to *remind* the church of this biblical emphasis, and in this way it has had a major impact on thinking about missions and its task. Here is an example of how one missions organization shaped its vision statement to reflect this understanding:

> Christar workers participate by planting churches in these least-reached communities, *where [God] is yet to be worshiped.*[4]

The goal of their organization is to plant churches in difficult areas so that people there might become worshipers of God.

And another missions organization similarly states as its purpose:

> *To Every Tribe* exists *to extend the worship of Christ* among all peoples by mobilizing the church, training disciple-makers, and sending missionary teams to plant churches among the unreached.[5]

Worship as the Fuel of Missions

Piper also makes the point that worship is not just the *goal* of missions. It is also the *fuel* of missions. He writes:

> Passion for God in worship precedes the offer of God in preaching. You can't commend what you don't cherish.[6]

In other words, you cannot go and tell others that "Great is the LORD, and greatly to be praised" (Ps 96:4) until you have first recognized the Lord's greatness in your own heart and have greatly praised him. You must first be a worshiper yourself before you can go and become an advocate for worship among the nations.

---

4. https://www.christar.org/ (emphasis added).
5. https://www.toeverytribe.org/ (emphasis added).
6. Piper, *Let the Nations Be Glad*, 3.

Amy Carmichael was a great missionary pioneer to India in the nineteenth century. The story is told (though undocumented) that once on her mission compound she had a new chapel built.

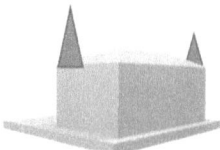

Someone asked her why there was a larger steeple at the front and a smaller one in the rear. She replied, "That's to remind us that worship must always precede service."

Truly fruitful service will grow out of a heart of worship, not just a sense of duty or responsibility. Jesus said, "Seek first the kingdom of God and his righteousness, and all these things will be added to you" (Matt 6:33).

Another mission agency summarized its ministry perspective in a similar way with the tagline:

- We *worship*.
- We love.
- We go.[7]

Worship Leads to Missions Leads to Worship!

And so in the purposes of God, worship and missions inevitably intertwine in this way. That is a *God-centered* view of the gospel, a God-centered view of building the church, a God-centered view of the work of missions. It is all ultimately for God, and about God and his glory. God earnestly desires his glory to be seen and acknowledged and lifted up among all the nations.

> Let the peoples praise you, O God;
> let all the peoples praise you!
> Let the nations be glad and sing for joy. (Ps 67:3–4a; see also Ps 148:11–13)

7. www.crossworld.org (emphasis added).

We are to be God's spokespersons, heralds, ambassadors, proclaiming:

> Praise the Lord, all nations!
> Extol him, all peoples! (Ps 117:1)

And thus we join in with God in his great purpose for the world:

> God is pursuing with omnipotent passion a worldwide purpose of gathering joyful worshipers for himself from every tribe and tongue and people and nation. . . . Therefore, let us bring our affections into line with His, and, for the sake of His name, let us renounce the quest for worldly comforts, and join His global purpose.[8]

Summary

Psalm 96 summarizes well the themes we have been considering as we looked at the relationship between worship and the gospel and missions:

O sing to the Lord a new song; sing to the Lord, all the earth! Sing to the Lord, bless his name;	*Worship . . .*
tell of his salvation from day to day. Declare his glory among the nations, his marvelous works among all the peoples!	*leading to missions . . .*
For great is the Lord, and greatly to be praised; he is to be feared above all gods.	*leading to worship*
For all the gods of the peoples are worthless idols, but the Lord made the heavens. (Ps 96:1–5)	*(turning from false to true worship)*

Great Commission and Great Commandment

Another way to see the dependent relationship between missions and worship is to compare the Great Commission and Great Commandment.

The Great Commission is of course the name we give to the resurrected Christ's final charge to his disciples in Matthew 28:

> All authority in heaven and on earth has been given to me. Go therefore and make disciples of all nations, baptizing them in the name of the Father and of the Son and of the Holy Spirit,

---

8. Piper, *Let the Nations Be Glad*, 32.

teaching them to observe all that I have commanded you. (Matt 28:18–20)

The Great Commandment was Jesus' response to the question asked him about the greatest commandment in the Old Testament law:

> You shall love the Lord your God with all your heart and with all your soul and with all your mind. This is the great and first commandment. (Matt 22:37–38)

When we compare these two statements (see the chart below) we see some striking differences.

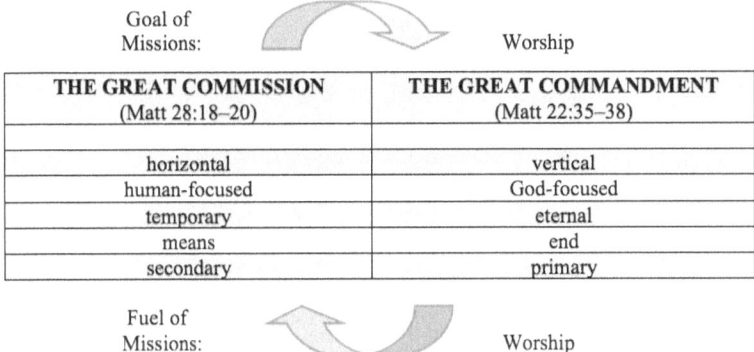

Goal of Missions:	→ Worship
THE GREAT COMMISSION (Matt 28:18–20)	**THE GREAT COMMANDMENT** (Matt 22:35–38)
horizontal	vertical
human-focused	God-focused
temporary	eternal
means	end
secondary	primary

Fuel of Missions: ← Worship

The Great Commission by definition is *horizontal* and *focused on people*. The Great Commandment, on the other hand, is purely *vertical* in its focus: we are to love God with all our being (which is simply another way to speak of worship). The Great Commission, like missions, is *temporary* and limited to this present age; the love for God of which the Great Commandment speaks will continue into eternity.

The culmination of the process of disciple-making is "teaching them to obey *all*" that Jesus commanded (which is the process of discipleship). And Jesus himself said that the *most important* of his commands was "to love the Lord your God with all your heart, soul, mind and strength." So in fulfilling the Great Commission, disciple-makers are ultimately leading their disciples to live according to the Great Commandment: to be worshipers first and foremost.

So we see that the Great Commission is a crucially important *means* to an even greater *end*: the fulfilling of the Great Commandment in the lives of people.

Not only that, but disciples who are growing in their obedience to not only the first but also the *second* greatest commandment (to "love your neighbor as yourself," Matt 22:39) will learn to see those neighbors as God sees them and will themselves become Great Commission disciple-makers.

And we might say that the end goal of evangelism is to *win more worshipers for God* (from among the nations); and that the final purpose of discipleship is to *build better worshipers of God*—those who love God with ever more of their heart, soul, mind, and strength. Missions, in both its evangelism and discipleship aspects, has as its *ultimate* aim that *more worship* be offered up to God, for his glory.[9]

> "Missions exists because worship doesn't."
> (John Piper)

For Reflection and/or Discussion

What is your reaction to this chapter's perspective on the relationship between worship and missions?

---

9. For more on the relationship of missions and worship, see chapter 38, "Worship and Culture in the Work of World Missions," in my book *Let Us Draw Near*.

9

THE CENTRALITY OF WORSHIP
IN ALL OF LIFE

In this chapter we want to look closely at John 4, one of the most important passages on worship in the New Testament. It is so important because in John 4 *Jesus himself* teaches about worship. (The word for worship is used *nine* times in verses 20–24.)

We see Jesus crossing traditional geographical, ethnic, and social barriers to enter Samaria (usually avoided by the Jews)[1] and lovingly confronting a Samaritan woman with her need for "living water" (4:10–15). Then we read:

> The woman said to him, "Sir, I perceive that you are a prophet. Our fathers worshiped on this mountain, but you say that in Jerusalem is the place where people ought to worship." Jesus said to her, "Woman, believe me, the hour is coming when neither on this mountain nor in Jerusalem will you worship the Father." (4:16–21)

---

1. The Jews despised the Samaritans: because they were Jewish/gentile half-breeds; because they rejected all but the first five books of the Old Testament; and because they had set up their own system of worship on Mount Gerizim. (That is why it was so radical for Jesus to make a "good Samaritan" the hero of his parable in Luke 10:29–37.) Jews traveling between Judea (in the south) and Galilee (in the north), or vice versa, would normally cross over the Jordan in order to bypass Samaria. Yet John tells us in 4:4 that Jesus "*had to* pass through Samaria." This was certainly because the Father had him on a mission to reach the woman and her town (see 4:24).

The woman refers to her people's worship on Mount Gerizim and the Jews' worship in Jerusalem, and is in effect posing the question: "Which is correct? Which group is worshiping in the right way and the right place?"

And, as he so often does, Jesus answers this question in an unexpected and surprising way. He says, "The hour is coming" (v. 21) and, in fact, "is now here" (v. 23) when *neither* place is the appointed venue for worship of the Father. Jesus says, in effect, "I am changing the rules. With my coming everything is different."

Worship "in spirit and truth"

> But the hour is coming, and is now here, when the true worshipers will worship the Father *in spirit and truth*, for the Father is seeking such people to worship him. God is spirit, and those who worship him must worship *in spirit and truth*." (John 4:23–24)

Jesus says that true worship will be worship "in spirit and truth." And the word "in" here is the same preposition as in verse 21, making the contrast even more clear: "neither *in* this mountain nor *in* Jerusalem will you worship the Father," but rather "the true worshipers will worship the Father *in* spirit and truth."

Jesus apparently is inaugurating a major lessening of the importance of *where* or *when* one worships, and a wholesale magnifying of the importance of *how* one worships: "in spirit and truth."

Worship "in spirit"

Many English translations render the word "spirit" in vv. 23 and 24 with a lowercase "s," while other versions capitalize the word. And this is representative of the fact that, two thousand years after the fact, there is still a lot of debate and no consensus on whether Jesus is referring here to the human "spirit," that is, to the inner, immaterial part of the human being, or whether the Holy Spirit is in view.

While the Holy Spirit certainly plays a key role in worship (as we will examine in chapter 25), the fact that Jesus is referring to the human spirit here seems to be supported by his words in v. 24: "God is *spirit*, and those who worship him must worship in spirit and truth." In other words, God is a spiritual, immaterial being, and therefore people will connect with him primarily on a spiritual, immaterial level.[2] "Worship in spirit" then would refer to the fact that true worship must come from the inside out, must be sincere and genuine and from the heart.

With "worship in spirit" Jesus may be drawing an implicit contrast with the Jewish leaders, whom he often criticized because of the merely *external* nature of their worship:

> You hypocrites! Well did Isaiah prophesy of you, when he said: "This people honors me with their lips, but their heart is far away from me. But in vain do they worship me, teaching as doctrines the precepts of men." (Matt 15:8–9; see also Matt 23:1–3, 5, 25–28)

God detests lip service in the absence of heart worship; he hates outward shows of religiosity without genuine and sincere inner devotion, the letter of the law without its spirit.[3] True worship must begin on the inside, and be genuine and sincere.

Worship "in truth"

But, Jesus says, worship must not only be "in spirit"; it must also be "in truth." That is, it must be *God's* way; as we saw in chapter 3, it must be a *response* to God's *revealed truth*.

Jesus may be intending here also an implicit criticism: in this case, of *Samaritan* worship. False worship, we have seen, comes from trying to worship God in the absence of, or ignoring, God's revelation. And, as we saw above, that is what the Samaritans had done. Jesus said to the woman:

> "You worship *what you do not know*; we worship what we know, for salvation is from the Jews." (4:22)

The Samaritans were very sincere, even enthusiastic, in their worship. But their worship was not a response to God's revelation. They had devised their own form and place of worship, while rejecting most of the Old Testament and God's revealed will concerning Jerusalem as the place where he was to be worshiped. (At least, Jesus says, the Jews had the advantage

---

2. A compelling, and perhaps conclusive, defense of this view on a grammatical basis may be found in Tim Ralston's paper "Ambiguity of 'in Spirit.'"

3. We see this also in the Old Testament prophets, where God condemns the rituals and sacrifices of the people (even though externally they are in accordance with the Mosaic law) because of their *externality* in the absence of heartfelt adoration. (See, for instance, Amos 5:21–24.)

of worshiping "what we know," because salvation was "from the Jews" as the recipients and caretakers of God's revelation.)

True worship must be in "truth," according to God's revelation. And of course, that means above all that true worship will be *through Christ*, God's ultimate revelation, who is himself *the Truth* (John 14:6).

Worship "in spirit *and* truth"

So worship must be sincere and from the heart ("in spirit"), but also according to God's revelation ("in truth"). Jesus is saying that *both* of those aspects are necessary.

That is true in our day as well. Our worship must be *in spirit*, genuine and sincere, heartfelt, from the inside out. For there are institutions and groups in our world that may have an outward veneer of Christian tradition and practice, may sing the great hymns of the faith, may perhaps even recite the Apostles' Creed weekly—but the people may not have accepted Christ as their Savior and do not pursue him with a genuine heart of devotion (though of course only God can judge that).

Our worship must also be *in truth*, according to God's revelation in Christ. For there are many people in our world who are very sincere in their religious beliefs and practices, but reject God's truth and God's Savior.

These are the twin dangers to true worship, as Eric Alexander puts it: "Zeal without knowledge, on the one hand, and knowledge without zeal, on the other; sincerity without truth, or truth without heart, in worship."[4] Both are necessary.

God Wants Our Lives

In the important worship verse we have already seen, Romans 12:1, we read:

> I appeal to you therefore, brethren, by the mercies of God, to present your bodies as a living sacrifice, holy and acceptable to God, which is your spiritual worship.

Paul seems to be here applying Jesus' teaching from John 4: it is not so much a matter of *where* or *when* you worship, but *how* you worship. If

---

4. Alexander, "Sermon #3 on John 4," in "Acceptable Worship."

worship in its deepest nature is in *spirit* and *truth,* and is not limited to a *place* like Mount Gerizim or Jerusalem—then worship must be *all of life.* For you can worship in any place, at any time, as long as it is in spirit and truth.

And so Paul says that as an appropriate *response* to all "the mercies of God" we have received through Christ (as he has just expounded in Romans 1–11), we are to offer up our "bodies" (that is, our entire lives) as a fitting sacrifice of worship. This is a crucial New Testament perspective on worship: that it is the response of *our entire lives* in thankful praise to the one who has redeemed us through Christ:

> So, whether you eat or drink, or whatever you do, do all to the glory of God. (1 Cor 10:31)

Note: this does *not* mean that there are no longer any holy times or holy places—but rather that *every* time and *every* place is holy to the Lord![5]

God wants a life and a lifestyle of worship. Christians need to realize that they should not depend on their pastor or worship leader to be solely responsible for providing them their weekly allotment of worship. Rather every believer is to be walking in a life and a lifestyle of worship all during the week. When we do that, we come to church with hearts already filled with love for God, and that will make the corporate gathering that much more powerful and special than if we come empty.[6] (Admittedly, all of us may sometimes come to church empty, and God in his grace will meet us there; but the *normal* pattern for the *healthy* Christian is a daily walk of worship, which then fills and strengthens and empowers the corporate gathering as well as our individual lives.)

The Father Is Seeking Worshipers

One important final observation. Jesus said to the woman:

> "But the hour is coming, and is now here, when the true worshipers will worship the Father in spirit and truth, for *the Father is seeking such people to worship him.*" (John 4:23)

---

5. Paraphrasing a point made in Carson, ed., *Worship by the Book,* 40.

6. *From the Field:* At Singapore Bible College one student (a missions mobilizer from the Philippines) testified to her change in perspective: "Thanks so much for the enriching time at class last week. It somehow made the difference when I went for church service last Sunday, nothing changed, really, just me ☺."

The Father is *seeking worshipers*. That is what he wants first and foremost from every one of us. As we have seen, that is why he created us and that is why he redeemed us.

Jesus never said, "the Father is seeking *pastors*," or "the Father is seeking *missionaries*," or "the Father is seeking *Christian businessmen and -women*." Jesus said, "the Father is seeking *worshipers*." That is what he wants first in every one of our lives.

Many young Christians are seeking after "God's will for my life." Here we see unequivocally God's will for your life: he wants you *to be a worshiper*! And if we will go hard after that, we can trust God to lead us into the areas of vocation and service he has for us.

> But seek first the kingdom of God and his righteousness, and all these things will be added to you. (Matt 6:33)

First, and above all, we must be *worshipers*. That is what the Father is seeking.

> The Father is seeking worshipers. (John 4:23)

For Reflection and/or Discussion

How will seeing worship as all of life
impact your churchgoing? Your daily walk?

10

THE CENTRALITY OF WORSHIP IN HEAVEN

In a great worship scene in Revelation 5, we see God the Father on the throne, along with the Lamb of God; then around them the angelic creatures referred to as the "four living creatures," the (probably) angelic beings called the "twenty-four elders," "myriads of myriads" of angels, and finally "every creature."

> Then I looked, and I heard around the throne and the living creatures and the elders the voice of many angels, numbering myriads of myriads and thousands of thousands, saying with a loud voice,
> "Worthy is the Lamb who was slain,
> to receive power and wealth and wisdom and might and honor and glory and blessing!"
> And I heard every creature in heaven and on earth and under the earth and in the sea, and all that is in them, saying,
> "To him who sits on the throne and to the Lamb
> be blessing and honor and glory and might forever and ever!"
> And the four living creatures said, "Amen!" and the elders fell down and worshiped. (Rev 5:11–14)

The Business of Heaven

These groups are gathered concentrically around the throne, and all are focused solely on praising God and the Lamb. This is the business of heaven: a *preoccupation* with God, his glory, and his worship. Nothing else is going on; there are no side conversations. All are focused on God and his glory. And that is a model for *our* worship as well. Our single-minded focus in worship should also be on the God of glory, as we prepare to one day join that great scene around the throne.

Heavenly Worship Now

But the New Testament gives us another perspective on heavenly worship: it is not only our future, but also *our present privilege*. We are not only on earth (as "strangers and exiles," Heb 11:13) but also positionally/spiritually already in heaven:

> [God] raised us up with [Christ] and seated us with him in the heavenly places in Christ Jesus. (Eph 2:6)

Paul tells us that "our citizenship is in heaven" (Phil 3:20).

My US passport carries these words:

> The Secretary of the United States of America hereby requests all whom it may concern to permit the citizen/national of the United States named herein to pass without delay or hindrance and in case of need to give all lawful aid and protection.

In other words, as a citizen of the United States I am due the rights and privileges that come from being a citizen of my country—and passports of other nations carry such verbiage also.

Now, since we are citizens of heaven, we have the rights and privileges that come from that status. That means that, in a very real sense, we can take part *now* in the worship of heaven—that land where we truly belong.

Corporate worship is not something that *begins* and *ends* at the appointed times; rather, when we gather we are *joining in* with that worship that is always going on around the throne.

> A preoccupation with God and his glory is the business of heaven.

For Reflection and/or Discussion

How might the concept of joining in with heavenly worship impact your experience of corporate worship?

11

WORSHIP IS CENTRAL

A Unifying Theme

And so we have seen what a huge, central, pivotal theme worship is in the Scriptures. In fact, worship ties the entire biblical story together.

God created us to worship him and to enjoy his presence. In the fall we refused to give him the worship that only he deserves, and turned to false worship of all kinds.

The biblical narrative relates God's work throughout human history to restore to himself the worship of all creation. He sent his Son to redeem us and thus enable us to become the worshipers of God that we were created to be, instead of the rebels against God that we had become. The gospel message may then be seen as a call to all humanity to turn from false worship to true worship of the Creator God.

Once we have turned to true worship through Christ, worship then encompasses the response of our entire lives to the glory of God.

And in the great scenes of worship in Revelation, we see the final consummation of God's purpose to receive unto himself the worship of all and the fulfillment of the angel's charge (and the entire Bible's command) to "worship *God*" (Rev 22:9).

> Worship is central because God is central.

For Reflection and/or Discussion

Do you see the Bible differently after considering the central and unifying theme of worship throughout its pages?

Part 4

Worship in the Old Testament[1]

12. Important Themes and Vocabulary in Old Testament Worship
13. Worship in Old Testament History: Pentateuch
14. Worship in Old Testament History: Pre-Exilic Israel
15. Worship in Old Testament History: Exilic and Post-Exilic Israel
16. The Psalms: Israel's Worship Book . . . and Ours

---

1. Two fine Old Testament scholars have produced comprehensive studies of biblical worship and, given their expertise, their works are naturally strongest and most detailed in their treatments of the Old Testament. See Allen P. Ross, *Recalling the Hope of Glory,* and Daniel I. Block, *For the Glory of God.* The reader is referred to these excellent works for further study of worship in the Old Testament.

12

IMPORTANT THEMES IN OLD TESTAMENT WORSHIP

Theme: **Worship as Response**

As we have already seen in chapter 3, the divine initiative is prominent throughout Scripture: "Acceptable worship does not start with human intuition or inventiveness, but with the action of God."[1] Thus we see this divine initiative operating in the Old Testament.

Worship as Response to Revelation

> Then Moses said to God, "If I come to the people of Israel and say to them, 'The God of your fathers has sent me to you,' and they ask me, 'What is his name?' what shall I say to them?" God said to Moses, "I AM WHO I AM." And he said, "Say this to the people of Israel: 'I AM has sent me to you.'" (Exod 3:13–14)

God is revealing his nature with this name: "I AM WHO I AM." That is, "I am the self-existent One. I have no cause, no beginning. I am God. There is no one like me, the Creator." The people's worship is going to be in *response* to this *revelation* of himself through Moses.

---

1. Peterson, *Engaging with God*, 26.

Worship as Response to Redemption

> [God] said, "But I will be with you, and this shall be the sign for you, that I have sent you: when you have brought the people out of Egypt, you shall *serve* God on this mountain." (Exod 3:12)

The Hebrew word here rendered "serve" is also often translated as "worship" in the Old Testament. God is saying, "When I bring you out of Egypt, in *response* to my redeeming work in your life as a nation, you shall worship me."

Worship as Response to Covenant Relationship

> "I will take you to be my people, and I will be your God, and you shall know that I am the LORD your God, who has brought you out from under the burdens of the Egyptians." (Exod 6:7)

God is going to form a special covenant relationship with this people. In fact, the phrase "the LORD our God" occurs 440 times in the Old Testament! Obviously this is a central concept. And in *response* to that covenant relationship, the people will give God their worship.

Theme: **God's Grace, Lovingkindness, Mercy**

Perhaps you have heard unbelievers (or even untaught believers) say something like: "The God of the Old Testament is a God of hate and violence, and the God of the New Testament is a God of love." But *God does not change*, and the Old Testament is full of demonstrations of God's grace and mercy, represented especially by a special, beautiful, and powerful Hebrew word:

ḥesed

The word *ḥesed* is use 248 times in the Old Testament. About half of those occurrences are in the Psalms, including twenty-six times in Psalm 136 alone (as part of a repeated refrain). Obviously a *very* important word, it is normally rendered (depending on the translation) as "steadfast love" or "lovingkindness" or "mercy." *ḥesed* combines the idea of love and loyalty. It speaks of God's faithfulness to those who are in covenant with him, his *loyal love*. And throughout the Old Testament we see God being faithful to his covenant people Israel, even though they repeatedly turn away from him.

Here are a few of the many instances of this key Old Testament covenant word:

> The LORD passed before him and proclaimed, "The LORD, the LORD, a God merciful and gracious, slow to anger, and abounding in *steadfast love* and faithfulness, keeping *steadfast love* for thousands, forgiving iniquity and transgression and sin." (Exod 34:6–7)

> Surely goodness and *mercy* shall follow me all the days of my life, and I shall dwell in the house of the LORD forever. (Ps 23:6)

> "But let him who boasts boast in this, that he understands and knows me, that I am the LORD who practices *steadfast love*, justice, and righteousness in the earth. For in these things I delight, declares the LORD." (Jer 9:24)

As can be seen in these references, God's *ḥesed* is *basic to who he is*. He is "abounding in steadfast love" to those in covenant relationship with him—including, of course, us!

David, when he was running for his life in the wilderness of Judah after his son Absalom had rebelled against him, composed a profound statement of trust in God. He proclaimed:

> Because your *steadfast love* is better than life,
> my lips will praise you. (Ps 63:3)

David's life was in danger, but still he could rejoice in God's *ḥesed*, because he held it to be "better than life" itself.

A crucial theme in the Old Testament is this concept of God's *ḥesed*, and is a powerful motivation for the response of praise.

Theme: **Worship of the Heart (Spiritual Sacrifices)**

When we think about worship in the Old Testament, our minds often go first to the tabernacle/temple and its sacrifices, rituals, ceremonies, and festivals—the *external* trappings of worship under the Mosaic covenant. However, these externals are of *secondary* importance when it comes to the worship that God desires from his people under the old covenant. He is looking for an *inner reality*, without which the *external* observances are of no value to him.

A Surprisingly Common Emphasis

This unexpected truth is plainly evident throughout the Old Testament. Here are just a few of the many examples that could be cited:

> "For the LORD sees not as man sees: man looks on the outward appearance, but *the Lord looks on the heart.*" (1 Sam 16:7)

> Do I eat the flesh of bulls or drink the blood of goats?
> Offer to God *a sacrifice of thanksgiving*
> and perform your vows to the Most High....
> The one who offers *thanksgiving as his sacrifice* glorifies me. (Ps 50:13–14, 23a)

> For you do *not* delight in sacrifice, otherwise I would give it; You are *not* pleased with burnt offering. *The sacrifices of God are a broken spirit; a broken and a contrite heart*, O God, you will not despise. (Ps 51:16–17)

> I will praise the name of God with song and magnify him with *thanksgiving*. And it will *please the Lord better* than an ox or a young bull with horns and hoofs. (Ps 69:30–31)

A Powerful Example

A remarkable passage along these lines: King Hezekiah (one of the declining number of kings in Judah who "did what was right in the sight of the Lord" [2 Chr 29:2]) led the people in a revival of devotion to God and reinstituted the Passover after generations of neglect. We read in 2 Chronicles 30:18a, however, that "a majority of the people . . . had not cleansed themselves, yet they ate the Passover *otherwise than as prescribed.*" They had not followed God's explicit instructions for ritual cleansing in preparation for taking the Passover. Yet Hezekiah boldly asks, "May the good LORD pardon everyone who *sets his heart to seek God* . . . even though not according to the sanctuary's rules of cleanness" (30:18b–19). And, astonishingly, God *does* forgive them (30:20), *overlooking his own rules* and thus demonstrating the priority he places on setting one's *"heart* to seek God."

The New Testament Witness

We see this priority upheld in the New Testament as well.

As we have noted already, Jesus often criticized the Jewish leaders because of the externality of their religious observances, performing rituals to be seen by others (Matt 6:5, 16; 23:5), in the absence of heartfelt devotion to God.

> And [Jesus] said to them, "Well did Isaiah prophesy of you hypocrites, as it is written,
> 'This people honors me with *their lips,*
> but *their heart* is far from me;
> *in vain* do they worship me,
> teaching as doctrines the commandments of men.'" (Mark 7:5–7; see also Matt 15:7–9)

Jesus condemned this kind of worship as being "in vain," i.e., worthless.

> Jesus looked up and saw the rich putting their gifts into the offering box, and he saw a poor widow put in two small copper coins. And he said, "Truly, I tell you, this poor widow has put in *more than all of them.*" (Luke 21:1–3)

Jesus remarkably stated that the widow "put in *more than all of them,*" because her gift of two small coins (all she had) expressed *the complete devotion of her heart.* Her offering was more: not in *quantity,* but rather in *quality.* God doesn't *need* our money; he desires that we give as an expression of our heart for him.

Heart Worship

External religion and outward expressions without an internal reality are meaningless to God. He is always mainly concerned about the worship of the heart.

It is, of course, all too possible for us to "go through the motions" in our public and even our private worship, when God is really looking for our heart. And in our worship debates also we must be mindful of this same principle. For most debates, disagreements, and conflicts concerning worship in our churches revolve around *external* things: practices, tradition, styles, instruments, etc. But God does *not* have favorite styles, songs, instruments, or building types! He is looking for hearts of worship. Indeed, "Man looks on the outward appearance, but the LORD looks on the *heart*" (1 Sam 16:7).

> **God is always more concerned about the worship of the heart than about its outward form.**

For Reflection and/or Discussion

How have you experienced God's loyal love (*ḥesed*) in your life? How might the realization of the priority God places on the heart in worship challenge and impact your own practice of worship?

13

WORSHIP IN OLD TESTAMENT HISTORY: Pentateuch[1]

We now want to survey the Old Testament, period by period, to see what we can learn about worship.

The Beginning Period (Genesis 1–11)

Creation (Genesis 1–2)

We have already seen in chapters 4 and 6 how God created humanity to worship him and reflect his glory.

The Fall (Genesis 3)

In chapter 6 we also saw that the central issue in the fall was the issue of worship. Worship, as the English term denotes, is recognizing and celebrating the "worth-ship" of God. That's what Adam and Eve refused to do. "Although they knew God, they did not honor him as God or give thanks to him . . . and [they] worshiped and served the creature rather than the Creator" (Rom 1:21, 25).

---

1. The term is used to refer to the first five books of the Old Testament (Genesis through Deuteronomy) collectively.

Cain and Abel (Genesis 4:1–17)

We see in the very next chapter after the fall that worship, and the family, have already been horribly corrupted by sin. The first murder in the Bible revolves around an act of worship.

When Cain and Abel bring their offerings, God accepts Abel's but not Cain's. And then Cain, in anger at this rejection, slays his brother.

Why did God accept Abel's sacrifice and not Cain's? Hebrews 11 gives us the answer:

> *By faith* Abel offered to God a more acceptable sacrifice than Cain. (Heb 1:4)

It was *the heart of faith* with which Abel made his offering that made it acceptable. (The implication is that Cain did not offer his gift in faith; and we see something of Cain's heart from his response of murderous anger, rather than remorse or shame before God.) This is another example of the priority God places on the *heart* attitude of the worshiper.

Noah and the Flood (Genesis 6–8)

The wickedness of humanity led God to destroy the world in a great flood, but he preserved the remnant of Noah and his family. And the first thing Noah did upon leaving the ark was to build an altar and offer sacrificial worship, in *response* to God's *rescue* of him and his family:

> Then Noah built an altar to the Lord and took some of every clean animal and some of every clean bird and offered burnt offerings on the altar. (Gen 8:20)

The Tower of Babel (Genesis 11)

Men and women in their pride, instead of filling the earth as they were commanded through Adam and Eve (Gen 1:28) and Noah (Gen 9:1), stayed in one place. In direct defiance of God's instructions, they said, "Come, let us build ourselves a city and a tower with its top in the heavens, and let us make a name for ourselves, lest we be dispersed over the face of the whole earth" (Gen 11:4). We see their sinful pride also in their aim to "make a name for ourselves."

So God responded in judgment: he "confused the language of all the earth. And from there the LORD dispersed them over the face of all the earth" (Gen 11:9). The result is the rise of cultures and languages. Yet John Piper brings a fascinating, redemptive perspective to this judgment:

> The praise that Jesus receives from all the languages is more beautiful, because of its diversity, than it would have been if there were only one language and one people to sing....
>
> "After this I looked, and behold, a great multitude that no one could number, from every nation, from all tribes and peoples *and languages*, standing before the throne and before the Lamb . . . and crying out with a loud voice, 'Salvation belongs to our God who sits on the throne, and to the Lamb!'" (Rev 7:9–10).
>
> It was the spectacular sin on the plains of Shinar that gave rise to the multiplying of languages that ends in the most glorious praise to Christ from every language on earth.[2]

God in his sovereignty can turn even humanity's sin and rebellion, and his resulting judgment, to ultimately multiply his praise!

The Patriarchal Period (Genesis 12–50)

Abraham

The Call of Abram

As we have seen, God by his own gracious initiative reveals himself to the pagan Abram and completely changes his life trajectory.

> Now the LORD said to Abram, "Go from your country and your kindred and your father's house to the land that I will show you. And I will make of you a great nation, and I will bless you and make your name great, so that you will be a blessing. I will bless those who bless you, and him who dishonors you I will curse, and in you all the families of the earth shall be blessed." (Gen 12:1–3)

If Abram will obey the command to go, God promises to:

- make a great nation out of him.
- bless him.

---

2. Piper, "Pride of Babel and the Praise of Christ" (emphasis added).

- make his name great.
- make him a blessing.
- bless those who bless him, and curse those who curse him.
- bless all the families of the earth through him (this last promise is sometimes called the "Great Commission" of the Old Testament).

And we learn in Isaiah 43 that God's intent for the nation descended from Abraham was that it be:

> "my chosen people,
> the people whom I formed for myself
> *that they might declare my praise*." (Isa 43:20–21)

God was seeking to form a unique worshiping people:

> that your way may be known on earth,
> your saving power among all nations. (Ps 67:2)

Unfortunately, Israel often forgot this part of its mandate; they were all too ready to enjoy their status as God's chosen people, but in their pride looked down on the benighted nations surrounding them.

The Response of Abraham

Abram obeys God's call (12:4); then upon arriving in the promised land he builds altars and calls upon the name of the Lord (12:7–8): he responds in worship.

God's Continuing Revelation to Abraham[3]

God continued to reveal himself to Abraham throughout his life, appearing and speaking to him, repeating his promises, and showing various facets of his nature by identifying himself by different names:[4]

---

3. When God formalizes his covenant with Abram in Genesis 17, he changes his name from Abram ("exalted father") to Abraham ("father of a multitude") (Gen 17:5).

4. It has been pointed out that all these and other descriptive names given to God in the Old Testament are subsumed and fulfilled by Jesus, "the name that is above every name" (Phil 2:9).

- *El Elyon* (God Most High [14:18–19])
- *El Shaddai* (God Almighty [17:1–2])
- *El Olam* (the Everlasting God [21:33])
- *Yahweh Jireh* (the LORD Who Sees/Provides [22:14])

Abraham's Life of Faith and Worship

Abraham was saved, and lived, by faith in the promises of God:

And [God] brought [Abram] outside and said, "Look toward heaven, and number the stars, if you are able to number them." Then he said to him, "So shall your offspring be." And he believed the LORD, and he counted it to him as righteousness." (Gen 15:5–6)

"Abraham believed God, and it was counted to him as righteousness"—and he was called a friend of God. (Jas 2:23)

And Abraham's life was also characterized by many private and public acts of worship—sacrifices (Gen 12:7, 8; 13:18; 22:7); prayer: praise and thanksgiving (12:8; 13:4), petition (24:12); intercession (18:22–23; 20:7); tithing (14:20); building of altars (in response to God's appearances) (12:7, 8; 13:3–4, 18; 22:9).

Isaac

We learn far less in Genesis about Isaac than we do about Abraham. But we do see in Genesis 26 that God appears to Isaac and repeats to him the promises that he had made to Abraham.

From there [Isaac] went up to Beersheba. And the LORD appeared to him the same night and said, "I am the God of Abraham your father. Fear not, for I am with you and will bless you and multiply your offspring for my servant Abraham's sake." (Gen 26:23–24)

And Isaac likewise *responds* by building an altar, calling on the name of the Lord, and worshiping.

So he built an altar there and called upon the name of the LORD and pitched his tent there. (Gen 26:25)

Jacob

Isaac's son Jacob is an interesting figure. In many ways he is a picture of the nation that will be named after him (after his name is changed to Israel, 32:28): like the later nation, Jacob is called and blessed by God but often chooses to do things his own way. However, God persists in working in Jacob's life, until by the end of his life he becomes a true worshiper of God (see Genesis 35 and Hebrews 11:21).

Jacob's Ladder (28:10-22)

A significant event in Jacob's life occurs in Gen 28. Jacob is on the run for his life (27:41–45) because he has cheated Esau out of his birthright (25:29–34) and out of his father's blessing (27:1–40).

Bartolomé Esteban Murillo (1617–1682), *Jacob's Dream*

One night along the way, as he sleeps:

> And he dreamed, and behold, there was a ladder [or flight of steps, or ramp] set up on the earth, and the top of it reached to heaven. And behold, the angels of God were ascending and descending on it! (Gen 28:11–12)

This account of "Jacob's ladder" has a fascinating parallel in John 1. Jesus is calling his disciples, and we read:

> Jesus saw Nathanael coming toward him and said of him, "Behold, an Israelite indeed, in whom there is no deceit!" Nathanael said to him, "How do you know me?" Jesus answered him, "Before Philip called you, when you were under the fig tree, I saw you." Nathanael answered him, "Rabbi, you are the Son of God!

You are the King of Israel!" Jesus answered him, "Because I said to you, 'I saw you under the fig tree,' do you believe? You will see greater things than these." And he said to him, "Truly, truly, I say to you, you will see heaven opened, and the angels of God ascending and descending on the Son of Man." (John 1:47–51)

The wording of Jesus' last phrase in verse 51 is *almost identical* with Genesis 28:12, with *one crucial difference*: the angels, instead of "ascending and descending" on a *ladder* are doing so "*on the Son of Man.*" Jesus is obviously alluding to Genesis 28 and is in effect saying, "*I* am the fulfillment of Jacob's vision. In a way that Jacob could not have imagined, *I* am the ladder; *I* am that connection between heaven and earth, between God and man." As both God and man, Jesus is uniquely positioned to be the bridge between God and man, and man and God. We will see more of the full significance of that *two-way mediation* for our worship in chapter 24.

God's Covenant Promises Repeated

In Jacob's dream God speaks to him and repeats to him the promises he had previously made to Abraham and Isaac:

> I am the LORD, the God of Abraham your father and the God of Isaac. The land on which you lie I will give to you and to your offspring. Your offspring shall be like the dust of the earth, and you shall spread abroad to the west and to the east and to the north and to the south, and in you and your offspring shall all the families of the earth be blessed. Behold, I am with you and will keep you wherever you go, and will bring you back to this land. For I will not leave you until I have done what I have promised you. (Gen 28:13–15)

Jacob's Response of Worship

Jacob's heart is stirred by the dream, and we see even at this point in his life the beginnings of a deeper life of worship to come.

> Then Jacob awoke from his sleep and said, "Surely the LORD is in this place, and I did not know it." And he was afraid and said, "How awesome is this place! This is none other than the house of God, and this is the gate of heaven." (Gen 28:16–17)

The Exodus (Exodus 1–19)

God acts by his own gracious initiative to call and send the sheepherder Moses (Exod 3) to lead his people out of slavery in Egypt.

God had three purposes in the Exodus:

1. *to show his power and the greatness of his name*: to Moses and the people of Israel (Exod 8:22; 10:1–2; 14:31; 15:11–13); to the Egyptians (7:5; 14:4, 17–18); to Pharaoh (7:17; 8:9–10; 9:14, 16, 29); to the nations (9:16; 15:13–16; Josh 2:8–11; 4:23–24);
2. *to judge the false gods and false worship of Egypt* (Exod 9:11; 12:12; Num 33:3–4);

and, above all,

3. *to redeem for himself a unique worshiping people* (Exod 7:16; 8:1, 20; 9:1, 13; 10:3; Ps 114:1–2).

> My chosen people,
> the people whom I formed for myself
> that they might declare my praise. (Isa 43:21)

The Mosaic (Sinai) Covenant (Exodus 20–Deuteronomy)

God entered into covenant with his people at Mount Sinai, through the mediation of Moses.

God's Commitment

In initiating the covenant with the people, God promised two main things as his side of the agreement:

1. His special *presence* among his people

   "Then the cloud covered the tent of meeting, and *the glory of the* Lord *filled the tabernacle.*" (Exod 40:34; see also Lev 26:11; 2 Chr 7:1)

2. A special *relationship* with his people

I will also walk among you and be your God, and you shall be my people. (Lev 26:12; see also Exod 6:6–7; Lev 11:45; 22:33; 25:38; 26:12; Num 15:41; Deut 29:13)

The People's Part

In response, God asked for the people's *worship*. Here are six aspects of the worship that God sought from the people:

1. Exclusive worship

"You shall have no other gods before me." (Exod 20:3)

2. Word-directed worship

The people's worship was to be according to God's instruction (verbal and written). They did not have to guess who God was or what he wanted. (As we have seen, false religions, lacking God's direct revelation, require a guess like that.)

"Moses came and told the people all the words of the Lord. . . . And Moses wrote down all the words of the Lord." (Exod 24:3–4)

3. Lifestyle worship

The people were to live as a nation under the direct rule of God: a *theocratic* nation. Their national lifestyle was to be one of worship and obedience, honoring God in all aspects of society by caring for the poor and widows, etc.

"You shall be to me a kingdom of priests and a holy nation." (Exod 19:6)

4. Ritual worship

Most often people associate Old Testament worship with the array of complex rituals, sacrifices, ceremonies, and festivals associated with the tabernacle (and later the Jerusalem temple). And indeed the tabernacle was the physical and spiritual center of the nation and its worship life.

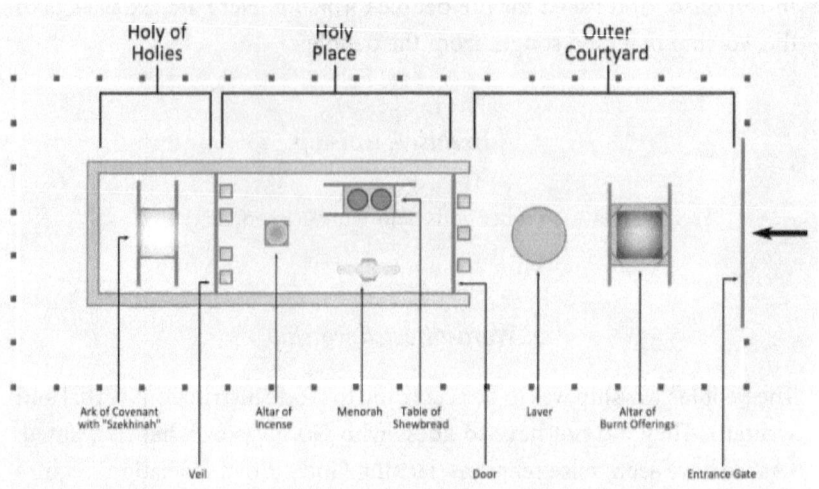

The sacrificial system of the Mosaic covenant was extremely complex. Chapter after chapter in Exodus and Leviticus communicate the regulations that the people were to follow: how to prepare, what to bring, what to do, etc. What did the system and its complexity communicate? Why did God institute such a complicated system? Here are some likely reasons:

1. To show *the holiness and purity of God* (he was set apart in the holy of holies).
2. To reflect *the beauty and majesty of God* (the grandeur of the tabernacle and its decorations).
3. To point to *the sinfulness of the people* (they could not come close).
4. To show *the seriousness of sin* (it was not a simple matter to deal with).
5. To demonstrate *the grace of God* (in providing a way to temporarily cover sin).

6. To produce *a growing frustration with individuals' and the nation's inability to keep the law of God.*

This last is a crucial aspect. Over time, a godly Jew would realize that after offering the *same* sacrifices *year after year* (Heb 9:25; 10:1–3, 11), the people were still not getting any better. In fact, the entire Old Testament chronicles the inability of people to live according to God's standards *in their own strength*—even God's chosen people, who had the advantage of the presence and revelation of God. The people rashly proclaimed when Moses came down from Mount Sinai and relayed to them God's commands: "All that the LORD has spoken we will do!" (Exod 24:3). Yet soon thereafter they were worshiping the golden calf (Exod 32)! And the rest of the Old Testament gives testimony to the large-scale devolution of that presumptuous and self-righteous pronouncement—beginning with the golden calf incident, continuing with grumblings and worse crimes during the wilderness period and the lawless period of the judges, and later with a host of bad kings and the shocking large-scale neglect (or ignorance) of the law and the Passover for sometimes generations at a time (see 2 Kgs 22:8–13; 2 Chr 30). *Idolatry was never far away from taking center stage in the nation's life.*

The book of Hebrews makes it clear that God intended the Old Testament system to be *temporary*, in preparation for the coming of Christ:

> For since the law has but a shadow of the good things to come instead of the true form of these realities, it can never, by the same sacrifices that are continually offered every year, make perfect those who draw near. (Heb 10:1)

Paul insists that the problem was *not* with the law (it was a perfect representation of the will of God), but rather with the people's *hearts* (Rom 8:2–4). So through the law and the sacrificial system, the devoted Jew would begin to see inadequacy of the system and to long for *a better way.* And indeed that better way is foretold in the prophets: a new covenant would come, and God would write his law on their hearts and put his Holy Spirit within them (Jer 31:31–33b; Ezek 36:26–27).

This new covenant (which would be instituted through Christ's death [Luke 22:20]) would bring with it divine enablement to live in obedience to God:

> For *God* has done what the law, weakened by the flesh, could *not* do. By sending his own Son in the likeness of sinful flesh and for

sin, he condemned sin in the flesh, in order that the righteous requirement of the law might be fulfilled in us, who walk not according to the flesh but according to the Spirit. (Rom 8:3–4)

The complex ritual system of the Mosaic covenant would thus help to prepare for the coming of Christ and the new covenant by demonstrating the people's helplessness and dire need for God to intervene in a decisive and redemptive way.

5. *Testimony worship*

Israel's worship was to be a testimony to the nations of how God would bless a people who would worship him as the one true God.

> May God be gracious to us and bless us
> and make his face to shine upon us,
> that your way may be *known* on earth,
> your saving power *among all nations*. (Ps 67:1–2)

Ironically, Israel's worship would also be a testimony to the nations when they turned to false worship and idolatry (as was so often the case). Because then God would discipline them, bringing hardship, defeat in battle, etc. This discipline would itself be a testimony to the nations: that God is *so holy* that he will judge *even his own people* when they turn away from him (Jer 22:8–9; Isa 5:16).

6. *Typological worship*

Finally, the nation's worship would be typological. That is, it would foreshadow and picture in various ways the coming work of Christ. This is seen most vividly (at least in retrospect) in the observance of the Day of Atonement. James Torrance summarizes this well:

> The high priest stands before the people as their divinely appointed representative, bone of their bone, flesh of their flesh, their brother, in solidarity with the people he represents. All that he does, he does in their name; this is symbolized by the fact that he bears their names engraved on his breastplate and shoulders as a memorial before God (Exod 39:7). He consecrates himself for this ministry by certain liturgical acts of washing and sacrifice. Then comes the great moment when he takes an animal, lays his hands on the victim and vicariously confesses the sins of

all Israel in an act of vicarious penitence acknowledging the just judgments of God; when the victim is immolated as a symbol of God's judgment, he takes the blood of the vessel, ascends into the Holy of Holies, and there vicariously intercedes for all Israel that God will remember his covenant promises and graciously forgive. He then returns to the waiting people outside with the Aaronic blessing of peace.

The New Testament writers saw this as a foreshadowing of the ministry of Christ, who comes from God to be the true Priest, . . . bearing on his divine heart the names, the needs, the sorrows, the injustices of all nations, to offer that worship, that obedience, that life of love to the Father which we cannot offer.[5]

Israel's *worship*—exclusive, word-directed, lifestyle, ritual, testimony, typological worship—was to be their *response* to the covenant that God had initiated with them.

Israel's covenant duty was worship.

For Reflection and/or Discussion

Does seeing the law as a *response* to redemption
(rather than as a *means* to redemption)
help you understand the grace of God better?

---

5. Torrance, "Christ in Our Place," 44–45.

14

WORSHIP IN OLD TESTAMENT HISTORY:
Pre-Exilic Israel (Joshua–2 Chronicles)

We will now overview a large swath of Israel's history—from the conquest to the Babylonian exile.

The Conquest (Joshua)

God had two purposes in the conquest of the promised land:

1. The Destruction of False Worship

God's command to go into the promised land and wipe out the Canaanites is troubling to many. But it is important to see it as the judgment of God upon the depraved worship of that land, which often included temple prostitution, child sacrifice, etc.

> Before they crossed the Jordan, God had warned the people of Israel that this conquest was not a tribute to their righteousness [Deut 9:4–7]. They do not deserve a land flowing with milk and honey. They are not destroying the inhabitants because of Israel's superior righteousness, but because of God's justice towards the nations and God's utterly undeserved grace toward Israel.[1]

---

1. Piper, *Providence*, 119–20.

2. The Establishment of True Worship

> One thing is clear about the conquest: the point was *pure worship*. God's objective was *not* that Israel would be the only people that worshiped him. His point was to insure *that He was the only God that they worshiped*.[2]
>
> The point of Israel's separation was not ethnic exclusiveness (there were all kinds of ways that foreigners could be incorporated into the worship community of Israel) but religious protection.[3]

In spite of God's repeated warnings, we read that Israel did not follow through on God's command to rid the land of its inhabitants. And, as predicted, the influence of their idolatry would repeatedly drag down the nation throughout the coming centuries and lead to harsh discipline at the hand of the Lord. (As noted earlier, God would deal justly even with his own people when they turned away from him.)

> They did not destroy the peoples,
> as the Lord commanded them,
> but they mixed with the nations
> and learned to do as they did.
> They served their idols,
> which became a snare to them. (Ps 106:34–36)

Cycles of True and False Worship (Judges–2 Chronicles)

The rest of the historical books of the Old Testament can be summarized as a series of cycles:

---

2. Hawthorne, "Story of His Glory" (emphasis added).
3. Wright, *Mission of God*, 257.

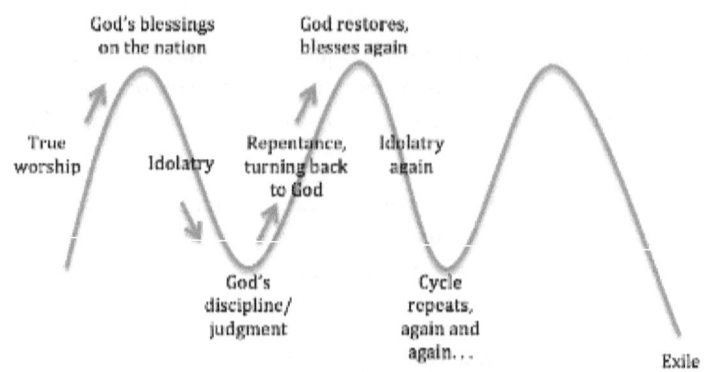

Israel's fate as a nation always followed its worship. When the people were worshiping God rightly, he would bless them as a nation. But, as happened time and time again, they would eventually turn to idolatry (infected by Canaanite worship because of their failure to totally remove the inhabitants of the land and their religious structures and practices), and God would bring discipline against his people (defeat in battle, failure of crops, etc.)—though *always* with a view to bringing them to repentance. And, repeatedly, when the people of Israel did cry out to the Lord and turn back in repentance, God in his great ḥesed (and "for his great name's sake," 1 Sam 12:22) would forgive them and restore their fortunes. But then the pattern of idolatry, discipline, repentance, and restoration would happen again—and again, and again.

Finally the sin of the people became so bad that God took them into exile; but even then it was only a temporary exile (for the Southern Kingdom), and God would allow them to return later.

We see from these cycles that when the people's worship was *right*, then God would *bless* and things would go right for them as a nation; and when the people's worship was *wrong*, then everything went wrong under the disciplining hand of God. *Israel's fate as a nation always followed its worship*, since it was the people's *worship* that God desired as their part of the covenant agreement.

King David

David is a crucial figure in the history of the worship of Israel, and in the history of worship in general, for three reasons:

1. David greatly developed the public worship of the nation

It is a remarkable fact that, after the establishment by God of the tabernacle and its accompanying worship system through Moses, as recorded in Exodus and Leviticus, there is virtually no mention of music being used in the public worship of Israel for many centuries. The worship of the tabernacle itself appears to have been practiced without musical praise.[4]

That situation changes drastically and dramatically with King David. When he establishes Jerusalem as the political and religious capital of Israel, the tabernacle and the ark of the covenant go from being portable, mobile worship sites to being stationary, established worship venues. Interestingly, David leaves the Mosaic tabernacle itself in Gibeon (1 Chr 16:39–43), and puts the ark in a newly constructed tabernacle in Jerusalem (1 Chr 15:1); the sacrifices continue (only) in Gibeon, and there is some musical worship there too (1 Chr 16:40–42), but Jerusalem becomes the doxological center of the nation, where daily praises as well as the nation's festivals are celebrated.

And David enriches those celebrations with a huge overhaul of the practice of public worship, most notably by assigning and organizing whole ranks of Levites to be full-time musical ministers, as singers and as instrumentalists, in the service of the people's worship. See especially chapters 15, 16, 23 and 25 of 1 Chronicles for descriptions of these developments.

> Then [David] appointed some of the Levites as ministers before the ark of the LORD, to invoke, to thank, and to praise the LORD, the God of Israel. Asaph was the chief, and second to him were Zechariah, Jeiel, Shemiramoth, Jehiel, Mattithiah, Eliab, Benaiah, Obed-edom, and Jeiel, who were to play harps and lyres; Asaph was to sound the cymbals, and Benaiah and Jahaziel the priests were to blow trumpets regularly before the ark of the covenant of God. Then on that day David first appointed that thanksgiving be sung to the LORD by Asaph and his brothers. (1 Chr 16:4–7)

---

4. This is the astute observation of Peter Leithart in *From Silence to Song*, 14, 54.

What gave David the right to tinker with and expand the Mosaic directives for Israel's worship? Leithart shows from 2 Chronicles 29:25 (at the later time of Hezekiah) that David had received some sort of revelation from the Lord to that effect, so that his expansive recasting of the Mosaic system was divinely inspired and sanctioned:

> And [Hezekiah] stationed the Levites in the house of the LORD with cymbals, harps, and lyres, according to the commandment of David and of Gad the king's seer and of Nathan the prophet, *for the commandment was from the Lord through his prophets.* (2 Chr 29:25)

The grandeur of David's worship reforms had huge implications not only for Israel, but also for the church up to our present day. For, as Leithart points out, "when Christians sing hymns and psalms in worship, when we play organs or pianos, guitars or trumpets, we are heirs of David's 'liturgical revolution.'"[5]

2. David was a tremendous example of a true worshiper

David was, of course, far from being a perfect man. He committed some serious sins in his life, with far-reaching consequences. And yet the overwhelming orientation of his life was that—whether he was going through good times (see Ps 23) or hard times (see Ps 63)—David knew *the answer was always God*. The Lord referred to him as "a man after his own heart" (1 Sam 13:14)—because he would turn to God, no matter what the circumstances.

We see a powerful example of this in Psalm 63. Our Bibles call this "A Psalm of David, when he was in the wilderness of Judah," referring to the time later in his life when his son Absalom rebelled against him, causing him to flee for his life to the desert. There David sees his bare and parched surroundings as an illustration to him of a life without God; and his heart cries out with longing for God and for the joy of his presence.

> O God, you are my God; earnestly I seek you;
> my soul thirsts for you;
> my flesh faints for you,
> as in a dry and weary land where there is no water. (Ps 63:1)

---

5. Leithart, *From Silence to Song*, 15.

In worldly terms, David has lost it all: his family, his throne, his reputation, his security. He is on the run, far from the tabernacle and the palace, in the dry, barren, dusty desert where he can take no creature comforts for granted. Yet, as Spurgeon put it, "There was no desert in his heart, though there was a desert around him."[6] Perowne similarly writes:

> It is remarkable that in this Psalm . . . there is no petition. There is gladness, there is praise, there is the most exalted communion with God, there is longing for His presence as the highest of all blessings; but there is not one word of asking for temporal, or even for spiritual good.[7]

David gives us this beautiful expression of a man thoroughly saturated with love and longing for God. He says in effect: "It's not water I need, not the comfort of my palace, not even the refuge of the tabernacle. I need God!" Though his life is in danger, he confesses to God in verse 3 that "your steadfast love [*ḥesed*] is *better than life.*"

Far from Jerusalem and hence removed from any possibility of fulfilling any of the Mosaic instructions for worship, David doesn't seek to perform a religious or ceremonial duty. Instead, he opens his heart to God, thirsts and yearns for him, and praises and worships him from his heart. As such he is a model for us of a true worshiper.

3. David was a composer of many songs for corporate worship

David, a musician himself, wrote many songs for use in private and public worship (including at least seventy-three of the psalms). Many of these texts we still set to music and use in worship.

King Solomon and the Temple

David's son Solomon built the temple in Jerusalem after the basic structure of the tabernacle, only it was much richer in its design and materials. When it was completed and the ark of the covenant was brought into the holy of holies, we read that, as had happened at the completion of the tabernacle (Exod 40:34), "the glory of the LORD filled the temple" (2

---

6. Spurgeon, *Treasury of David*, on Psalm 63:1.

7. Perowne, *Book of Psalms*, 505.

Chr 7:1). As with the tabernacle, this signified God's continuing presence among his people.

The temple in Jerusalem was one of the most ornate and beautiful buildings of its day, dedicated to the worship of the God of glory (1 Kgs 8:27–29). The rituals and the ceremonies were even more elaborate than at the tabernacle, building upon David's reforms of Israel's worship and his expansion of the musical component.

The Downward Spiral of Idolatry

Under Solomon's son Rehoboam, the kingdom split into northern and southern kingdoms. Idolatry got worse and worse. Finally, the Northern Kingdom was conquered by the Assyrians and disappeared from history. The Southern Kingdom lasted a little longer, with occasional revivals, notably under Hezekiah (2 Kgs 18–19) and Josiah (2 Kgs 22–23); but it likewise got worse and worse until God sent them into exile too.

In the books of 1 and 2 Kings and 1 and 2 Chronicles, when the writers talk about the different rulers of the Northern and Southern Kingdoms, the reign of each king is always evaluated *according to his worship*. For example:

> In the third year of Hoshea son of Elah, king of Israel, Hezekiah the son of Ahaz, king of Judah, began to reign. . . . And *he did what was right in the eyes of the* LORD, according to all that David his father had done. He removed the high places and broke the pillars and cut down the Asherah. (2 Kgs 18:1–3)

> Manasseh . . . reigned fifty-five years in Jerusalem. And *he did what was evil in the sight of the* LORD, according to the abominations of the nations whom the LORD drove out before the people of Israel. (2 Chr 33:1–2)

Doing *"right in the sight of the Lord"* meant that the king *worshiped God rightly*, and led the people in doing that also. Doing *"evil in the sight of the Lord"* meant that he *fell into idolatry*, and led the people down that path as well. So every king is evaluated *according to his worship*: It was his *worship* that made his reign successful or unsuccessful. When his worship was right, the nation's worship was right. When his worship was wrong, the nation's worship was wrong.

Also during this period we have the ministry of many of the prophets, calling the people to repentance and/or warning of impending judgment.

> The LORD, the God of their fathers, sent persistently to them by his messengers, because he had compassion on his people and on his dwelling place. But they kept mocking the messengers of God, despising his words and scoffing at his prophets, until the wrath of the LORD rose against his people, until there was no remedy. (2 Chr 36:15–16)

Israel's fate as a nation always followed its worship.

For Reflection and/or Discussion

What do the cycles in Israel's history tell you about human nature?

15

WORSHIP IN OLD TESTAMENT HISTORY: Exilic and Post-Exilic Israel

Exilic Worship

The Destruction of Jerusalem and the Temple

God allows the Southern Kingdom to be sent into exile at the hands of the Babylonians, and Jerusalem is destroyed in 586 BC (see 2 Chr 36:17–20).

The temple, one of the most magnificent buildings in the world, built by Solomon for the worship of God, is destroyed. God allows the building that was built for his praise to be razed. And why? Because God did not care about a building if he didn't have the *hearts* of the people.

As we have seen, the testimony of this tragic state of affairs would be:

> And many nations will pass by this city, and every man will say to his neighbor, "why has the LORD dealt thus with this great city?" And they will answer, "Because they have forsaken the covenant of the LORD their God and worshiped other gods and served them." (Jer 22:8–9)

God had made a covenant with his people, and promised his presence among them and a special relationship with them. And in response he asked for their worship: exclusive, wholehearted, faithful worship. Yet they often would turn away to idolatry; and after many cycles of discipline/repentance/restoration/true worship/renewed idolatry (and enduring patience and *ḥesed* on God's part), as we have seen, God finally sends his people into exile.

The glory of God had filled the holy of holies in the tabernacle (Exod 40:34) and later the temple (2 Chr 7:1–3), signifying God's gracious presence among his people. After the exile, Ezekiel sees a tragic vision of God's glory leaving the temple and then departing from Jerusalem (Ezek 10:15–19; 11:22–25). Thus far have the people fallen: they have lost God's special presence among them.

Exilic Worship in the Synagogue

Exiled to Babylon, the people had no temple, and thus no way to participate in the sacrificial worship God had established. But they would still gather in smaller groups for worship. Many biblical scholars consider this to be the origin of the Jewish *synagogue*.

> The focus shifted from animal sacrifices, which could only be properly performed at the Temple, to the study and teaching of the Torah—the Jewish Bible—which became the focal point of worship in the synagogues.[1]

In these meetings, the great *Shema* ("Hear, O Israel: The LORD our God, the LORD is one . . ." [Deut 6:3]) would be recited, and prayers would be lifted up to God. And, significantly, the Law ("Torah") would be read aloud, after which *someone would expound on the meaning of the text read*.

This exposition of the word of God would have enormous implications for the future, continuing in synagogue observances for centuries and into New Testament times; and it then became a model and foundation for Christian preaching, as it extended its influence into the ministry of Jesus Christ, into Paul's missionary activities, and into the regular ministry of the church (see Luke 4:16–21; Acts 2:42; 13:16–41; 14:1; 17:2–3, 17; 18:4, 19; 19:8; Rom 10:14–15; 2 Tim 4:2). So this aspect of exilic worship had a profound effect on Christian worship.

---

1. Markey, "What Effects Did the Babylonian Exile Have on the Jewish Religion?"

Post-Exilic Worship

The Rebuilding and Restoration

God allowed his exiled people to return to Jerusalem after seventy years of captivity (2 Chr 36:20–23). The story of rebuilding the walls and the buildings of Jerusalem and the temple is related in the books of Ezra, Nehemiah, and Haggai.

After the rebuilding of the temple, the priesthood and sacrificial system were reinstituted. However, sadly, we never read about the glory of God filling this new temple (as it had the tabernacle and the first temple). The next time we read of the glory of God dwelling in the midst of his people is *in the person of Jesus Christ*:

> And the Word became flesh and *dwelt among us*, and we have seen *his glory*, glory as of the only Son from the Father, full of grace and truth. (John 1:14)

Importantly, the synagogue system continued even after temple worship was resumed. Both of these will later influence Christian worship.

The Development of Traditions and Legalism

During the rest of the period leading up to the New Testament, the Jewish leaders developed a complex system of traditions, rules, and regulations superimposed on the Mosaic law. Jesus would decry this system of rules because, as he put it, they were "'teaching as doctrines the commandments of men.' . . . And he said to them, 'You have a fine way of rejecting the commandment of God in order to establish your tradition!'" (Mark 7:7b, 9). As a result, Jesus said, their worship was "in vain" (Mark 7:7a).

The law itself was not the problem, but rather all that was presumptuously added to it by the Jewish leaders. Jesus said, "Do not think that I have come to abolish the Law or the Prophets; I have not come to abolish them but to fulfill them" (Matt 5:17). But to do so he had to clear away the tangled brush that had been allowed to grow around the law and choke out its spiritual intent.

The Sabbath observance, itself commanded in the law, bore much of the brunt of the Jewish leaders' heavy-handed regulations. They specified thirty-nine different activities that they claimed amounted to "work" and were therefore forbidden on the Sabbath. For example:

> On a Sabbath, while [Jesus] was going through the grainfields, his disciples plucked and ate some heads of grain, rubbing them in their hands. But some of the Pharisees said, "Why are you doing what is not lawful to do on the Sabbath?" (Luke 6:1–2)

The Pharisees considered this to be an act of "threshing."

Jesus detested this sort of legalistic pickiness, as it missed the whole point of the observance:

> And he said to them, "The Sabbath was made for man, not man for the Sabbath. So the Son of Man is lord even of the Sabbath." (Mark 2:27–28)

The rules for Sabbath-keeping were so minute and burdensome that the conscientious Jew would be so concerned about transgressing one of these small matters that the day could no longer be restful! As a result, its intended purpose—that of being a day of rest and worship that was "made for man"—would be thwarted.

The entire system piled a heavy burden of legalism upon the people, as Jesus would complain about the scribes and Pharisees:

> They tie up heavy burdens, hard to bear, and lay them on people's shoulders. (Matt 23:4)

Jesus came to relieve the people of this kind of unnecessary burden, as he expressed in his beautiful invitation:

> Come to me, all who labor and are heavy laden, and I will give you *rest*. Take *my* yoke upon you, and learn from me, for I am gentle and lowly in heart, and you will find rest for your souls. For my yoke is easy, and my burden is light. (Matt 11:28–30)

Four Hundred Years of Silence

After the close of the book of Malachi, there is no more revelation from God for four hundred years. The *next direct word from God* that Israel receives is when the angel Gabriel appears to Zechariah in the temple in Luke 1 and foretells the birth of John the Baptist. God is moving again among his people, and events quickly escalate from that point on as the coming of Christ approaches.

Key Worship Takeaways from Old Testament History

Worship was always in *response* to God's gracious initiative in *revealing* himself and acting on behalf of his people.

1. God's priority in worship was always the *heart*.

2. God's *ḥesed* (loyal love) was the defining characteristic in all his dealings with his covenant people.

3. The entire Mosaic system was only a preparation for and "a shadow of the good things to come" (Heb 10:1).

4. A big part of this preparation was the indisputable demonstration of the inability (and unwillingness) of the human heart to obey and worship God as he deserved (Exod 24:3).

5. In this way, the need was made clear for a "new covenant," through which God was to provide divine enablement for living by writing his law on the people's hearts and putting his Holy Spirit within them (Jer 31:33; Ezek 36:27).

6. Thus God prepared to bring his Son into the world, to fulfill the law as the great Sacrifice to which it pointed; and to show the way, and be the means, of true worship.

> God does not care about a building if he does not have the hearts of the people.

For Reflection and/or Discussion

What are some examples of legalism you see in the church today? In your personal life?

16

THE PSALMS:
Israel's Worship Book . . . and Ours

We cannot leave our study of worship in the Old Testament without a closer look at the book of Psalms. It is the great worship book of the Old Testament, and a marvelous gift to the people of God of all ages. Martin Luther wrote of the Psalms: "If my purpose were to choose the best of all the edificatory books . . . my choice would inevitably fall on our present book."[1]

The Uniqueness of the Psalms

A very important understanding of the Psalms comes from the early church:

> It is reported that Athanasius, an outstanding Christian leader of the fourth century, declared that the Psalms have a unique place in the Bible because most of Scripture speaks *to us*, while the Psalms speak *for us*.[2]

The Psalms can help give expression to our feelings, needs, and prayers in a unique way. They address honestly and directly before God all types of

---

1. Luther, "1528 Preface to the Psalms," 37.
2. Anderson, *Out of the Depths*, x (emphasis added).

life situations, both good and bad. "Psalms are the language we use when we need a voice other than our own."[3]

The Focus Point of the Psalms

Psalms 146–50 all begin and end the same way: with "Praise the LORD!"—or in Hebrew, *Hallelujah!* The Hebrew is actually two words, *Hallelu-Yah*: *Hallelu* is a plural command, "praise"; and *Yah* is a shortened form of the name of God *Yahweh*. We often use "Hallelujah" as an exclamation of praise, but actually it is a *command* to all of God's people: a command to "praise the LORD."

This Hebrew word for "praise" is actually used thirteen times in Psalm 150 (at least twice in every verse); and as such this psalm serves as a sort of exclamation point concluding the entire book of Psalms, and summarizes the call of the entire book to "Praise the LORD!"[4]

> Let *everything* that has breath praise the LORD. Praise the LORD!
> (Ps 150:6)[5]

The Authors of the Psalms

The Psalms are a collection of a number of different writers. Seventy-three of the psalms are attributed to David in their titles. Other authors identified are: Asaph (twelve); Sons of Korah (eleven); Solomon (two);

---

3. Plantinga and Rozeboom, eds., *Discerning the Spirits*, 160.

4. Surprisingly, the Psalms say little about animal sacrifices. Rather there is the preponderant emphasis on *heart worship* (which, as we have seen, needed to underlie acceptable sacrifice anyway). *From the Field*: I was teaching at a conference in Nepal. My translator was the head of the ministry sponsoring the conference, and his name was Anugraha. As he was translating my lectures, I often heard him say "Anugraha." I thought it was pretty strange that he would bring his own name in so often—until I learned that *anugraha* is Nepali for "praise"!

5. "The title of the book of Psalms in Hebrew is *Tehillim*, 'praises.' This is so even though the largest single category of psalms are the psalms of lament. Praise in the Old Testament was not just about being happy and thankful but about acknowledging the reality of the one living God in the whole of life—including the tough times. So even in those psalms which are mostly in a troubled mode, there is a movement toward praise. Even the whole book of Psalms moves from the predominant lament and petitionary psalms in the early sections to the almost complete dominance of praise in the final section" (Wright, *Mission of God*, 132).

Moses (one); Hernan (one); and Ethan (one). The authors of forty-nine of the psalms are not identified.

The Content of the Psalms

Some psalms were intended for private worship, and some for public worship. The various types of psalms have been classified according to their characteristics and forms:

- Salvation History psalms (trace God's faithfulness in the history of Israel)
- Laments (Community and Individual)
- Songs of Thanksgiving
- Hymns of Praise
- Festival Songs and Liturgies
- Songs of Trust and Meditation[6]

In addition, we have David's psalm of *confession*, Psalm 51 (after his sin with Bathsheba had been exposed):

> Have mercy on me, O God,
> according to your steadfast love;
> according to your abundant mercy
> blot out my transgressions. (51:1)

And then there is David's great psalm of *forgiveness* (after that sin had been confessed and forgiven):

> Blessed is the one whose transgression is forgiven,
> whose sin is covered. (32:1)

David's intensely personal psalm of trust and rest in the Lord, Psalm 23, has of course been appropriated by countless believers over the centuries:

> The Lord is my shepherd; I shall not want. (23:1)

In addition to these personal and private expressions, many other psalms have found an important place in the corporate praise of the church, for example:

> Make a joyful noise to the Lord, all the earth!

---

6. Anderson, *Out of the Depths*, 170–71.

Serve the Lord with gladness!
Come into his presence with singing! (100:1–2)

The wide variety of moods and emotions expressed in the Psalms makes it possible for believers to find a vehicle for their prayers in the different circumstances of life.[7]

The Tone of the Psalms

C. S. Lewis makes a fascinating observation about the psalmists' outlook on life and faith:

> I want to stress what I think that we (or at least I) need more [than instruction about sacrifice]: the joy and delight in God which meet us in the Psalms. . . . These poets knew far less reason than we for loving God. They did not know that he offered them eternal joy; still less that he would die to win it for them. Yet they express a longing for him, for his mere presence, which comes only to the best Christians or to Christians in their best moments. They long to live all their days in the Temple so that they may constantly see "the fair beauty of the Lord" (Ps 27:4). Their longing to go up to Jerusalem and "appear before the presence of God" is like a physical thirst (42). . . . Lacking that encounter with him, their souls are parched like a waterless countryside (63:1). They crave to be "satisfied with the pleasures" of his house (65:4). . . . One day of those "pleasures" is better than a lifetime spent elsewhere (84:11–12).
>
> I had rather—though the expression may seem harsh to some—call this the "appetite for God" than the "love of God."[8]

The Poetry of the Psalms

A defining characteristic of Hebrew poetry is its use of a kind of "rhyme" quite unlike what we are used to. Instead of rhyming the sounds at the end of lines, this poetry uses what we might call "concept rhyming": it uses

---

7. *From the Field:* Often in teaching this material, I would ask each class member to share his or her favorite psalm. It was always a rich time, as students shared about how a particular psalm had lifted them up at an important juncture in their life; and it was remarkable that just about every student would have a *different* favorite psalm!

8. Lewis, *Reflections on the Psalms*, 50–51. I heard a pastor add that these amazing expressions of trust and rest in the Lord came long before the invention of anesthetics!

content parallelism to compare and contrast lines of the text. Three main types of parallelism have been identified in the book of Psalms. They are:

1. *Synonymous parallelism*: the second line restates the content of the first line in a slightly different way

   > Therefore the wicked will not stand in the judgment,
   > nor sinners in the congregation of the righteous. (Ps 1:5)

2. *Antithetical parallelism*: the second line draws a contrast with the first line

   > For the LORD knows the way of the righteous,
   > but the way of the wicked will perish. (Ps 1:6)

3. *Synthetic parallelism*: the second line develops further the thought of the first line

   > As a father shows compassion to his children,
   > so the LORD shows compassion to those who fear him. (Ps 103:13)

A tremendous implication of this sort of poetry is that the parallelisms *can be translated effectively into any language*, in a way that would be impossible with sound rhyming. Thus God in his sovereignty made possible the beauty of this book to be made available to all the nations and cultures of the world!

The Balanced Perspective of the Psalms

We live in a day when in many churches, not to mention in society as a whole, people have sought to throw off what they consider to be outmoded and stifling formality, and have opted for more relaxed, informal forms, practices, dress, etc. The worship and music likewise reflect a more relational age, and the immanence of God is valued and invoked.

This is a healthy departure from a lifeless traditionalism where God is admired from afar but kept at a distance. Yet a more informal approach to worship should not degrade into a casual one. The Psalms give us a balance by showing us the exalted Lord of glory:

> O Lord, our Lord,
> how majestic is your name in all the earth! (Ps 8:1)

—but also giving glimpses of a deeply personal God:

> The Lord is *my* shepherd. (Ps 23:1)

Let us not forget in our worship that our God who has come close is still the transcendent One. He is close, but he is also glorified and holy. He is our friend, but he is also our Lord. We may come with confidence and joy, yet with reverence and awe. Let us boldly "draw near to the throne of grace" (Heb 4:16), but bow our knee to him who sits upon it.

How simply and powerfully the psalmist in 2:11 expresses the delicate balance between God's transcendence and immanence as we come to him in worship:

> *Rejoice . . . with trembling.*[9]

Hallelu-jah! Praise the Lord!

For Reflection and/or Discussion

What is your favorite psalm? Why?
What does it teach you about worship?

---

9. See Man, "Rejoice with Trembling."

Part 5

Worship in the New Testament

17. Similarities and Differences between Old and New Testament Worship
18. Important Themes in New Testament Worship
19. Significant New Testament Worship Passages: Gospels and Acts
20. Significant New Testament Worship Passages: Epistles
21. Eternal Praise: The Great Scenes of Worship in the Book of Revelation
22. Worship in the Book of Hebrews
23. The Holy Spirit and Worship
24. Jesus Christ and Worship

17

SIMILARITIES AND DIFFERENCES BETWEEN OLD AND NEW TESTAMENT WORSHIP

This is an interesting topic to reflect on. There are some profound continuities between the worship of the two Testaments, but also some crucial differences.

After reflection, refer to the footnote for some examples of these similarities and differences.[1]

Then, having considered both the many continuities *and* discontinuities between worship in the Old Testament and worship in the New,

1. *Similarities*
1. Same God (Creator)
2. Centrality of the glory of God
3. Worship as response to God's revelation
4. Importance of the Scriptures
5. God's gracious provision of redemption
6. Need for a mediator
7. Sacrifice/priesthood
8. Singing
9. Prayer
10. Giving

Differences
1. Many sacrifices/once-for-all sacrifice of Christ
2. Many priests/one high priest, mediator; priesthood of all believers
3. Animal sacrifices/spiritual, living sacrifices
4. Worship centrally located (tabernacle/temple)/worship no longer centralized
5. Indwelling Holy Spirit (under the new covenant)

you may want to listen to a chapel message given by Dr. Mark Bailey, the former president of Dallas Theological Seminary. In "Dispensational Expressions of Worship," he goes even further to detail biblically how the requirements and nature of worship have changed during different periods of biblical history.[2] Even those who do not hold to the dispensational system of biblical interpretation will find in this message many keen observations about how God's standards and expectations for worship have changed during the various epochs of the history of salvation.

Here is a summary of Dr. Bailey's main points in chart form:

	Time	*Place*	*Person*	*Sacrifice*
Pre-Law	any time	anywhere	anyone	different types
Law	prescribed (daily; feast)	only at tabernacle or temple	only the priests	prescribed
Now (John 4)	any time	anywhere; heavenly tabernacle	through Christ/ we are all priests	spiritual sacrifices, mediated through Christ (selves, praise, works, giving)
Millennium	1,000 years	restored temple	Christ as priest/ king in Jerusalem (Zech 6)	memorial sacrifices, feasts (Ezek 45)
Heaven	forever	God/Christ *are* the temple	angels and believers (Rev 4, 5, 6)	praise

> From more form to more freedom.

For Reflection and/or Discussion

What similarity between Old and New Testament worship
seems most profound to you?
What difference is most meaningful to you?

---

2. Mark Bailey, "Dispensational Expressions of Worship." A video of this message can be found on YouTube under the same title.

18

IMPORTANT THEMES IN NEW TESTAMENT WORSHIP

Theme: **Inward Worship**

John Piper zeroes in on this theme.

> What we find in the New Testament is an utterly stunning degree of indifference to worship as an outward form and an utterly radical intensification of worship as an inward experience of the heart.[1]

As we saw in chapter 9, the Samaritan woman at the well in John 4 asks Jesus to speak to the competing claims of legitimacy of the Jewish system of worship (in Jerusalem) and that of the Samaritans (on Mount Gerizim). Jesus pronounces that under the new regime he is inaugurating, place will no longer be the issue at all. It will no longer be a matter of *where* or *when* you worship, but *how* you worship. Worship must originate in one's "spirit," in the internal, immaterial part of a person, and must be in "truth," that is, according to God's revelation. The New Testament writers align themselves with Jesus' pronouncement about the priority of worship "in spirit," of worship from the *heart*.

However, we saw in the Old Testament that there too God placed priority on the worship of the heart. What then is distinctive about the New Testament? Quite simply, that under the old covenant heart worship

---

1. Piper, "Pursuit of God."

was demonstrated by one's obedient adherence to the stipulations of the tabernacle/temple system. But in the New Testament, that system having been done away with through the work of Christ, the outworking of heart worship is to take place in *all of life* rather than through a detailed prescription for public worship. That is the next theme.

Theme: **Whole-Life Worship**

As we also saw in chapter 9, the apostle Paul seems to build upon Jesus' declaration in John 4 that worship will be "*neither* in this mountain *nor* in Jerusalem . . . *but* in spirit and truth" (John 4:21, 23). Paul makes a logical application of Jesus' sense when he states in Romans 12:1 that our appropriate response ("therefore") to God for all that he has done for us and given to us in Christ ("by the mercies of God," as detailed in the first eleven chapters of the epistle) is "to present your bodies as a living sacrifice, holy and acceptable to God, which is your spiritual worship." In other words, since worship is not to be limited by time or place it should be all-pervasive: our whole lives as a grateful response to his magnificent grace. "You are not your own, for you were bought with a price. So glorify God in your body" (1 Cor 6:19–20).

For the believer, there is no secular place or pursuit, no separation of life into religious and nonreligious areas. *Every* time and *every* place is holy to the Lord. ("Whether you eat or drink, or whatever you do, do all to the glory of God" [1 Cor 10:31].)

The implications of this truth are profound for individual believers. It means that each one of us is responsible for a daily walk of worship that allows the presence and influence of God to pervade all our activities and projects and thoughts and dealings with others. We are "to do all to the glory of God" by living for him, and in his power. Worship is not to be confined to a morning quiet time or to a Sunday morning gathering.

Corporate worship is an event that builds upon, rather than replaces, the individual worship walks of the people. It is simply not fair to place on the shoulders of pastors or worship leaders the responsibility for "providing worship" for the people of God (still less for "leading them into the presence of God").

For churchgoers, a more relevant question than "What did I get out of the service today?" might well be "What did I bring to the service today?" When believers come with hearts brimming with gratitude and devotion from a week of walking with and worshiping God, our corporate worship can become, by the Spirit's enablement, something truly powerful, and more than the sum of its parts.

Theme: Freedom of Form

It is an amazing fact that the New Testament is virtually silent on the matter of form for the church's worship. John Piper makes this astonishing (but true) observation):

> There is no authorization in the New Testament for worship buildings, or worship dress, or worship times, or worship music, or worship liturgy or worship size or thirty-five-minute sermons, or Advent poems or choirs or instruments or candles .... Almost every worship tradition we have is culturally shaped rather than biblically commanded.[2]

This last sentence, however, does *not* mean that our worship traditions are wrong. After all, we do need to make many decisions about what worship in our churches is going to look like (in Piper's terms, about our buildings, our worship times, our worship music, the length of the service and the sermon, etc.). But the clear implication is that the New Testament's silence on so many of the details and the absence of specific commands means that we are allowed *considerable freedom* in the structuring of worship in our churches. Not *total* freedom, not "anything goes": there *are* biblical principles (such as we are seeing in this book) to guide us. But there is a considerable amount of flexibility. That explains the huge diversity of different worship forms and practices around the world and down through the centuries.

We will examine this subject in more detail in chapter 28, as we consider its implications for the intersection of worship and culture.

Theme: Access

The old covenant system of worship, despite its gracious provisions for relating to the covenant-keeping God of Israel (through a temporary covering of sin [Rom 3:24–25] in anticipation of Christ's atoning work), nevertheless was a system that demonstrated strongly the distance that

---

2. Piper, "Our High Priest Is the Son of God Perfect Forever."

sin had put between God and even his own chosen people. Access to the presence of God (represented in the architecture of the tabernacle/temple) was severely proscribed. The common people were allowed to enter only the courtyard of the tabernacle/temple; one had to be a priest to enter the holy place; and entry into the holy of holies was reserved for the high priest alone, who himself could enter only once a year, on the Day of Atonement (see Lev 16).

The book of Hebrews clearly demonstrates how all the barriers of the old covenant system were destroyed, and "the new and living way" into the presence of God made fully available, by the redeeming death of Christ on the cross:

> Therefore, brethren, since we have confidence to enter the holy places by the blood of Jesus, by the new and living way that he opened for us through the curtain . . . let us draw near with a true heart in full assurance of faith. (Heb 10:19–22)

That opening was powerfully dramatized by the tearing of the veil in the Jerusalem temple (the one barring access into the holy of holies, i.e., into the presence of God) at the precise moment of Christ's death (Matt 27:51; Mark 15:38; Luke 23:45). The barrier of sin was removed by the perfect sacrifice of Christ.

Christ died, and reigns, to make this access possible:

> For Christ also suffered once for sins, the righteous for the unrighteous, that he might bring us to God. (1 Pet 3:18)

> Let us then with confidence draw near to the throne of grace, that we may receive mercy and find grace to help in time of need. (Heb 4:16)

Every new covenant believer has direct access into God's presence through Christ.

> One of the great distinctives and privileges of New Testament worship is the direct access every believer has into the presence of God through Christ.

For Reflection and/or Discussion

Does the freedom of form in worship allowed by the New Testament concern you? Excite you? Why?

19

SIGNIFICANT NEW TESTAMENT WORSHIP PASSAGES: Gospels and Acts

The Rest of Worship (Matt 11:28–30)

As we saw at the end of chapter 15, during the intertestamental period the Jewish leaders added to the Mosaic law many additional rules and regulations—legalistic provisions about Sabbath observances and numerous other aspects of religious and daily life. Jesus had no tolerance for this.

> "The scribes and the Pharisees . . . tie up heavy burdens, hard to bear, and lay them on people's shoulders." (Matt 23:2, 4)

Jesus came to extend grace, rest, and release from spiritual burdens and strivings.

> "Come to me, all who labor and are heavy laden, and I will give you *rest*. Take my yoke upon you, and learn from me, for I am gentle and lowly in heart, and you will find *rest* for your souls. For my yoke is easy, and my burden is light." (Matt 11:28–30)

Because of the finished work of Christ, we can rest in God's unmerited favor, and offer God our thanksgiving and praise with wonder, joy, freedom, and assurance. We do not need to worry about whether our worship is "good enough." When we come in and through and, indeed, *with* Christ, the Father is *always* pleased with our worship, because he is always pleased with his *Son*. (Much more on this in chapter 24.) Hence *worship is not a work*, not something by which we strive to make ourselves somehow acceptable to the Father. The great work has been done!

Seeing Things God's Way (Mark 12:28–34)

The scribes and Pharisees were the object of Jesus' most scathing denunciations (see the whole of Matt 23; Mark 12:38–40). Jesus condemns them especially for the *externality* of their religion: practicing their rites for public view (Matt 6:1–6; 23:27–28). And they are also often seen in the Gospels trying to criticize, entrap, or trick Jesus (see Mark 12:13), and turn the people away from him (though Jesus invariably turns the tables on them!).

But in this account we see a rarity: a scribe coming to Jesus with an honest question, and with a spiritual perspective that Jesus himself commends.

> And one of the scribes came up and heard them disputing with one another, and seeing that he answered them well, asked him, "Which commandment is the most important of all?" Jesus answered, "The most important is, 'Hear, O Israel: The Lord our God, the Lord is one. And you shall love the Lord your God with all your heart and with all your soul and with all your mind and with all your strength.' The second is this: 'You shall love your neighbor as yourself.' There is no other commandment greater than these." And the scribe said to him, "You are right, Teacher." (Mark 12:28–32a)

In some ways, the scribe's reply is quite humorous: *of course* he's right—he's *Jesus*!

At any rate, the scribe is not taken aback by Jesus' answer (as so often the Jewish leaders were by his responses), but rather fully endorses Jesus' point of view. And then the scribe goes on to add this profound commentary on the significance of the two Great Commandments that Jesus has just cited:

> "You have truly said that he is one, and there is no other besides him. And to love him with all the heart and with all the understanding and with all the strength, and to love one's neighbor as oneself, is *much more* than all whole burnt offerings and sacrifices." (Mark 12:32b–33)

Jesus then commends the scribe's deep spiritual understanding:

> And when Jesus saw that he answered wisely, he said to him, "You are not far from the kingdom of God." (Mark 12:34)

What a commendation indeed! Why is the scribe not far from the kingdom? Because the scribe is *looking at things the way God does*; he has a spiritual perspective in keeping with kingdom values. He sees the spiritual priority of love for God and for neighbor over all outward expressions of worship.

One could only wish Mark had told us what happened with the scribe, whether in fact he became a believer in and follower of Jesus. It seems likely, because of the spiritual trajectory he was already on, which Jesus himself identifies. This is surely a sign that the Holy Spirit was already at work in his heart, teaching him this most important of spiritual realities.

Lavish Worship (Mark 14:3–9)

An alabaster flask of ointment of pure nard.

This beautiful account is framed by signs of the mounting opposition to Jesus during the last week of his earthly life, both from without:

> It was now two days before the Passover and the Feast of Unleavened Bread. And the chief priests and the scribes were seeking how to arrest him by stealth and kill him. (Mark 14:1)

—and even from within the band of disciples:

> Then Judas Iscariot, who was one of the twelve, went to the chief priests in order to betray him to them. (Mark 14:10)

Against that backdrop of hostility and treachery, Mark recounts an incident of striking contrast, a beam of light that shines all the brighter for the growing darkness surrounding it. It is the account of a remarkable act of love and worship. As G. Campbell Morgan wrote, "There was He, in a dark and desolate land; and lo! out of the heart of a woman, a spring of fresh water sprung for the thirsty Christ! He valued it."[1]

Action (14:3)

> And while he was at Bethany in the house of Simon the leper, as he was reclining at table, a woman[2] came with an alabaster flask of ointment of pure nard, very costly, and she broke the flask and poured it over his head. (Mark 14:3)

Reaction (14:4–9)

"Some"

> There were some who said to themselves indignantly, "Why was the ointment wasted like that? For this ointment could have been sold for more than three hundred denarii and given to the poor." And they scolded her. (Mark 14:4–5)

Matthew 26:8 identifies these as the disciples, and John 12:4–5 even zeroes in on Judas as the spokesman.

Jesus

Jesus' response was quite different:

> But Jesus said, "Leave her alone. Why do you trouble her? She has done a beautiful thing to me. For you always have the poor with you, and whenever you want, you can do good for them. But you will not always have me. She has done what she could; she has anointed my body beforehand for burial. And truly, I say

---

1. Morgan, *Gospel According to Mark*, 290.
2. This incident is found in all four Gospels. In Luke 7:37, the woman is termed "a sinner," while John 12:3 identifies her as Mary, the sister of Martha and Lazarus.

to you, wherever the gospel is proclaimed in the whole world, what she has done will be told in memory of her." (Mark 14:6–9)

Far from seeing Mary's act as wasteful or inappropriate, he commends her and her instinctive act of selfless devotion. He calls it a "beautiful thing." Mary had a unique opportunity to serve the Lord and express her love for him—and she took full advantage of it. She didn't spend a week praying about it or seeking God's will. She did "what she could"—literally, Jesus is saying, "what she had, she did"—and he rejoiced in her spontaneous display of devotion.

Jesus adds that Mary's act had a far deeper significance than even she realized, as she "anointed my body for burial." God rewarded her faithfulness with a very special place in the unfolding story of redemption, and a continuing role as well: "wherever the gospel is proclaimed in the whole world, what she has done will be told in memory of her." And so we fulfill Jesus' words and honor her every time this story is related (including as you read it right now!) about one who gave her best, from the heart, for her Lord.

A Worthy Example

We need to not only honor Mary, but to follow her example. It would have fulfilled all the demands of Middle Eastern hospitality for Mary to have anointed the head of Jesus with a few drops of the precious ointment. But her heart was so full of adoration that she just gave it all. She broke the bottle, and poured it all out. She held nothing back.

Undoubtedly Mary's act of total commitment and love meant so much to Jesus because it was itself so *Christlike*—it was suggestive of what *he* was about to do: to allow himself to be "broken and spilled out" for the sins of the world. What *he* had, he did: he gave of himself fully for the salvation of humanity. He held nothing back.

And Mary's act also was a faint reflection of what the Father *himself* was about to do: to give the very best *he* had—*his only Son*—for the salvation of the world (John 3:16).

A Lavish Gift of Worship

Mary's act was, above all, an act of *worship*. The disciples thought it was a wasteful expression, and in a certain sense that's true. Worship doesn't produce much that is tangible. But it is worship that puts *everything else* in its proper perspective. And so Marva Dawn calls worship a *"royal waste of time."*[3] Worship allows us to let God take his proper place as King over our lives.

God has lavished his grace upon us (Eph 1:7–8) and deserves a lavish response of worship in return. How few of us are fit to stand with Mary! Are we more like the disciples, with their haughty composure and stale moderation? What Mary had, she did. Hers was a heart brimming with grateful devotion, and she gave her very best.

May we learn to live like her, give like her, worship like her!

The Priority of Heart Worship (Luke 21:1–4)

(Please see the treatment of this passage in chapter 12.)

Worship in Spirit and Truth (John 4:19–26)

(Please see the treatment of this key passage in chapter 9.)

Ascended on High (Luke 24:50–51; Acts 1:9–11)

> And [Jesus] led them out as far as Bethany, and lifting up his hands he blessed them. While he blessed them, he parted from them and was carried up into heaven. (Luke 24:50–51)

The ascension of Jesus Christ is too quickly skipped over (or ignored) in many churches. Yet it is an event with enormous implications for our lives and for the life of the church. The implications of Jesus' ascension include:

- Jesus has been exalted and has taken his place of *rulership* at his Father's right hand (1 Tim 3:16; Col 3:1; Eph 1:20–21).
- Jesus serves now as our *Advocate and Intercessor* in the Father's presence (1 John 2:1; Heb 7:25).

---

3. Dawn, *Royal Waste of Time*.

- For the first time, *humanity dwells in the Father's presence* in heaven, guaranteeing that we will also follow Jesus there one day (John 14:2–3; 1 Cor 15:23).
- Jesus went and sent the *Holy Spirit* to dwell in us and with us (John 7:39; 16:7).
- Christ our Mediator in his continuing humanity and eternal priesthood (1 Tim 2:5; Heb 4:14, 15; 5:6; 6:20; 7:17, 21; 8:1; 10:21) serves the heavenly tabernacle (Heb 8:1–2) and actively *leads his people into the Father's presence in worship* (Heb 2:12; 10:19–22).

This last truth is the most important for our purposes here, and will be developed much more fully in chapter 24.

> The ascension is the foundation of the Bible's theology of worship. . . .
> The God whom we meet in worship and whom we serve in all our lives is the risen, ascended, exalted, and glorified Lord Jesus Christ who reigns over all. . . . In the specific context of corporate worship, it implies that public liturgy must maintain elements of grandeur and majesty fitting for the King of Kings and Lord of Lords, for the one who calls us and leads us in worship is none other than the resurrected and ascended Lord of glory.[4]

The Worship of the Earliest Church (Acts 2:42–47)

(Please see the treatment of this passage in chapters 27 and 28.)

> "You shall worship the Lord your God, and him *only* shall you serve." (Matt 4:10)

For Reflection and/or Discussion

Are you inspired by the worship of the woman with the alabaster vial in Mark 14?

---

4. Farley, "Jesus' Ascension," 2–3. For more helpful resources on the ascension, see Calvin Institute of Christian Worship, "Ascension Resource Guide"; Milligan, *Ascension and Heavenly Priesthood*; Atkins, *Ascension Now*; and Dawson, *Jesus Ascended*.

20

SIGNIFICANT NEW TESTAMENT WORSHIP PASSAGES: Epistles

Worship and the Fall (Romans 1:20–25)

(Please see the treatment of this key passage in chapter 6, and a fuller exposition in Ron Man, "False and True Worship.")

Paul's Doxology (Romans 11:33–36)

Paul's explanation in Romans of the ramifications of the fall (1:18–32) and the ensuing darkness of sin that has engulfed the human race (3:9-18, 23) makes the gospel shine all the more brightly as he expounds on it in the ensuing chapters. He shows how the gospel is indeed "the power of God for salvation to everyone who believes" (1:16), for through it God has showered upon believers:

- The righteousness of God through faith in Jesus Christ (3:22; 5:19)
- Justification by his grace as a gift (3:24, 26; 4:5; 5:1)
- Redemption (3:24)
- Propitiation (3:25)
- Peace with God (5:1)

- Grace (5:2; 5:15)
- Reconciliation (5:11)
- Salvation as a free gift (5:17; 6:23)
- Life (5:18)
- Eternal life (5:21)
- Newness of life (6:4)
- Resurrection life (6:5)
- Deliverance from condemnation (8:1)
- Life in the Spirit (8:1–11)
- Adoption (8:15)
- Mercy (11:30)

Paul also expounds in chapters 9–11 on the mystery of God's purposes for Israel and the gentiles, and how his grace, mercy, and sovereignty infuse these purposes as well.

After this profound theological treatise in chapters 1–11 on the gospel and God's work in the world (and before turning to practical applications in chapters 12–16), Paul bursts forth in praise to the wise and utterly sovereign God whose ways he has been privileged to plumb so profoundly:

> Oh, the depth of the riches and wisdom and knowledge of God! How unsearchable are his judgments and how inscrutable his ways!
> "For who has known the mind of the Lord,
> or who has been his counselor?
> Or who has given a gift to him that he might be repaid?"
> For from him and through him and to him are all things.[1] To him be glory forever. Amen (11:33–36).

Paul has turned from *theology* to *doxology*, and shown us the intimate and necessary connection between the two. As the late John Stott eloquently put it (partially cited already in chapter 3):

> Theology (our belief about God) and doxology (our worship of God) should never be separated. On the one hand, there can be *no doxology without theology*. . . . All true worship is a response

---

[1] "God created the world, holds it in existence, and governs all of it for his purposes" (Piper, *Providence*, 698).

> to the self-revelation of God in Christ and Scripture.... It was the tremendous truths of Romans 1–11 which provoked Paul's outburst of praise in verses 33–36 of chapter 11....
>
> On the other hand, there should be *no theology without doxology*. There is something fundamentally flawed about a purely academic interest in God. God is not an appropriate object for cool, critical, detached, scientific observation and evaluation. No, the true knowledge of God will always lead us to worship, as it did Paul. Our place is on our faces before him in adoration.
>
> As I believe Bishop Handley Moule said at the end of the last century, we must "beware equally of an undevotional theology and of an untheological devotion."[2]

After the most profound theological exposition ever written, Paul bows the knee in faith and love, and breathlessly exclaims that "from him and through him and to him are all things. To him be glory forever. Amen" (11:36).

Lifestyle Worship (Romans 12:1)

(Please see the treatment of this key passage in chapter 9.)

Worship for and from the Nations (Romans 15:8–12)

> For I tell you that Christ became a servant to the circumcised to show God's truthfulness, in order to confirm the promises given to the patriarchs, and in order that the Gentiles might glorify God for his mercy (15:8–9a).

John Piper offers an important perspective on this passage, and on God's purposes for the nations in general.

> The aim of the gospel among the nations is not man-centered. Paul does not say, "Christ became a servant in order that the Gentiles might *receive* mercy." He says, "Christ became a servant in order that the Gentiles might *glorify God* for receiving mercy."
>
> The ultimate aim of the gospel is God.... Don't fall short of the ultimate aim when you preach the gospel.... Offer them

---

2. Stott, *Romans*, 311–12.

the greatest gift: a merciful God, and that God glorified for his mercy. . . .

This is the essence of worship: heartfelt, hope-filled joy in the God of mercy overflowing in fitting outward expressions. . . . When we call the nations to worship the true God in Christ, that is what we call them to.[3]

"In remembrance of me": The Lord's Supper (1 Corinthians 11:23–26)

(Please see the treatment of the Lord's Supper in chapter 27.)

"Decently and in Order": The Gathering (1 Corinthians 14)

Priorities

As pointed out previously, there is precious little in the New Testament by way of specific instructions about how to practice corporate worship in the church. Of the little that one does find, most of it has to do with Paul correcting abuses or imbalances. Such is the case in 1 Corinthians 14. Here we have Paul giving preference to love (v. 1), spirit and mind (v. 15), and peace (v. 33)—as well as setting as priorities for the assembly: prophecy over tongues (vv. 2–5, 19, 23–25), church edification over self-edification (vv. 4, 5b, 12, 26, 31), intelligibility over unintelligibility (vv. 9–11, 16–17, 19), and order over confusion (vv. 27–31, 33, 40).

The Needed Balance

N. T. Wright speaks helpfully to the balance Paul is calling for:

> I am innately suspicious of one standard reading of this passage [1 Corinthians 14], that which discovers here a priority of free-form, non-liturgical worship as the genuine Spirit-led phenomenon as opposed to liturgical or set forms, deemed to be less fully spiritual. . . . Of course, the passage does indeed give us a picture of the early worshipping church as enjoying considerable freedom; Paul's arguments against chaotic worship would

---

3. Piper, "Gospel Worship."

be irrelevant unless there was an openness to fresh revelations of the Spirit which could in principle lapse into complete disorder. But his argument for unity despite diversity of gifts in chapter 12 . . . , and his argument for order rather than chaos in chapter 14, indicate as well that as far as he is concerned genuine Spirit-led worship will have framework and body to it, not just free-floating and unstructured outbursts of praise and prayer. . . . The order he envisages is an order within which all sorts of new and unexpected things can and should happen. But we should also note the emphasis on mission: one of the key criteria for authentic worship will be that if an outsider enters, he or she will be confronted, not with chaos and apparent gibberish, but with the clear and convicting message of the gospel [vv. 25–26].[4]

"Yes" and "Amen": God's Program in Two Words (2 Corinthians 1:20)

The Gospel in Miniature

Nestled in the opening strains of Paul's second epistle to the Corinthians is a statement that plumbs the depths of God's redemptive work through Christ and the relationship with him that we enjoy because of it:

"Yes!"

For all the promises of God find their Yes in him [Christ]. (1:20a)

The promises inherent in God's creation of humans in his image for fellowship with himself, and the promises extended to fallen humans in the messianic and redemptive prophecies of the Old Testament: all of these promises find their fulfillment, receive a resounding *Yes!*, in Christ. He is the Yes to all that God in his grace has intended for us.

"Amen!"

God has planned it all and brought it to fruition through the saving work of his Son; it is left for us simply to respond and receive and adore.

---

4. Wright, "Worship and the Spirit in the New Testament." (unpaginated).

> That is why it is through him [Christ] that we utter our Amen to
> God for his glory. (2 Cor 1:20b)

"That is why" emphasizes that our part is completely dependent on God's part: he has initiated and consummated his saving purposes on our behalf.

Our response to God's *Yes* to us in Jesus is summarized by Paul as "our *Amen*." All of our prayer and praise and worship are expressions of grateful assent and surrender to God's loving purposes for us in Christ.

More than that, our *entire lives* (which is the true New Testament scope and realm of worship, as we have seen in John 4:23 and Romans 12:1) are to be a confirmation and reflection of the wondrous work God has wrought in us. Our *Amen* is the full-orbed response of love, with all our heart, soul, mind, and strength (Mark 12:30), to God's *Yes* to us in Jesus, expressed through life-pervading worship.

All of Christ

It should be noticed that Jesus is also *the active agent* in our response of worship to God for all he has done for us in his Son. Our Amen is actually *"through* him" (1:20b); he is the operative force both in the God-to-human movement of Yes and in the human-to-God response of Amen.

We will see much more about this dual role of Christ later in chapter 24.

To the Glory of God

God's sovereign and gracious Yes to us in Jesus Christ and our humble and never-ending response of Amen work together "for his glory" (1:20b).

"To the praise of his glory": God's Purpose in Redemption (Ephesians 1:3–14)

After his opening greeting, Paul launches into this epistle by praising God ("Blessed is the God and Father of our Lord Jesus Christ") because he "has blessed us in Christ with every spiritual blessing" (1:3). He then enumerates a number of these blessings that makes him worthy of praise, namely:

- Election 1:4
- Love 1:4

- Adoption 1:5
- Redemption 1:7
- Forgiveness 1:7
- Knowledge of his will 1:9
- Inheritance 1:11
- Sealing with the Spirit 1:12

All these blessings, the "riches of his grace" (1:7), he has "lavished upon us" (1:8).

He has accomplished and bestowed all these things for our good, but ultimately for his honor. Three times Paul reminds us that what God did in Christ, he did "to the praise of his glorious grace" (1:6), "to the praise of his glory" (1:12, 14). God is deserving of all praise and blessing and worship for what he has done for us in Christ.

> His aim is the God-exalting, soul-satisfying praise of the glory of his grace. . . . Grace is the consummate expression of God's glory.[5]

The Ministry of Song (Ephesians 5:18–20)

There is not nearly as much about musical ministry in corporate worship in the New Testament as there is in the Old. However:

> That the singing or chanting of hymns was an integral part of the worship of New Testament churches is clear from Paul's instructions about worship in 1 Cor 14:26. Paul says, "When you come together, each one has a hymn." In Col 3:16 and Eph 5:19 he encourages his readers to sing "psalms, hymns and spiritual songs to God." James also calls on his readers to "sing songs of praise" (5:13).[6]

Ephesians 5:18–20 does provide a helpful foundation:

> And do not get drunk with wine, for that is debauchery, but be filled with the Spirit, addressing one another in psalms and hymns and spiritual songs, singing and making melody to the Lord with all your heart, giving thanks always and for everything to God the Father in the name of our Lord Jesus Christ.

---

5. Piper, "Gospel Worship" (emphasis added).
6. Gloer, "Worship God!," 38.

In this passage we see at least eight aspects that should characterize our corporate ministry of song.

A *Spirit-Filled* Ministry

> And do not get drunk with wine, for that is debauchery, but *be filled with the Spirit*, ...

When someone is drunk, that person is controlled by the influence of alcohol. Paul says that we should be controlled rather by the Spirit of God.

With all the debates about the filling of the Spirit, it's intriguing that here the result of being filled by the Spirit is singing!

> For we are the real circumcision, who *worship* by the *Spirit of God* and glory in Christ Jesus and put no confidence in the flesh. (Phil 3:3)

A *Mutual* Ministry

> ... addressing *one another* ...

There is an important *horizontal* aspect to our ministry of song in corporate worship: it is something we do *together*. Personal and private worship is an important part of our walk with God, but in the gathering of the church we need to be focused on one another as well as on God. Congregational worship is to provide a mutual benefit, rather than primarily an individual benefit; hence, the ubiquitous "What's in it for me?" or "What do I get out of it?" attitude with which so many approach corporate worship shows a severe misunderstanding of why we come together. We minister to one another and encourage one another and draw strength from one another as we sing.

A *Diverse* Ministry

> ... in psalms *and* hymns *and* spiritual songs, ...

The exact designations of these three categories of song have been widely debated for the past two thousand years, with no indisputable outcome. However, it is quite certain at least that Paul is saying that we should use *different* kinds of songs in our corporate praise. Let's draw from musical riches across stylistic, generational, and national boundaries.

A *God-Focused* Ministry

> . . . singing and making melody *to the Lord* . . .

Ultimately, of course, our song is directed toward the One who alone is worthy of our praise. We do not sing for our own enjoyment or benefit (though those may happen also), but for God's pleasure and glory.

An *Internal* Ministry

> . . . with your *heart,* . . .

Our songs must well up from the inside. We are to make melody in our hearts before a song ever reaches our lips. We have seen that God is far more concerned about the inner attitude of worship than about the external form it takes. For worship to be God-honoring and God-pleasing, it must be an expression of a devoted heart.

> "Man looks on the outward appearance, but the Lord looks on the *heart.*" (1 Sam 16:7)

A *Responsive* Ministry

> . . . *giving thanks* always and for everything to God the Father . . .

We have a song to sing only because of God's initiative in revealing himself to us and showing himself mighty in saving acts on our behalf. All worship is a grateful response to God's gracious self-revelation.

A *Christ-Empowered* Ministry

> . . . *in the name of our Lord Jesus Christ.*

Our song pleases God because we come to worship in and through our great high priest, whose song subsumes and perfects our own. Praying and worshiping in Christ's name is far more than just tacking on Christ's name at the end for maximum effect. Rather, it is acknowledging that it is only in Christ and through Christ, by Christ's priesthood and dressed in Christ's righteousness, that we can draw near to God at all. (Much more on this in chapter 24.)[7]

A *Trinitarian* Ministry

> Be filled with the *Spirit*, . . . and give thanks for everything to God the *Father* in the name of our Lord *Jesus Christ*.

The normal New Testament pattern of worship is seen here: we bring our praise *to the Father, through the Son, in the power of the Holy Spirit*.[8]

> This, indeed, is one of Paul's more strikingly trinitarian passages, reminiscent of 1 Corinthians 12:4–6, but this time giving not just a parallel between the three members of the Godhead but also a shape and a mutual relation: the Spirit enables worshippers to give thanks to the Father in the name of the Lord Jesus.[9]

---

7. *From the Field*: She was a small, unassuming woman, librarian of the Presbyterian seminary sponsoring the conference I was speaking at in Nigeria. At the end of one of the sessions, the moderator asked this woman to close the time in prayer. I will never forget how she started her prayer: she said, "In Jesus' name," and then went on with her prayer to the Father.

I was struck at what a profound theological insight that simple practice (her regular practice, as I got to hear later) demonstrated. We habitually tack on "in Jesus' name" at the end of our prayers, all too often in a rote manner and without reflection on what we are really saying. But prayer in Jesus' name (and worship in Jesus' name too) is based on the conviction that it is only in, through, and by Christ that we enter into the Father's presence with our prayers and our praises. We can come confidently and boldly and with assurance precisely because he has opened and shown us *"the new and living way"* to the Father (Heb 10:19–22). And not only that, but in fact Jesus *takes us with him* into the Father's presence! We can be sure that our petitions and praises are always accepted when we come in Christ.

What a bold way to acknowledge these amazing truths, by *beginning* prayer with "in Jesus' name"! It is recognizing that his name—that is, his person and his saving work—is the "key" that opens the door into the Father's presence; his name is the "password" that gives us entrance.

8. See also: "Making Our Worship More Trinitarian," part 6, chapter 1 in Man, *Worship Reader*.

9. Wright, "Worship and the Spirit" (unpaginated).

"All, and in all": Christ, His Word, and Our Song (Colossians 3:16)

Colossians 3:16 shows marked similarities to Ephesians 5:19 (especially the mention of "psalms, hymns, and spiritual songs"), but also provides some unique perspectives on our corporate life and worship.

The Context: Living in Christ

Paul calls on the Colossian believers (and us) to live with a heavenly perspective, in line with their newness of life in Christ (Col 3:1–10). Their new identity in Christ gives them a unity in Christ that supersedes human categories:

> Here there is not Greek and Jew, circumcised and uncircumcised, barbarian, Scythian, slave, free; but Christ is all, and in all. (Col 3:11)

All those distinctions are now meaningless because they are in Christ, and are Christ's: for them he "is all," the ground of their being and the fullness of their new existence.

Living out this reality as a unified church (the "one body" into which they have been called in Christ [3:15b]) will call for a number of different qualities (which, if they came naturally, Paul would have no need to command!): compassion, kindliness, humility, meekness, patience, mutual forbearance, forgiveness, love, and gratitude (3:13–15).

The Call: Worshiping through Christ

> Let the word of Christ dwell in you richly,
>   with all wisdom
>   teaching and admonishing one another
>   with psalms, hymns and spiritual songs;
>   with grace
>   singing to God
>   in your hearts.[10]

---

10. Layout of v. 16 from the grammatical and exegetical study of Detwiler, "Church Music and Colossians 3:16."

It is surely no accident that in this context, where Paul calls for this kind of unity in the church, he highlights *singing*. For corporate song is ideally suited to illustrating and expressing the *unity in diversity* that is to characterize the body of Christ: many distinct voices (different ranges, tone qualities, etc.), yet joined together in a harmonious chorus of praise to God that is certainly more than the sum of the parts.

It is also deeply significant that Paul identifies this singing as a worthy conduit and reflection of the "word of Christ" dwelling in the congregation's midst. Christ continues to speak to us through his word and by means of human preachers, teachers, readers—and musicians (see chapter 24). The entire context and content of worship should be word-centered and word-filled; that will make even our singing be a rich source of teaching and admonishment and wisdom. Matt Merker states:

> Singing is part of the ministry of God's Word. When a congregation verbalizes truth in song, the Holy Spirit unleashes the double-edged sword of Scripture in our midst.[11]

A Royal Priesthood Offering Spiritual Sacrifices (1 Peter 2:5, 9)[12]

It is interesting to see how the New Testament authors did not shy away from using terms connected to the Old Testament sacrificial system, though investing those terms with more internal, spiritualized meanings. Such is the case here in 1 Peter 2:

> You yourselves like living stones are being built up as a spiritual house, to be a holy priesthood, to offer spiritual sacrifices acceptable to God through Jesus Christ. (2:5)

> But you are a chosen race, a royal priesthood, a holy nation, a people for his own possession, that you may proclaim the excellencies of him who called you out of darkness into his marvelous light. (2:9)

Of course, there are key differences between national, ethnic Israel and the global, multiethnic church. But in these verses the church is described by Peter with terms and functions highly reminiscent of Israel:

---

11. Merker, *Corporate Worship*, ch. 7 (unpaginated).
12. For this section, see Merker, *Corporate Worship*, chapter 7.

a holy priesthood, spiritual sacrifices, a chosen race, a royal priesthood, a holy nation, a people for his own possession. And like Israel, a "people whom I formed for myself that they might declare my praise" (Isa 43:21), the church is to "proclaim the excellencies of him who called you out of darkness into his marvelous light."

This is one more example of the ubiquitous revelation and response pattern in Scripture. God has taken the initiative to reveal his excellencies in his gracious work of calling us out of darkness into light; and our appropriate response is to gratefully proclaim those excellencies he has revealed.

> "For from him and through him and to him are all things. To him be glory forever. Amen."
> (Rom 11:36)

For Reflection and/or Discussion

What is your reaction to the truth of God's "Yes" to you in Christ? What might your "Amen" look like in your life? (2 Cor 1:20)

21

ETERNAL PRAISE: The Great Scenes of Worship in the Book of Revelation

> There is no book in the New Testament in which worship plays so prominent a role. The reason for this prominence is found in John's conviction that the question of worship is the fundamental and ultimate question of human existence in time and in eternity.[1]

Revelation 1

John "was in the Spirit on the Lord's Day" (Rev 1:10), and sees many amazing visions, as we read throughout the book—but none greater than the vision in chapter 1 of the glorified Christ himself. Indeed, John starts his account by telling us that what he writes is the "revelation of Jesus Christ" (1:1).

Jean-Jacques von Allmen wrote, "The place of worship is essentially the place where Christ is found."[2] Revelation 1 is such a place of worship.

---

1. Gloer, "Worship God!," 47.
2. Allmen, *Worship*, 241.

> One like a son of man, clothed with a long robe and with a golden sash around his chest. The hairs of his head were white, like white wool, like snow. His eyes were like a flame of fire, his feet were like burnished bronze, refined in a furnace, and his voice was like the roar of many waters. In his right hand he held seven stars, from his mouth came a sharp two-edged sword, and his face was like the sun shining in full strength. (Rev 1:13–16)

What a picture of glory! And as mentioned earlier in this book, this picture is one we need to be reminded of in an age when much emphasis in corporate worship is on being relaxed and informal, and even casual. If the Lord Jesus were to physically appear in our worship service, he would certainly not be dressed in blue jeans, but in shining white robes as we see here. And, rather than chumming it up with him, we would fall at his feet, as did John. We would "rejoice with trembling!" (Ps 2:11)

> To him who loves us and has freed us from our sins by his blood and made us a kingdom, priests to his God and Father, to him be glory and dominion forever and ever. Amen. (Rev 1:5–6)

Revelation 4

In this chapter John gets to look into the very throne room of God in heaven.

> After this I looked, and behold, a door standing open in heaven! . . . At once I was in the Spirit, and behold, a throne stood in heaven, with One seated on the throne. And he who sat there had the appearance of jasper and carnelian, and around the throne was a rainbow that had the appearance of an emerald. (Rev 4:1–3)

John has reached the very limits of human language in trying to describe the wonder of what he sees: God himself on his throne! John also observes groups of angelic creatures that he calls the "twenty-four elders" (4:4) and "four living creatures" (4:6–7).

The second group is involved in a remarkable activity:

> And the four living creatures, each of them with six wings, are full of eyes all around and within, and day and night they never cease to say,
> "Holy, holy, holy, is the Lord God Almighty,
> who was and is and is to come!" (Rev 4:8)

They praise God, who is holy, who is Lord, who is Almighty, who is the Eternal One.

Then we read:

> The twenty-four elders fall down before him who is seated on the throne and worship him who lives forever and ever. They cast their crowns before the throne, saying,
> > "Worthy are you, our Lord and God,
> > to receive glory and honor and power,
> > for you created all things,
> > and by your will they existed and were created." (Rev 4:10–11)

The angelic beings, as they bow and worship and cast their crowns, speak of God's supreme worthiness; they consider God worthy of eternal "glory and honor and power" because he is the *Creator*.

Revelation 5

In Revelation 5, God is given eternal praise because he is also the *Redeemer*.

> And between the throne and the four living creatures and among the elders I saw a Lamb standing, as though it had been slain. (Rev 5:6)

Here we see something of the wonder and mystery of the incarnation: one who is Lion and Lamb, who is God and human, who died yet who is alive forevermore.

Though Jesus in his humanity is actively involved in leading us in our worship of the Father (more on that in chapter 24), as God he is of course also worthy of *being worshiped*, and that is what we see here in Revelation 5. He is worthy of eternal praise because:

> You were slain, and by your blood you ransomed people for God from every tribe and language and people and nation. (5:9)

The tremendous scene continues:

> Then I looked, and I heard around the throne and the living creatures and the elders the voice of many angels, numbering myriads of myriads and thousands of thousands, saying with a loud voice,
> > "Worthy is the Lamb who was slain,
> > to receive power and wealth and wisdom and might and honor and glory and blessing!"

And I heard every creature in heaven and on earth and under
the earth and in the sea, and all that is in them, saying,
"To him who sits on the throne and to the Lamb
be blessing and honor and glory and might forever and ever!"
And the four living creatures said, "Amen!" and the elders fell
down and worshiped. (5:11–14)

Revelation 7

John sees a "great multitude" with a single, unified message: *eternal praise* to God and to the Lamb.

> After this I looked, and behold, a great multitude that no one could number, *from every nation, from all tribes and peoples and languages*, standing before the throne and before the Lamb, clothed in white robes, with palm branches in their hands, and crying out with a loud voice, "Salvation belongs to our God who sits on the throne, and to the Lamb!" (Rev 7:9–10)

What a sight and sound that will be! We can only imagine: a huge mass of humanity, as far as the eye can see, of incredible diversity, yet all unified in lifting their loud praises to God and to the Lamb! To which the angelic host add their exclamations of eternal praise:

> And all the angels were standing around the throne and around the elders and the four living creatures, and they fell on their faces before the throne and *worshiped* God, saying, "Amen! Blessing and glory and wisdom and thanksgiving and honor and power and might be to our God forever and ever! Amen." (Rev 7:11–12)

In this passage we observe:

- a "great *multitude*" ("that no one could number")
- a great *diversity* ("every nation, all tribes and peoples and languages")
- a great *sound* ("crying with a loud voice")
- a great *salvation* ("Salvation belongs to our God who sits on the throne, and to the Lamb!")
- a great *praise*: ("blessing and glory and wisdom and thanksgiving and honor and power and might")
- a great *God* who is praised ("be to our God forever and ever")

Note that the multitude does *not* cry, "We're saved! We're saved!" Instead, they acknowledge that salvation is all of God, and all of grace: "Salvation *belongs to our God* who sits on the throne, and *to the Lamb!*" True worship will always be God-centered and *focus more on the Giver than the gift*.

Revelation 14

Here we see the gospel's call to worship go out one more time to all the earth.

> Then I saw another angel flying directly overhead, with an *eternal gospel* to proclaim to those who dwell on earth, to *every nation and tribe and language and people*. And he said with a loud voice, "Fear God and *give him glory*, because the hour of his judgment has come, and *worship him* who *made heaven and earth, the sea and the springs of water.*" (Rev 14:6–7)

The call is for all peoples to worship and give glory to the Creator, the only one worthy of worship.

Revelation 19

This climactic scene is punctuated repeatedly with cries of "Hallelujah!" in praise for God's great work of final judgment, for his final consummation of the "marriage of the Lamb," and for the irruption of his eternal rule.

> After this I heard what seemed to be the loud voice of a great multitude in heaven, crying out,
> "*Hallelujah!*
> Salvation and glory and power belong to our God,
>   for his judgments are true and just;
>   for he has judged the great prostitute
>   who corrupted the earth with her immorality,
>   and has avenged on her the blood of his servants."
> Once more they cried out,
> "*Hallelujah!*
> The smoke from her goes up forever and ever."
> And the twenty-four elders and the four living creatures fell down and *worshiped* God who was seated on the throne, saying,
> "Amen. *Hallelujah!*". . .

Then I heard what seemed to be the voice of a great multitude, like the roar of many waters and like the sound of mighty peals of thunder, crying out,
> "*Hallelujah!*
> For the Lord our God the Almighty reigns.
> Let us rejoice and exult
> and give him the glory,
> for the marriage of the Lamb has come,
> and his Bride has made herself ready." (19:1–7)

Revelation 21–22

And finally, in the new heavens and new earth, we see that the worship of God will be complete.

> The throne of God and of the Lamb will be in it, and his servants will worship him. (Rev 22:3)

And the glory of God will fill all in all:

> And the city has no need of sun or moon to shine on it, for the glory of God gives it light, and its lamp is the Lamb. (Rev 21:23)

> And night will be no more. They will need no light of lamp or sun, for the Lord God will be their light, and they will reign forever and ever. (Rev 22:5)

And, as we saw previously in our study, the angel's stern imperative to John (in the last chapter of the Bible) applies to the *entire* narrative of the Bible, to all of humanity and to all of creation:

> "Worship *God!*" (Rev 22:9)

Ascriptions of Praise to God in Revelation

Created beings, both human and angelic, give praise to God (or are called to do so) with the following terms:

- Glory (1:6; 4:9, 11; 5:12, 13; 7:12; 14:7; 19:1, 7)
- Dominion (1:6)
- Honor (4:9, 11; 5:12, 13; 7:12)

- Thanks (4:9; 7:12)
- Power (4:11; 5:12; 7:12; 19:1)
- Wealth (5:12)
- Wisdom (5:12)
- Might (5:12,13; 7:12)
- Blessing (5:12, 13; 7:12)
- Salvation (7:10; 19:1)

Often they are heaped one upon another (e.g., "Blessing and glory and wisdom and thanksgiving and honor and power and might be to our God forever and ever!" [Rev 7:12]), as if the ascribers are at a loss to find enough descriptors to give God his due.

Indeed, there can never be enough ways to praise our great God!

"Worship God!" (Rev 22:9)

For Reflection and/or Discussion

What perspectives on your own walk of worship
do these great scenes of worship in the book of Revelation give you?

22

WORSHIP IN THE BOOK OF HEBREWS

Revelation and the Letter to the Hebrews have more to teach us about worship than any other books of the New Testament. Hebrews also offers unique insights into the past and present priestly ministry of Jesus Christ; in fact, the letter is so richly christological that Noel Due has maintained, "If we take Christ out of Hebrews, we are left with nothing."[1]

It is commonly held that Hebrews was written to Jewish believers who were in danger of reverting to Judaism because of persecution for their faith. So the writer goes to great lengths to demonstrate the superiority of Christ and of the new covenant over anything found under the old covenant. The message to these wavering believers is: "You have so much more in Christ. Why would you ever go back?"

Christ through his atoning death has removed the barrier of sin and opened "the new and living way" into the very presence of God for every believer, by which we can "draw near" to God with confidence and assurance (10:19–22). This access is one of the uniquely precious aspects of the new covenant.

The writer of Hebrews shows us how in Christ and in the new covenant we have a vastly *better way*, a *better mediator*, and a *better worship*.

---

1. Due, *Created for Worship*, 156.

A Better Way

The writer of Hebrews displays a whole raft of benefits the original readers (and we) have under the new covenant, as contrasted with the Old. We have a better:

1:2–14	spokesman for God (the Son)
2:2–3	message (salvation)
3:3	rest
4:15	high priest (tempted but sinless)
7:7, 15–17	priestly order (of Melchizedek)
7:19	hope
7:21	priesthood (eternal)
7:22	covenant (with a better guarantor)
7:27; 9:26	sacrifice (the priest himself)
7:28	priest (perfect)
8:2; 9:11	tabernacle
8:6	ministry (better covenant)
8:6	covenant (better promises)
8:6	promises
8:10; 10:16	law (written on heart, mind)
8:11	knowledge of the Lord
8:19	access (to the holy place)
9:12; 12:24	blood
9:12	redemption (eternal)
9:14; 10:22	cleansing (of the conscience)
9:14–15	inheritance (eternal)
9:23, 28	sacrifice
9:24	holy place (in heaven)
9:26; 10:12, 14	frequency (once for all)
12:22	mountain/city (Zion)
12:28	kingdom (cannot be shaken)
13:9	food (grace)
13:10	altar (Christ)

All of these things are *better* because of Christ and his work.

A Better Mediator

All the "better ways" of the new covenant are built on the foundation of the covenant instituted by a better *mediator*: Jesus Christ.

Christ's Dual Role (Hebrews 1:1—3:1)

In chapters 1 and 2, the writer focuses on the two natures and roles of Jesus Christ. Hebrews 1 speaks of the worship *of* the Son, in his deity (1:1–3, 6) and authority (1:8, 12–13). Hebrews 2 speaks of the worship *by* the Son in his humanity (2:7, 11) and priesthood (2:12b, 17).

These two roles of Christ seen in chapter 1 (as God's spokesman/revealer) and in chapter 2 (as our priest, making propitiation and leading our worship) are then summarized in 3:1:

> Therefore, holy brethren, you who share in a heavenly calling, consider Jesus, the *apostle* and *high priest* of our confession.

As God, Jesus perfectly communicates God's purpose and message (which is what an apostle does; he is one who is literally "sent" to do this). As a human, he is our high priest, offering a propitiating sacrifice on our behalf and leading us to the Father in worship. In this way we see the pattern of revelation and response displayed and fulfilled in the person and work of Jesus Christ himself:

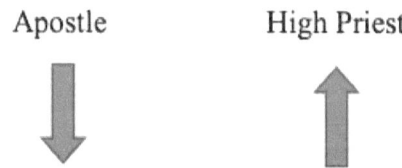

The Superior Priesthood of Christ (Hebrews 5–10)

The writer of Hebrews contrasts the old covenant priesthood (the Levitical priesthood or order of Aaron) with the new covenant priesthood of Christ (in the so-called "order of Melchizedek"), developing at length the obvious superiority of the latter in every way.

Levitical Priesthood/Order of Aaron	Priesthood of Christ/Order of Melchizedek
Descended from Levi, Aaron (7:5, 11)	Descended from Judah (7:14)
Sinful (5:3; 7:27)	"holy, innocent, unstained, separated from sinners" (7:26)
Weak (5:2; 7:28)	Perfect (5:9; 7:28; 10:14)

Levitical Priesthood/Order of Aaron	Priesthood of Christ/Order of Melchizedek
Many, because mortal/temporary (7:2)	One, permanent priesthood (lives forever) (7:24)
Could only purify the flesh (9:13)	Can purify the conscience (9:14)
Had to offer for own sins (5:3; 7:27; 9:7)	Sinless (7:26)
Had to offer same sacrifices repeatedly (5:1; 7:27; 9:25; 10:1, 3, 11)	One sacrifice (7:27; 9:12, 26, 28; 10:10, 12, 14)
Offered blood of animals (9:18–22; 10:4)	Offered himself, own blood (7:27; 9:12, 25–26); "better sacrifices" (9:23)
Offerings could not make perfect or perfect the conscience (5:9; 7:11, 18; 9:9; 10:1)	Can purify conscience (9:14), perfect those sanctified (10:14)
Served shadow tent/tabernacle (8:5; 9:23–24)	Serves true tabernacle (8:2; 9:11, 23–24)
Could not take away sins (10:11)	Redeems from sins committed under old covenant (9:15); grants eternal redemption (9:12); saves forever (7:25)
Served an imperfect covenant (8:7)	"guarantor of a better covenant" (7:22; 8:6)
Inferior ministry based on inferior promises (8:6)	Better ministry based on better promises (8:6)

Christ Entering the Heavenly Tabernacle as Priest

> Christ . . . through the greater and more perfect tent (not made with hands, that is, not of this creation) . . . entered once for all into the holy places, not by means of the blood of goats and calves but by means of his own blood. (Heb 9:11–12)

Christ's Ongoing Ministry in the Heavenly Tabernacle as Priest (His Session and Ongoing Ministry)

> We have such a high priest, one who is seated at the right hand of the throne of the Majesty in the heaven, a minister in the holy places, in the true tent that the Lord set up, not man. (8:1–2)

> Let us then with confidence draw near to the throne of grace, that we may receive mercy and find grace to help in time of need. (4:16)
>
> He always lives to make intercession for them. (7:25)
>
> Who is to condemn? Christ Jesus is the one who died—more than that, who was raised—who is at the right hand of God, who indeed is interceding for us. (Rom 8:34)

Summary: A Better Priesthood

> And every priest stands daily at his service, offering repeatedly the same sacrifices, which can *never* take away sins.
> But when Christ had offered for *all* time a *single* sacrifice for sins, he sat down at the right hand of God. . . . For by a *single offering* he has perfected for *all* time those who are being sanctified. (Heb 10:11–14)
>
> The former priests were many in number, because they were prevented by death from continuing in office, but he holds his priesthood *permanently*, because he continues forever.
> *Consequently*, he is able to save *to the uttermost* those who draw near to God through him, since he always lives to make intercession for them. (Heb 7:23–25)

This last statement tells us that Jesus' ongoing intercessory ministry on our behalf guarantees our eternal salvation!

A Better Worship

Hebrews 10:19–22 begins the final, applicational section of the letter. This passage itself summarizes important themes as it builds on what has gone before.

> Therefore, brothers, since we have confidence to enter the holy places by the blood of Jesus, *by the new and living way* that he opened for us through the curtain, that is, through his flesh, and since we have a great priest over the house of God, *let us draw near* with a true heart in full assurance of faith, with our hearts sprinkled clean from an evil conscience and our bodies washed with pure water.

> "Therefore..."

This word shows that the author is turning now to the practical implications of what has gone before concerning the superiority of Christ and his priesthood and of the new covenant as a whole.

> "... *let us draw near* with a true heart in full assurance of faith" (Heb 10:22a)

The supreme distinctive and benefit of the new covenant is found in these words: the *access* that every believer has into the very presence of God through the work of Christ. Other passages that speak of that access:

> Let us then with confidence *draw near* to the throne of grace, that we may receive mercy and find grace to help in time of need. (4:16)

> Consequently, he is able to save to the uttermost those who *draw near* to God through him, since he always lives to make intercession for them. (7:25)

> Through him we have also obtained *access* by faith into this grace in which we stand, and we rejoice in hope of the glory of God. (Rom 5:2)

> For through him we both have *access* in one Spirit to the Father. (Eph 2:18)

> This was according to the eternal purpose that he has realized in Christ Jesus our Lord, in whom we have boldness and *access* with confidence through our faith in him. (Eph 3:11–12)

Our access, our invitation to draw near, is possible because of both the *past* work of Christ ("since we have confidence to enter the holy place by the blood of Jesus" [Heb 10:19]) *and* the *present* work of Christ ("and since we have a great priest over the house of God" [Heb 10:21]).

> "Therefore, *brethren*, since *we* have confidence... and since *we* have a great priest... let *us* draw near..." (Heb 10:19, 21–22)

Together we have been called, and together we are members of one another and of his body (Heb 2:11, 13b, 17; 3:1, 12; 13:22).

Indeed, the invitation is "let *us* draw near." While every believer has individual access to God in worship and prayer and fellowship, the immediate context of Hebrews 10:19–22 seems to focus on the corporate gathering:

> And let us consider how to stir up one another to love and good works, not neglecting to meet together, as is the habit of some, but encouraging one another, and all the more as you see the Day drawing near. (Heb 10:24–25)

> "Therefore, brethren, since we have *confidence* to enter the holy places . . . let us draw near . . . in full *assurance* of faith . . ." (Heb 10:19–22)

We can draw near freely and without fear because of the gracious saving work of Christ (Heb 4:16; Eph 3:11). The writer contrasts the Israelites' fearful approach to Mount Sinai (Heb 12:18) and our confident and joyful approach to Mount Zion and the presence of God (Heb 12:22–23).

Such confident, abundant access can only elicit responses of thankfulness and reverent worship (Heb 12:28; 13:15).

Conclusion

The writer brings his entire argument into focus in the last chapter of the letter:

> *Through him* [Christ] then let us continually offer up a sacrifice of praise to God, that is, the fruit of lips that acknowledge his name (Heb 13:15).

The intense *Christ-centeredness* of the letter comes to a head here. *In Christ* we have life. *With Christ* we can boldly approach the Father. *Through Christ* we offer our worship.

"Let us draw near": through Christ, in Christ, with Christ.

> "*Let us draw near* in full assurance of faith."
> (Heb 10:22)

For Reflection and/or Discussion

What new insights into worship have you gained from this study of the book of Hebrews?

23

THE HOLY SPIRIT AND WORSHIP

A Complementary Role

The members of the Trinity—Father, Son, and Holy Spirit—are all equally God and equally glorious. Yet, remarkably, the different members of the Trinity voluntarily perform different roles:[1] The Father gives (John 3:16) and sends the Son (a major theme in the Gospel of John: 4:34; 5:24, 36–38; 6:29; 7:16; etc.); the Son obeys and submits to the Father (John 4:34; Luke 22:42); and the Spirit, as we will see in this chapter, always points to and glorifies Christ (John 16:14).

It is remarkable that the members of the Trinity are so eternally secure in their relationship with one another that there is never any sense of competition. They willingly perform their different roles in order to fulfill the purposes of their one, unified divine will.

A Beautiful Role

Scripture does not tell us as much about the Holy Spirit as it does about the Father and the Son, but that is in keeping with the Spirit's own priority to glorify the person of Christ, instead of drawing attention to himself:

---

1. This truth is reflected to a certain extent in Christian marriage: husband and wife are both equal before God spiritually, but perform different roles.

> "When the Spirit of truth comes, he will guide you into all the truth, for he will not speak on his own authority, but whatever he hears he will speak, and he will declare to you the things that are to come. *He will glorify me*, for he will take what is mine and declare it to you." (John 16:13–14)

In fact, theologians have sometimes referred to the Spirit as "the shy member of the Trinity," exactly because of this self-effacing aspect of his ministry. His work is usually unseen and therefore somewhat mysterious, and is often understood only in retrospect. J. I. Packer highlights this beautiful aspect of the Spirit's work:

> Think of it this way. It is as if the Spirit stands behind us, throwing light over our shoulder, on Jesus, who stands facing us. The Spirit's message is never, "Look at me; listen to me; come to me; get to know me," but always, "Look at him, and see his glory; listen to him, and hear his word; go to him, and have life; get to know him, and taste his gift of joy and peace."[2]

The question is often asked whether it is appropriate to worship the Holy Spirit. Indeed, the New Testament never speaks of the Holy Spirit being worshiped, only the Father and the Son, even though the Spirit is equally divine. The primary pattern of worship in the New Testament is that of *worshiping the Father through the Son in the power of the Holy Spirit*. But because the Spirit is also God, it is certainly not wrong to offer him worship and praise. Accordingly, while there are very few hymns and contemporary songs focusing on the Spirit solely, there are some where each member of the Trinity is honored in successive verses. And, of course, the Holy Spirit normally receives more attention in worship on Pentecost Sunday.

Yet an ongoing focus on worship of the Spirit would seem to be excessive and not in line with the biblical pattern (or with the Spirit's wishes!). In fact, it could be said that the clearest sign that the Holy Spirit is vibrantly at work in a church is not where the Spirit is the main focus of what is said or sung, but rather where *the person and work of Christ is being exalted* (in line with the Spirit's own priority).

---

2. Packer, *Keep in Step*, 66.

Glorifying Christ

The fact is that we never see the Holy Spirit in the New Testament apart from being intimately connected with Christ and his work: "There is no separate activity of the Holy Spirit in revelation or salvation in addition to or independent of the activity of Christ."[3]

How does the Holy Spirit glorify Christ?

1. The Holy Spirit glorifies Christ by acting throughout Christ's earthly ministry.

- The Spirit and Christ's Conception (Luke 1:35).[4] (Mary conceived Jesus by the Holy Spirit.)
- The Spirit and Christ's Baptism (Luke 3:21–22; see also John 1:32–33). (The Spirit descended on Jesus like a dove.)
- The Spirit and Christ's Temptations (Luke 4:1–2, 14). (The Spirit led Jesus into the wilderness to be tempted, and afterwards led him back to Galilee.)
- The Spirit and Christ's Ministry (Matt 12:28; Luke 4:18; 10:21; Acts 10:38). (Jesus ministered in the power of the Spirit.)
- The Spirit and Christ's Death (Heb 9:14). (Jesus gave himself over to death by the Spirit.)
- The Spirit and Christ's Resurrection (Rom 1:4; 1 Pet 3:18)

---

3. Torrance, *Christian Doctrine*, 196.

4. The Holy Spirit shows up throughout the nativity narratives of Luke 1–2, also working in Elizabeth (1:41), Zechariah (1:67), Simeon (2:25–27), and (prophetically) John the Baptist (1:15). Sadly, "The Holy Spirit is the forgotten participant in the Christmas drama. This omission is seen not only in the Christmas card selection at Hallmark, but also in music for the season. There are dozens of shepherd carols, magi carols, angel carols, and Mary and Joseph carols, but precious few that acknowledge the work of the Spirit" (Witvliet, "Singing Our Prayers").

2. The Holy Spirit glorifies Christ by *continuing* Christ's earthly ministry.

Jesus promises to send *"another* Helper" who in many ways will continue Christ's work, only now through his church (John 14:16, 26; 15:26; 16:13–14; Acts 1:1).

3. The Holy Spirit glorifies Christ by bringing us to faith in Christ.

It is the Holy Spirit that draws us and brings us into a saving relationship with Christ (John 16:8; 3:5; Titus 3:4–5).

4. The Holy Spirit glorifies Christ by giving us assurance of our relationship to God in Christ.

The Spirit works in our hearts to give us confidence in our salvation (Rom 8:15; Gal 4:6).

5. The Holy Spirit glorifies Christ by motivating and empowering our worship of the Father through Christ.

> For we are the circumcision, who worship *by the Spirit of God* and glory in Christ Jesus and put no confidence in the flesh. (Phil 3:3)

The Spirit can be seen as the connective tissue between the revelation and response poles of the biblical pattern of worship we have seen throughout this book. It is the role of the Holy Spirit to take the revelation of God from our *minds* into our *hearts* and to draw forth our response:

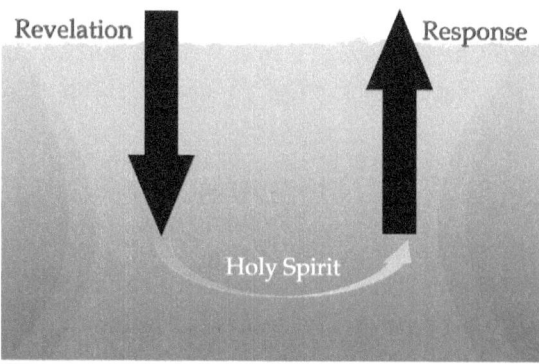

He does that in bringing us to salvation: we hear the gospel, the truth about what Christ has done for us. And then the Holy Spirit takes that information (which, after all, people can hear and not respond to) into our hearts and makes it real and precious to us and draws us into the response of saving faith.

And in our Christian life, the Spirit takes the truth of God again from our head into our heart. As we learn truths about God, the Holy Spirit brings comprehension.

> Now we have received not the spirit of the world, but the Spirit who is from God, that we might *understand* the things freely given us by God. (1 Cor 2:12)

The Spirit takes the *objective* truth about God in Christ and makes it *subjectively* precious to us: objective revelation, subjective response. And then he draws forth our response of praise and worship and thanksgiving.

We can say that we *can* come to the Father in worship because of the ministry of *Christ*, but we *want* to come to the Father because of the ministry of *the Holy Spirit*!

> 6. The Holy Spirit glorifies Christ by producing growth
> in Christlikeness in us individually and as a church,
> and giving gifts for the building up of the body.

It is significant that the Bible never says we're to grow in "*Spirit-likeness*"; it says we are to grow in *Christlikeness*. And that again is the result of the behind-the-scenes ministry of the Holy Spirit. We often are not consciously aware of the Spirit working in our hearts and lives, but we can look back and see how the Holy Spirit has worked quietly within us—showing us Christ, making us more like him, and drawing forth our worship (Rom 8:2–4; Gal 5:25; 2 Cor 3:18; Eph 2:22; Phil 3:3).

Conclusion

And so we see through all of this *the utter Christ-centeredness of all the Spirit's work*: always pointing us to Christ, wooing us to Christ, rooting us in Christ, growing us in Christ, drawing forth our worship in and through Christ. No wonder Paul and Peter both refer to the third person of the Trinity as "the Spirit of Christ" (Rom 8:9; 1 Pet 1:11).

> Notice the utter Christ-centeredness of all the Spirit's ministry.

For Reflection and/or Discussion

How do you respond to the beauty of the Holy Spirit's quiet, humble, and self-effacing work within us?

24

JESUS CHRIST AND WORSHIP

With this subject we reach the most profound depths (and heights) of worship. We will examine some truly transformative truths about the spiritual dynamics of worship.

We begin by considering: What makes worship in the church *good*? Is it the right song or song set? Or the right anointed worship leader? Or the right group of talented musicians? Or the right amount of sincerity?

We are going to see that it is *none* of those things. In fact, this chapter should lead us to repent of the sin of trying to do worship *in our own strength*. We simply cannot reach a standard that makes our worship wholly acceptable and pleasing to God—not through our own efforts, however diligent or committed or talented we may be. We need, and have, *Christ's enablement* to make our worship acceptable and pleasing to God; he has provided "the new and living way" to the Father (Heb 10:20).

God's Grace for Our Salvation, Sanctification, and Worship

Grace is God doing for us what we could never do for ourselves. In the early church, in his argument against the heretic Pelagius, Augustine insisted that "what God requires, he provides."[1] This tremendous truth of God's grace is unique out of all the religious systems of the world: every

---

1. A paraphrase at Augustine, *Confessions*, 10.29.40.

religion requires something of its followers, but only Christianity claims that what God requires, *he actually provides.*

And God does so, Peter tells us, so that God himself will receive all the glory.

> As each has received a gift, use it to serve one another, as good stewards of God's varied grace: whoever speaks, as one who speaks oracles of God; whoever serves, as one who serves by the strength that God supplies—*in order that in everything God may be glorified* through Jesus Christ. (1 Pet 4:10–11)

As John Piper likes to put it, "We get the *grace*; and God gets the *glory.*"

- God requires perfect holiness in order to enter heaven. We do not have that in ourselves, but in his grace, Christ has provided that holiness for us: that is *God's grace for our salvation* (Eph 2:8–9).
- God wants us to live a holy life on earth (1 Pet 1:15–16). We certainly cannot do that ourselves, but God has promised to help those who are in Christ in that quest: that is *God's grace for our sanctification* (Rom 8:26; Phil 2:12–13; 1 Cor 15:10; Col 1:29; 1 Thess 5:21–24; Titus 2:11–12; Heb 13:20–21).
- God deserves, and demands, perfect worship. What we will see below is God's wonderful provision for us in that arena as well: what God requires of our worship, he provides for us in Jesus Christ. That is *God's grace for our worship.*

Jesus, Our Mediator

Two-Way Mediation in the Old Testament

In the Old Testament, one finds a double agency of mediation back and forth between God and man, which reflects the foundational biblical pattern of revelation and response.

God spoke to Moses on the mountain, and his job was to go down and faithfully communicate the Lord's revelation to the people of Israel; he was God's chosen mediator from himself to the people. Moses' brother Aaron (the first high priest) was to represent, through the sacrificial system, the people in their response of worship back to God; he was the appointed mediator from the people to God.

Later in Israel's history one sees a similar pattern: the prophet was to serve as God's mouthpiece, communicating his revealed message to the people, as mediator between God and them. The priests continued as mediators between the people and God, representing them in their worship response.

Two-Way Mediation Fulfilled by Christ

In the New Testament, we learn the wonderful truth that Jesus Christ now fills *both* of those mediatorial roles. As the unique God-man, he mediates both between God and humans (in his deity), and between humans and God (in his humanity).

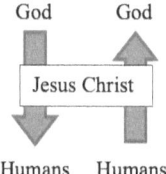

We saw the suggestion of this in chapter 14, as we considered Jesus' apparent allusion to Jacob's dream in Genesis 28:

> "Truly, truly, I say to you, you will see heaven opened, and the angels of God ascending and descending on the Son of Man" (John 1:51).

The incarnate Jesus is that unique bridge and connection between God and humanity, between heaven and earth.

Hebrews 2:12

This two-way mediation as it relates to our worship is beautifully and concisely portrayed in Hebrews 2:12.[2] Here the writer is quoting from Psalm 22:22,[3] though he states that these are *the words of Christ himself*, speaking to his Father:

> I will tell of your name to my brethren;
> in the midst of the congregation I will sing your praise.

This remarkable verse takes us to the very heart of worship under the new covenant. It shows that Jesus Christ in his present ministry is *the ultimate climax and fulfillment of the revelation and response pattern of Scripture* with which we began our study.

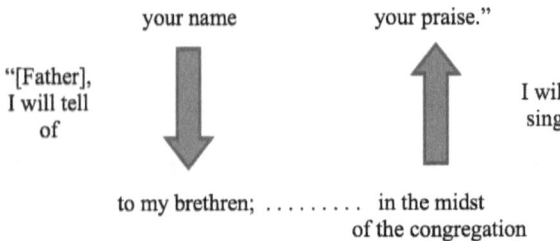

Jesus, as God, is the ultimate *revealer* of the Father; as a human, he is the ultimate *responder* to the Father.

Let us consider separately the two halves (and directions) of this verse.

---

2. For a fuller treatment of this passage and its implications for our worship, see my *Proclamation and Praise*.

3. This familiar psalm foretells the crucifixion of Christ, as he appropriates for himself the opening cry of verse 1 as he hangs on the cross ("My God, My God, why have you forsaken me?" Matt 27:46; Mark 15:34). Verse 22, quoted in Hebrews 2:12, is the first verse of the second section of the psalm, which looks beyond the suffering of the Messiah to the victory to follow (see Man, *Proclamation and Praise*, 8–12).

2:12a "I will proclaim your name to my brethren . . ."

Jesus' Earthly Mission

The New Testament (especially the Gospel of John) makes it clear that the thrust of Jesus' earthly ministry was to reveal the Father (his "name," that is, his nature) and to faithfully communicate his message to humanity.

> No one has ever seen God; the only God, who is at the Father's side, he has made him known. (John 1:18; see also Matt 11:27; John 17:6)

Jesus' Continuing Ministry

But there are also a number of Scriptures that speak of or imply the *continuation* of Jesus' ministry of revealing the Father *after* his glorification.

> "I made known to them your name, and *I will continue to make it known*, that the love with which you have loved me may be in them, and I in them." (John 17:26; see also John 16:12–15, 25)

Jesus, on the night before his crucifixion, is looking beyond the cross to an *ongoing* role of revealing the Father:
And in Acts 1:1 we read,

> In the first book, O Theophilus, I have dealt with all that Jesus *began* to do and teach. (Acts 1:1)

Luke's clear implication is that in his second volume (the book of Acts, the first volume being, of course, the Gospel of Luke), he will relate what Jesus *continues* "to do and to teach" (only now through the Holy Spirit, through his chosen apostles, and through his church).

Not Our Teaching Ministry

This all means that for any of us who are involved with teaching or preaching the word of God, we need to realize that it is in fact *Jesus' ministry, not ours*. We are speaking for and representing *him*, whose role it is to reveal the Father. What a high and holy and humbling privilege!

> "... and in the midst of the congregation I
> will sing your praise" (Heb 2:12b)

Jesus, Our Worship Leader

Even more remarkable, perhaps, are the implications of the second half of Hebrews 2:12. As our great high priest, Jesus represents us before the Father. He not only mediates our response of praise, he participates in it! This concept plumbs one of the most profound depths of the mystery of the incarnation: that Jesus Christ, who as God deserves and *receives worship* (Heb 1:6), should also as a human *be a worshiper himself!* When believers gather for worship, Jesus has promised to be in our midst, lifting up his own praise and leading us in ours.

Not Our Worship Ministry

As we saw, for those who teach and preach the word, so for those of us who plan and lead worship: we need to recognize that it is *not our worship ministry*. We are not really the worship leaders—*Jesus is!* He is the one who leads our singing and presents our worship to the Father.[4]

His Priesthood Our Access

The writer maintains that we can "draw near" (Heb 10:22) because of the *past* work of Christ ("*since* we have confidence to enter the holy places by the blood of Jesus" [Heb 10:19]) *and* because of his *present* work ("*since* we have a great priest over the house of God" [10:21].

As we saw in chapter 22, Christ's continuing priesthood is a major theme in Hebrews (5:6; 6:20; 7:17; 8:1–2). A crucial function of a priest is to worship and to lead the people in worship. "A priest not worshipping, is indeed a contradiction. And God hath sworn and will not repent

---

4. *From the Field:* In 2023 I gave a seminar for church leaders in Jordan, where I introduced the concept of Jesus as the leader of our worship and of our singing. (The occasion was the release of the Arabic translation of my book *Proclamation and Praise*.) Afterwards a young man approached and through a translator told me that he was from Iran. With a concerned look on his face, he explained that in his church in his home country they could not sing, because of the danger of being overheard. "So," he asked, "does that mean we are not worshiping?" It broke my heart to hear that, and I assured him that the Lord certainly understood their limitations and that of course they *were* worshiping.

that Jesus is a Priest forever."[5] A priest who leads worship must himself be a worshiper: true and full mediation (and incarnation) must certainly include this aspect. That he leads the congregation in its praise is not explicitly stated in Hebrews 2:12, but is clearly implied in harmony with the rest of Hebrews and the New Testament. It stands to reason that our high priest is the one who must lead us in offering our sacrifice, which is now identified as a "sacrifice of praise" (Heb 13:15, which explicitly states that we make that sacrifice *"through him"*). It is a natural conclusion that our praises would be in conjunction with, motivated by, empowered by, and even led by Christ's praises "in the midst of the congregation" (Heb 2:12b).

His Worship Our Worship

When Christ our model and brother praises the Father, he leads the way (*"the new and living way,"* Heb 10:19) for us. Because we are in union with him, his worship is our worship. Through him we come into the Father's presence in worship; we come clothed in his righteousness, and he bears up our weak offerings of worship and makes them one with his own perfect offering of praise. James Torrance has aptly summarized Jesus' role: "The real agent in all true worship is Jesus Christ."[6]

In its essence, New Testament worship centers in Jesus Christ and his two-way mediating ministry. Our worship is in, through, with, and by Jesus Christ:

> *Through him* then let us continually offer up a sacrifice of praise to God, that is, the fruit of lips that acknowledge his name. (Heb 13:15)

Implications for Our Worship

There are crucial implications and correctives for our understanding and practice of worship from the truths we have been examining in this chapter.

---

5. Tait, *Meditationes Hebraicae*, 16.
6. James Torrance, *Worship, Community*, 17.

1. New covenant worship is trinitarian worship.

As John Witvliet puts it:

- The Father *receives* our worship,
- The Son *perfects* our worship,
- and the Spirit *prompts* it.[7]

2. As much as we rightly focus on the past, finished work of Christ, we dare not neglect his *present* ministry ("since we *have* a great priest over the house of God" Heb 10:21).

The book of Hebrews has more to say about Jesus' continuing work than any other book in the New Testament.

- He leads our worship. (2:12; 3:1; 8:1–2, 6; 10:21; 13:15)
- He intercedes for us and comes to our aid. (2:18; 4:14–16; 7:25; 9:24; 13:21)
- He guarantees our eternal salvation. (7:25)

3. The living Christ is present in our midst when we gather for worship ("*in the midst of the congregation* I will sing your praise" Heb 2:12b).

4. Christ is the essence, enabler, empowerer, channel, guide, activator, offerer, mediator, and perfector of all true worship.

Worship and prayer are energized, transported, sanctified, and perfected by Christ as the basis for acceptance by the Father. This is a much more active understanding of the dynamics of worship and prayer than we often acknowledge. Our living and active Savior has not just opened or pointed out the way for us into the Father's presence (Heb 10:19–20); he

---

7. Witvliet, "Trinity Sunday" (emphases added). He also expands on this idea in his "Prism of Glory," 298.

takes us with him! In the words of Christopher Cocksworth: "The invitation of the book of Hebrews is *to go where he goes*"![8]

Worship is possible only in him and through him, by his grace and in his name. He is the "one mediator between God and men, the man Christ Jesus" (1 Tim 2:5). He is the ladder between heaven and earth (Gen 28:12; John 1:51), the bridge across the great divide.

5. Jesus is the only Way, but he is an all-sufficient Way.

As Bob Kauflin importantly reminds us:

> No worship leader, pastor, band, or song will ever bring us close to God. . . . Worship itself cannot lead us into God's presence. *Only Jesus himself* can bring us into God's presence.[9]

In spite of a huge diversity in worship styles and practices, in music and dress and architecture and forms and customs, from church to church, culture to culture, continent to continent, century to century throughout the history of the church—the fact remains that there is a constant wherever true worship is taking place: it is *the role of the living Christ in the midst of his people, leading their worship*. James Torrance stresses that "there is *only one way* to come to the Father, namely through Christ in the communion of saints, whatever outward form our worship may take."[10]

In light of Jesus' unique role as worship leader,[11] perhaps then a new title is needed for those of us who lead the people's praise—"worship facilitator"?[12]

---

8. Cocksworth, *Holy, Holy, Holy,* 157 (emphasis added). And Luther, writing on Hebrews 10:19–22, calls Christ the "ferryman" who takes us to the Father (*Lectures*, 226).

9. Kauflin, *Worship Matters*, 74.

10. Torrance, "Doctrine of the Trinity," 6.

11. The greatest compliment I ever got as a worship leader was: "You seemed to disappear, and we only saw Jesus!"

12. *From the Field:* In teaching a group of young worship leaders in Bangladesh in 2022, I emphasized this truth that they were not really worship leaders, but rather something more like worship facilitators. I was gratified several months later to see that the ministry that had invited me was advertising another training event—for "worship facilitators"! But a missionary friend working in France shared an even better idea. She wrote me: "I'm doing some practical workshops for a church in northern France this weekend. They call their group of musicians and leaders their '*serviteurs du*

> 6. Both the proclamation and exposition of God's word *and* the corporate praises of the congregation are done through and by (and are therefore both important aspects of) the effectual mediating ministry of Jesus Christ.

Some pastors and others consider preaching to be the real focus and goal of the service, and all other parts as only preliminary or preparatory. The Lord Jesus Christ would seem to disagree with that assessment! He thinks the public praises of God's people are so important that *he has committed himself to be right in the middle of that practice also*, initiating and empowering it and infusing it with the glory of his presence. We do not come to church to simply hear a sermon; rather we come to dialogue with the Father through Christ, to learn of God and be changed by him, to respond with heart and lips and lives of worship and obedience and service.

> 7. Our worship is pleasing and acceptable to God not because of its own inherent excellence, but because of (and only because of) the excellence of his Son.

God accepts and delights in our worship, not because of even our best efforts (we can't impress him with our artistry or even with our spirituality), but because of the Son's continual offering of worship in our place and on our behalf. He gathers up our imperfect expressions of worship into his own perfect one. It is not the excellence of our worship (quality, quantity, or form) that makes it acceptable and pleasing to the Father, but the excellence of his Son, with whom he is eternally well-pleased (Matt 3:17; 17:5; 2 Pet 1:17).[13]

We, as worshipers and as worship leaders, do not have to come to public (or private) worship fearing if it will be *"good enough,"* if it will be *acceptable* to God. When we come through and in dependence upon

---

culte' (worship servants), which is both original and quite appropriate!" Appropriate indeed! *Worship servants*: serving God in worship, and serving his people in worship!

13. *From the Field:* A student at Singapore Bible College commented on her newfound freedom in worship gained from the course and especially from the truths expounded in this chapter: "My view of worship was radically changed upon reading this book. I admit that I was rebuked by how I worship God before. Furthermore, my fear of attending this class because I cannot sing or I am out of tune was replaced with excitement to worship God and to know more on how to worship Him with reverence and joy as I learn more during our class."

Christ, our worship will *always* be good enough! And that is indeed *true freedom* for those of us involved in worship planning and leading, as well as for all of us as worshipers. We must repent of trying to do worship in our own strength and depend on Christ to do what only he can do!

Robert Webber wrote these powerful words:

> Who can love God with his heart, mind, and soul? Who can achieve perfect union with God? Who can worship God with a pure and unstained heart?
>
> Not me! . . . Not you. Not Billy Graham. . . . Not Matt Redman. Not anybody I know or you know.
>
> Only Jesus can. And He does for me and for you what neither of us can do for ourselves.
>
> This is the message that is missing in the literature of contemporary worship.[14] It is too much about what I ought to do and too little about what God has done for me. God has done for me what I cannot do for myself. He did it in Jesus Christ. Therefore my worship is offered in a broken vessel that is in the process of being healed, but is not yet capable of fullness of joy, endless intense passion, absolute exaltation, and celebration. But Jesus, who shares in my humanity yet without sin, is not only my Savior—he is also my complete and eternal worship, doing for me, in my place, what I cannot do. . . .
>
> He is eternally interceding to the Father on our behalf. And for this reason, our worship is always in and through Christ. . . .
>
> Thanks for Jesus Christ, who is my worship. We are free! And in gratitude, we offer our stumbling worship in the name of Jesus with thanksgiving.[15]

And so, as Hebrews 10:19–22 encourages us, we can "draw near with a true heart *in full assurance of faith,*" having "*confidence* to enter the holy places by the blood of Jesus."

Conclusion

God's Grace for Our Worship

God expects, deserves, and commands perfect worship. None of us is capable of that, but in his grace, God has provided for us in Christ "the

---

14. And, I would maintain, it is also missing in much of the literature of *traditional* worship as well!

15. Webber, "Blended Worship Response," 130.

new and living way" (Heb 10:19) to offer up that perfect worship. This is *God's grace for our worship*.

He does not intend for us to operate on a performance basis in our worship any more than in our salvation or sanctification. While we should of course offer our best to God in worship (through studying, practicing, and praying), ultimately that is not the ground of our acceptance before him. We cannot impress him with our worship! And we do not need to.

Worship Is Not a Work

We do not offer up our services, our sets, and our songs in hopes that by saying or singing or doing the right thing God will be obligated to "show up" and bless us. Instead we rest and bask in the status we enjoy with him as his beloved children, because we are in Christ by his mercy.

It is profoundly important to see that *worship is not a work*, not something we do entirely in our own strength. It is a grateful and humble gift that we offer to God in response to the grace that he has lavished on us, a response made perfectly acceptable as we offer it to God through Christ.

God receives great glory by *providing for us what he demands from us*. The all-sufficiency of Christ envelops, enriches, fulfills, and perfects our worship. *The power of true worship*, in all its wonderfully varied manifestations, is *the living Christ in our midst*.

Christ!

> *Through him* then let us continually offer up a sacrifice of praise to God, that is, the fruit of lips that acknowledge his name. (Heb 13:15)

Here is a moving account of this beautiful reality:

> Johann von Staupitz, Luther's mentor, asked him once, "Luther, what happens if all this works, if you have your Reformation? What happens to the devotions, and to the pilgrimages, and to the relics, and to all the wonderful things of the Church; and to the marvelous, majestic liturgy, with all of its pomp and ceremony; all these things that we've grown up with and that we

love so dearly and that are so close to our hearts? What will be left when you're through?" And Luther said, "Christ!"[16]

Christ! He is all we need. He is the author of life (Acts 3:15); the one mediator and bridge between God and humanity (1 Tim 2:5; John 1:51); the founder and perfecter of our faith (Heb 12:2); our great high priest (Heb 4:14). And he is the leader of our worship (Heb 2:12). Amen![17]

Jesus Christ is the leader of our worship.

For Reflection and/or Discussion

Do you feel liberated by the understanding
that worship is not a work, and is fully acceptable
to God through Christ as its leader?

16. Cited in Horton, "Worship." *From the Field:* In 2005, the first time I taught this material at Jordan Evangelical Theological Seminary (an amazingly strategic ministry in the heart of the Middle East), I finished with this anecdote, and the entire class immediately *erupted in applause!* The truth of the centrality and sufficiency of Christ was just so precious to them. (The prayer tower at the seminary has engraved on it, in Greek in order to be a little less confrontational than if it were in Arabic, the words from Colossians 1:27: "Christ in you, the hope of glory." What a powerful testimony in that part of the world! And it can lead to good discussions when visitors ask what the words mean!)

17. *From the Field:* A missionary friend shared with me this thrilling account:
> In one of the seminaries where I taught, Biblical Seminary of the Philippines, I had several Chinese Filipino students. These were Chinese people who have made the Philippines their home because of business and educational reasons. One such student, Vincent, was the associate pastor in a leading Chinese church, United Evangelical Church of the Philippines. In the Chinese churches, as in line with the traditions, the older people led the church. Their worship styles and manners were traditional, which the younger generations found it hard to appreciate. So, Vincent tried to bring in some changes and faced strong opposition from the elders. The elders' key objection was that Jesus never sang songs and therefore singing should never be part of worship. Unaware of Vincent's struggles, I shared in the class about Ron's book *Proclamation and Praise*, with key emphasis on Hebrews 2:12 where the prophecy concerning the Lord was recited: "I will proclaim your name to my siblings; in the midst of the church *I will hymnalize* you" (my translation). Vincent came and asked me for a copy of Ron's book. He shared the book and the concept of the Lord *hymnalizing* in the midst of his people with the elders. Soon after that the elders said, "If the Lord *sings* among his congregation, then our people can also sing songs." The result was a revived church, full of vibrant Chinese young people who sing praises and lift petitionary prayers.

Part 6

Worship in the Church

Having considered the broad topic of worship from many different angles, and having taken an intentionally nonsectarian approach to the lessons we can learn from the Scriptures, we turn now finally to focus on the practice of worship on the local church level.

This is, of course, a perilous undertaking, because it is here that we inevitably run into the issues of taste, preference, and culture that lead to so much of the debate and (sadly) dissension and even division in our churches today. There is obviously an incredible diversity of worship styles, approaches, and practices in our own local contexts, not to mention across the world and down through the centuries! In this part we will seek to carefully distinguish between biblical *nonnegotiables* and allowable *negotiables* as we take a broad view of worship practices across the church of Jesus Christ. We will definitely need the Scriptures to help us navigate this minefield!

25. The Nature and Priority of Worship in the Church
26. The Importance of Worship in the Church
27. The Content of Worship in the Church
28. Worship and Culture

25

THE NATURE AND PRIORITY OF WORSHIP IN THE CHURCH

Jewish Roots

While we do not have a lot of historical information about worship in the very earliest churches, we can observe that there were influences from Christianity's Jewish roots: both from the *synagogue* (especially the practice of the reading and expounding of the Scriptures) and from the *temple* (especially the remembrance of the once-for-all sacrifice of Christ in the celebration of the Lord's Supper).

The New Testament Witness

There is a little information to be found in the New Testament. In Acts 2, Luke tells us that at the conclusion of Peter's Pentecost sermon, "those who received his word were baptized, and there were added that day about three thousand souls" (2:41). And then *in the very next verse* Luke tells us what these new believers regularly did when they got together: "And they devoted themselves to the apostles' teaching and the fellowship, to the breaking of bread and the prayers" (2:42). And a few verses later we read that they were also "praising God" (2:47). They "devoted" themselves to these activities:

- the apostles' teaching (of the Old Testament, at that time)
- the fellowship
- the breaking of bread (or the Lord's Supper)
- the prayers
- praising God

It seems likely that Luke mentions these elements *immediately* after the account of the conversion of the first Christians (and emphasizes that they regularly "devoted" themselves to them) in order to suggest that these were *normative* activities for the church. And, in fact, if we consider what elements of worship are found in virtually *every* Christian tradition, across denominations and down through the centuries, we see that these are indeed consistent features (though fleshed out in widely diverse ways):

- the word of God (now the entire Bible)
- fellowship
- Communion or Lord's Supper
- prayer
- praise

These seem to be nonnegotiable *constants* for worship to be truly Christian.[1] Historically, around these elements often developed very complex structures; nevertheless, it is important to recognize these consistent elements.

Elsewhere in the New Testament, the element of singing is mentioned (Eph 5:18–20; Col 3:16; 1 Cor 14:26).

An Early Description

The earliest extant account of a Christian worship service, outside of the New Testament, dates from about the year 155:

---

1. *From the Field:* When teaching overseas, I would often assign as an overnight exercise for the students to consider just that question about what elements of worship are found in *every* Christian tradition. The students would invariably come up with a list virtually identical to the list above—another indication that Acts 2 is indeed signifying normative worship activities for the church.

> On the day called Sunday, all who live in cities or in the country gather together to one place, and the memoirs of the apostles or the writings of the prophets are read, as long as time permits; then, when the reader has ceased, the president verbally instructs, and exhorts to the imitation of these good things. Then we all rise together and pray, and, as we before said, when our prayer is ended, bread and wine and water are brought, and the president in like manner offers prayers and thanksgivings, according to his ability, and the people assent, saying Amen; and there is a distribution to each, and a participation of that over which thanks have been given, and to those who are absent a portion is sent by the deacons. And they who are well to do, and willing, give what each thinks fit; and what is collected is deposited with the president, who succours the orphans and widows, and those who, through sickness or any other cause, are in want, and those who are in bonds, and the strangers sojourning among us, and in a word takes care of all who are in need.[2]

A Later Characterization

Gordon Lathrop makes these observations about the commonalities of many (if not most) Christian gatherings up to this day.

> An assembly of people gathers. The gathering place may be very simple—a hut, a room, a house—or quite elaborate, one of the buildings developed over time from the large public buildings of the late Roman Empire. Singing enables these people to come together, and prayer, often spoken by one who acts as a presider, sums up the sense of the song, interpreting that coming together as being before God. Then, as if this were the principal reason for the gathering, ancient texts are read by one or more readers. Frequently the readings are interspersed with further song. The presider speaks about the meaning of the readings and the meaning of the gathering, and the people respond with yet more song or with an ancient credal text, corporately recited. Another person in the assembly leads prayers for a variety of needs throughout the world. Then gifts of money (and sometimes food) that have been brought by persons in the assembly are collected. Some of the people set a central table—perhaps a simple

---

2. Justin Martyr, "First Apology of Justin," 185–86. It has been noted that, interestingly, Justin here makes no mention of music; but he does speak of hymns elsewhere in this document.

piece of furniture, perhaps a massive stone—with food, linens, and candles as if for a feast, adding to the growing sense in the meeting that the other principal reason for the gathering is to be this meal. The food set out, however, is simply bread—in one or another form—and a cup of wine. In dialogue with the assembly, the one who presides speaks or sings a formal thanksgiving over the food, and, most commonly aided by others, distributes the food to the assembly for all to eat and drink. Concluding prayers and songs follow, and the assembly is dismissed.

Such a gathering, widely practiced in most of the Christian churches as the principal act of worship, has been especially associated with Sunday, though sometimes it may also occur on other days. It has been practiced, more or less in this form, for a long time, being traceable to the earliest centuries of the Christian movement. In the diverse churches the outline of the assemblies' actions may differ slightly, being intensified with more or less ceremony, led by a single person or by many people, interspersed with more or less communal song, and partly or wholly obscured because of the overlay of rich secondary patterns of action. In all of the churches, other events may be inserted into this outline, especially that washing with water whereby the community adds people to its number. Still, something like this assembly occurs weekly throughout the churches and is treasured as the very heart of Christianity.[3]

The Ultimate Goal

As we saw in chapter 9, John Piper shook up the evangelical world and the missions community with his insistence that:

> Missions is not the ultimate goal of the church. Worship is. Missions exists because worship doesn't.

Piper has in mind worship in its broadest understanding, such as we have been focusing on for most of this book. Nevertheless, he sees *corporate worship in the church* as a crucial expression of the inner worship of the heart. In fact, he goes as far as to state that:

> Of all the activities in the church, only one is an end in itself: *worship*.[4]

---

3. Lathrop, *Holy Things*, 1–2.
4. Piper, "Worship Is an End" (emphasis added).

This is a strong statement, indeed!

You will recall the treatment in chapter 8 comparing the Great Commission and the Great Commandment:

> We might say that the end goal of evangelism is to win *more* worshipers for God (from among the nations); and that the final purpose of discipleship is to build *better* worshipers of God—those who love God with ever more of their heart, soul, mind, and strength.

The same conclusion can be brought down to the level of the local church. One could say that the end goal of all the evangelistic/outreach activities of the church (including missions) is to win *more* worshipers for God, and that the end goal of all discipleship activities in the church (everything from children's ministry, to youth groups, to adult small groups and Bible studies, and even preaching itself) is to build *better* worshipers for God. We minister to children, to youth, to adults to help them become worshipers and then to grow in their love for and worship of God. Adapting Piper's phraseology, we could say that:

- Sunday School exists because worship doesn't.
- Youth groups exist because worship doesn't.
- Evangelism teams exist because worship doesn't.
- Discipleship programs exist because worship doesn't.
- Preaching exists because worship doesn't.

Worship is an end in itself! It is not a means to any other end (except the glory of God).

The Purpose of the Church

What we see from this is the importance of recognizing *a worship-directed, God-centered purpose for the church*. Through the church's ministries we seek to reach, help, encourage, and disciple people. But ultimately, we do all that *so that* they can reach their created potential as worshipers and lovers of God.

This important perspective should influence the crafting of churches' mission statements: instead of focusing solely on the Great Commission (as important as it is) as the church's primary purpose, proper place should be given to worship and the glory of God as ultimate ends. Here is one example of such a balanced statement:

> The mission of the church is to glorify God through joyful worship, to show God's love to all people, to lead them to faith in Jesus Christ, to make them his disciples, and to call them to his service.

Ministry for God

Every person in ministry (staff or volunteer) should have an ultimate *vertical* purpose to his or her ministry: a purpose of seeking to reflect and demonstrate and display the glory of God in the lives of people; a purpose of building into others (as they seek to also build into their own lives) a preoccupation with God, a loving of him with all the heart, soul, mind, and strength, a cherishing of him and his glory in lives of worship.

Others' Testimony to This Perspective

> A. W. Tozer: "The Christian church exists to worship God first of all. Everything else must come second or third or fourth or fifth."[5]

> William Nicholls: "Worship is the supreme and only indispensable activity of the Christian Church. It alone will endure, like the love for God which it expresses, into heaven, when all other activities of the Church will have passed away."[6]

> "Of all the activities in the church, only one is an end in itself: worship." (John Piper)

For Reflection and/or Discussion

Has this book, and this chapter, caused you to reorient your life more around worship?

---

5. Tozer, *Whatever Happened to Worship?*, 56.
6. Nicholls, *Jacob's Ladder*, 9.

26

THE IMPORTANCE OF WORSHIP IN THE CHURCH

Though, as just stated, worship (including worship in the church) is an end in itself, we can identify a number of other values and benefits for the people of God.[1]

1. Worship in the church honors the Father.

This is the ultimate purpose of corporate worship. It serves no higher purpose than this; it is a means to no other end.

God seeks, delights in, and indeed demands our worship. In the corporate gathering we "ascribe to the Lord the glory due his name" (Ps 96:8), as we acclaim him as Creator and Ruler; we celebrate his supreme worthiness, majesty, and attributes; and we proclaim our wonder at his grace and his great plan for the redemption of humanity (Eph 1:3–14).

2. Worship in the church celebrates Christ.

We exalt in the person and work of Christ. We bask in the glory of the gospel, as we tell, again and again, the "old, old story of Jesus and his

---

1. The following points are adapted from Allmen, *Worship*, 111–26; and Dawn, *Reaching Out*, chapters 6 and 7.

love." And we commemorate his death on the cross and remind ourselves of our part in his redemptive work as we celebrate the Lord's Supper.

3. Worship in the church draws us into fellowship with Christ and with the Father.

In corporate worship we draw near to God through, in and with our Mediator, the Lord Jesus Christ. He grants us access to the Father and takes us with him into the Father's presence (Heb 10:19-22) as he actively leads us in our expressions of praise (Heb 2:12).

4. Worship in the church foreshadows the kingdom.

Corporate worship reflects the worship of heaven as it looks forward to the time when all creation will continually praise its Maker, when we will "see him as he is" (1 John 3:2), and when we will eat and drink anew with Christ (Luke 22:30). It is a reflection of (and participation in—see chapter 10) the worship that even now goes on around the throne of God in heaven (Rev 4 and 5), and of that ultimate, unending worship of the future.

5. Worship in the church is used by the Holy Spirit.

In corporate worship the Spirit can act in believers' hearts through the truth proclaimed and sung and prayed, encouraging and engendering a deeper commitment to and growth in the Lord. And unbelievers can also be drawn by the Spirit as they see Christians in worship (1 Cor 14:24-25).

6. Worship in the church gives identity to the church.

The church is truly and identifiably *the church* when it is gathered for corporate worship. It is there that we are reminded that though we are *in* the world, we are not *of* the world (John 17:14-16)—we are set apart (2 Tim 2:21). And we celebrate our unity in the removal of sociological and ethnic barriers (Gal 3:28).

Yet we are indeed not gathered all the time, but have a necessary missionary aspect to our lives in the world. A helpful image is that of breathing: we breathe in (like the church gathering), and we breathe out (like the church scattering into the world). The process repeats itself over and over again. A healthy body must breathe both in and out; so too a healthy church body must both gather and scatter.

7. Worship in the church testifies to the world.

Corporate worship is a *challenge* to a world system that denies the relevance or even the existence of God. We proclaim in our gatherings what is true reality, the hope of the present and the world's future.[2]

But the testimony of corporate worship is not just a *challenge* to the world, but also an *invitation,* for all are invited to come and "taste and see that the LORD is good" (Ps 34:11), to find redemption and meaning.

8. Worship in the church nurtures the character of the believer.

"We become like that which we worship," goes the saying (see Ps 115:4–8). Corporate worship in spirit and truth feeds and nourishes us in the Lord, and motivates our growth in and commitment to him.

9. Worship in the church builds Christian community.

We do not gather to each have our own little private worship time with the Lord (there are other places and times for that), but together we build ourselves up (Heb 10:24): as we exercise our gifts for the common good (Eph 4:13–16); as we demonstrate love, kindness, humility, etc., towards one another in the corporate gathering (Col 3:12–15); and as we "let the word of Christ dwell in [us] richly, teaching and admonishing one another in all wisdom, singing psalms and hymns and spiritual songs" (Col 3:16). We are also reminded that we are part of the universal body

---

2. *From the Field:* Once while teaching in Moldova, I attended a Baptist church with an odd feature: the church roof was simply flattened off where a steeple would normally be. I was told that when Moldova was still part of the Soviet Union, the authorities gave permission to the church to build this building, but with the stipulation that it could not have a steeple; this was so that the church would not be too visible to surrounding neighborhoods. It was recognized to be a challenge to the atheistic Soviet system.

of Christ, joining with believers from across the world and across the centuries.

10. Worship in the church reorients believers to their true center.

After a week of bombardment by competing worldviews and a panoply of false "worships," corporate worship among God's people reminds us of who, and whose, we are.

11. Worship in the church prepares hearts for the preaching of the word.

Of course preaching is part of worship as well, but of a different kind. As hearts are filled with wonder from the rehearsal of familiar truths through Scripture readings, songs, and prayers, and they become more ready to be challenged through the word preached to ascend to new levels of understanding and commitment.

> Corporate worship gives identity to the church.

For Reflection and/or Discussion

What aspects of the importance of worship
in this chapter inspire you the most?

27

THE CONTENT OF WORSHIP IN THE CHURCH[1]

In this chapter we will unpack the normative elements of the corporate gathering mentioned by Luke in Acts 2:42, 46–47.

The Word of God ("the apostles' teaching")

In chapter 3 we already considered the importance of the word in worship.

The word is foundational for our worship in all its aspects, including our corporate worship in the church. When Christians gather, it is logical that the word of God should play a central and dominant role. For since worship involves focusing our thoughts and hearts and voices on the praise of God, in response to his self-revelation and his gracious saving initiative, our worship can duly honor God only if it accurately reflects what he shows us about himself in his word.

---

1. *Baptism* is an important, but usually not a weekly, feature of corporate worship, and will not be dealt with here. It is of course also a subject that has engendered much debate and controversy. The reader is referred to the balanced and fair treatment in Wayne Grudem's *Systematic Theology*, chapter 49; there are also many fine comparative studies.

The Word Neglected in Worship

The astounding observation has been made as to how little use is made of Scripture in the worship services of many evangelical churches. The irony, of course, is that those who claim to most strongly stand on the Bible have so little of it in their worship! In too many churches the entire first part of the service consists just of music—albeit songs about God and songs reflective of biblical truth (a minimum requirement for songs for worship)—but no Scripture is read at all. I have experienced this often in both traditional and contemporary services—the problem is pervasive.[2]

At the beginning of the service the people should hear/read (and/or see flashed on a screen) verses of Scripture chosen to give a clear signal that: "We have come to worship God. The word is how we know about God, and therefore it is the foundation for all that we do here and for our understanding of why we have come together." Without such a declaration—launching into songs without any context of revelation being set—worshipers make the faulty assumption (consciously or unconsciously) that we invite ourselves into God's presence, when in actuality it is only by virtue of his invitation (and his opening the way through the work of Christ) that we may come before him at all.

Ligon Duncan highlights the centrality of the Scriptures in Christian worship by urging us to "read the Bible, preach the Bible, pray the Bible, sing the Bible and see the Bible."[3]

The Word Read in Worship

> Until I come, devote yourself to the public reading of Scripture, to exhortation, to teaching. (1 Tim 4:13)

How rarely this command is obeyed in our churches!

As mentioned before, in Anglican, Catholic, and Orthodox churches, Scripture is prominent because it is built into their liturgies. Churches in the free church tradition must be more intentional to "let the word of Christ dwell richly among you" (Col 3:16); it necessitates more effort and focused attention.

---

2. *From the Field:* And I have personally experienced this problem in churches all over the world.

3. Duncan, "Foundations," 65. To "see the Bible" refers to the Lord's Supper.

Chapter 3 gives numerous ways in which the word of God can be given its proper place in the corporate gathering.

The Lord's Supper/Communion ("the breaking of bread")

In obedience to Jesus' command (Luke 22:19), his church has always made the ritual remembrance of his substitutionary sacrifice on the cross a central part of gathered worship.[4] In fact, in most traditions the Lord's Supper was celebrated weekly for the first 1,500 years of the church. Some groups continue this practice, though many groups now opt for a monthly observance, while others do it quarterly or even less often. (As will be seen later in chapter 28, in the absence of specific biblical instruction as to frequency, there is freedom in this respect.)

Remembrance

An understanding of the biblical nuance of "remembrance" (Greek *anamnesis*) is key to our understanding of the Lord's Supper. Biblical remembrance is not just commemorating an event long past, but rather recognizing the present implications and impact of that event. This was true of the Jewish Passover, and is true of the Lord's Supper.

> At the Last Supper, we do not merely remember the Passion of our Lord as an isolated date from 1900 years ago. Rather we remember it in such a way that we know that *we* are the people for whom our Saviour died and rose again. We are what we are today by the grace of God because of what God did for us then.[5]

---

4. Most Protestants recognize this as one of two "ordinances" (along with baptism), as ritual observances ordained by Christ himself as signs and symbols of divine grace effected by God internally in the life of the believer. Other Christian groups add more rituals to these two, and identify them as "sacraments" (i.e., acts that *in themselves* impart divine grace).

5. Torrance, "Place of Jesus Christ in Worship," 355–56.

The Scope of the Lord's Supper

Time (Past-Present-Future)

As seen above, at the Table we acknowledge that when Jesus died, he died for each of us—thus bringing the significance of the *past* event into our *present* experience. There is also a crucial *future* aspect as well. Paul writes: "For as often as you eat this bread and drink the cup, you proclaim the Lord's death *until he comes*" (1 Cor 11:26). We look ahead to when we will eat, drink, and enjoy table fellowship with our Savior in the kingdom (Luke 22:16, 18).

Senses

Of all Christian worship practices, the Lord's Supper is the most multi-sensory: we hear "the old, old story of Jesus and his love"; we see, touch, smell, and taste the elements.

Emotions

The Lord's Supper is a serious time, but ultimately not a sad one. It is *not* a funeral service for Jesus! Rather we somberly remember the price paid for our redemption (1 Cor 6:20), yet acknowledge that the work is finished (John 19:30) and that Jesus is our victorious and risen Savior (Rom 1:4), having conquered sin and death (Rom 8:2). So there is room in the celebration for *serious* reflection, but also for overwhelming *joy* and *gratitude*.

Personal but Corporate

Participating in the Lord's Supper offers the opportunity for *personal* reflection about one's former state and the glorious reality of all that we are and all that we have because we are in Christ by his redeeming work; and about the precious truth that in Christ *all* our sins (including our latest ones!) are forgiven thanks to his shed blood. Yet at the same time the Lord's Supper is a uniquely *corporate* observance. Many of the activities of worship we can also do when we are alone (Bible study, prayer, even singing), but the Lord's Supper is something we do *together* in the body of Christ.[6]

Much more could be said about the wide range of doctrinal understandings and practices of the Lord's Supper among various Christian groups, and there are many books that address these issues. For a balanced overview, see chapter 50 in Wayne Grudem's *Systematic Theology*.

Prayer ("the prayers")

Corporate prayer is an important unifying and focusing activity for the people of God, yet too little time and attention is given to this aspect of worship in many churches.

The pastor or other leader who is going to lead the church in prayer should be diligent to make adequate *preparation* in advance. Public prayer deserves planning, as does the sermon or the music. There is a place for written-out (or at least thought-out) prayers, as well as spontaneous prayers. Always praying extemporaneously can lead to repetitiousness and triteness.

Elements to include in prayer include (though not necessarily all in one prayer) praise, thanksgiving, confession, and intercession. Intercessory prayer should include known needs within the congregation (as well as its missionaries elsewhere), but should also look outside the walls of the church and bring important global, national, and local issues and leaders before God in prayer (1 Tim 2:1–2). The news can inform our congregational prayer. If it is something that is on the minds of the people, bring it before the Lord in prayer! It has often been observed that congregational prayers (and in fact, services as a whole) were affected dramatically on the Sunday after 9/11.

Silent prayer can provide a rich opportunity for the Spirit to work in the lives of the congregation. It can be especially important to give people the opportunity to silently reflect and respond at the conclusion of the sermon, when the message from the word is freshest in people's minds and hearts.

---

6. Churches should consider ways to give attention to this corporate aspect during the celebration of the Lord's Supper, perhaps by singing together as the elements are served, perhaps by serving one another the elements, perhaps by looking at our neighbor and reminding him or her as we partake that "this is the body/blood of Christ, given for you."

Bidded prayer (borrowed from the Anglican tradition) is one way to make congregational prayer more participatory. The leader will introduce a petition, and then give the congregation time (perhaps thirty seconds) to silently pray for that matter; then the leader introduces another item for silent prayer, and so on.

Music/Singing ("praising God"; "psalms, hymns and spiritual songs," Eph 5:19, Col 3:16)

(Please see also the extended treatment of "The Ministry of Song" in chapter 20.)

So important is this aspect of the corporate gathering that Jesus Christ himself is committed to leading the people's song (Heb 2:12)! (See chapter 24.)

It must always be remembered that church music is a "functional art."[7] Luther called music "the handmaid of theology": it must serve the truth that it proclaims.

> The Reformers recognized and took advantage of the power of music as a vehicle for communicating truth. So effective were Luther's musical reforms . . . that one outraged Jesuit churchman remarked, "The hymns of Luther have killed more souls than his sermons."[8]

The potential of music to amplify and intensify what is sung means that we have a great responsibility to ensure that what we are singing is infused with biblical truth. That means that song texts (when not directly from Scripture) must be carefully evaluated in terms of theological accuracy. And the musical vehicle chosen should complement (not overwhelm or contradict) the text that it delivers, and should be presented to the best of our ability, with care and diligent preparation (though musical excellence is not the ultimate goal).[9]

---

7. Hustad, *Jubilate II*, 22.
8. Fromm, "New Song."
9. See Man, "Music for Worship."

Readings Other than Scripture

Church history provides many rich instances of biblically faithful expressions that may be profitably used for solo, unison, or responsive readings in the worship service.

The Great Creeds of the Church

Powerful expressions of basic orthodox beliefs shared by Christians through the centuries can give a real sense of historical continuity and community (read in unison, of course). For instance: the Nicene Creed (AD 325); the Apostles' Creed (fourth century); the *Te Deum* (ca. AD 387).

Catechisms

Catechisms were primers in Christian beliefs, used for instruction of children and new believers. The question-and-answer format lends itself to use in responsive readings. For instance, individual questions and answers from the Heidelberg Catechism (1563) can be used that focus on the work of Christ, the Trinity, the Holy Spirit, etc. For example:

> Question 1: What is your only comfort in life and death?
> Answer: That I am not my own, but belong with body and soul, both in life and in death, to my faithful Saviour Jesus Christ. He has fully paid for all my sins with His precious blood, and has set me free from all the power of the devil.

Book of Common Prayer (1549, with multiple later revisions)

This is the liturgical guide for the Church of England. Largely written by Thomas Cranmer, it is richly poetic and prayerful, and packed with biblical truth. Again, portions can be profitably read by a leader or by the entire congregation. For example:

> Almighty God, unto whom all hearts are open,
> all desires known, and from whom no secrets are hid:
> Cleanse the thoughts of our hearts by the inspiration of thy Holy Spirit,

that we may perfectly love thee, and worthily magnify thy holy Name;
through Christ our Lord. Amen.

Excerpts can be used in different parts of the service, for instance in introducing Communion:

> We do not presume to come to this thy Table, O merciful Lord, trusting in our own righteousness, but in thy manifold and great mercies.
> We are not worthy so much as to gather up the crumbs under thy Table.
> But thou art the same Lord whose property is always to have mercy.
> Grant us therefore, gracious Lord, so to eat the flesh of thy dear Son Jesus Christ, and to drink his blood, that we may evermore dwell in him, and he in us. Amen.

The Valley of Vision: A Collection of Puritan Prayers and Devotions

This is a recent compilation of deep and rich prayers from the seventeenth, eighteenth, and nineteenth centuries. The readings are organized thematically in the collection, which allows them to be excerpted for special service focuses. For instance, consider this one for New Year's:

> I launch my bark [boat] on the unknown waters of this year,
>   with Thee, O Father, as my harbour;
>   Thee, O Son, at my helm;
>   Thee, O Holy Spirit, filling my sails.
> Give me Thy grace to sanctify me,
>   Thy comforts to cheer,
>   Thy wisdom to teach,
>   Thy right hand to guide,
>   Thy presence to stabilize.

New and Old

The above resources are just a few examples of the multitude of different gems from the centuries of the church. The main point here is to bring into our worship "what is new and what is old" (Matt 13:52). (This goes for songs too, of course.) In this way we express continuity with the "faith of our fathers" and we can thus honor the devotion of, and declare our solidarity with, those who came before us.

The word of God must be central in the worship of the church.

For Reflection and/or Discussion

What elements of worship could be stronger in your life?
In your church's worship life?

28

WORSHIP AND CULTURE

How do we balance the need for biblical fidelity with the need for cultural sensitivity and relevance in our worship? Churches all over the world face that ongoing and persistent challenge.

But this is not a new issue by any means. The early church faced its own set of cultural and cross-cultural challenges. Early churches often included Jews, Greeks, Romans, barbarians, master, slaves, etc., in the same body. Undoubtedly these groups brought widely different cultural perspectives, preferences, and expectations with them. And yet, unlike today in many parts of the world, there was not the option for a discontented Christian to find another church more to one's liking. There was *the* church at Ephesus, *the* church at Corinth, etc. Believers had to hang in there and work things out—not a bad idea in our time, either! Ultimately it was the Holy Spirit's role to forge unity out of their (and our) diversity (Eph 4:3).

Culture

Churches are not immune from the influences of culture. Every one of us lives in, and is in many respects a product of, the culture in which we live. It is "the air we breathe."

Culture has been defined as "the behaviors and beliefs characteristic of a particular social, ethnic, or age group."[1] Yet a simple way to think of it is simply as *"the way we do things around here."*[2]

As Aidan Kavanaugh has put it, Christian worship "swims in creation as a fish swims in water."[3] What a person feels to be appropriate or helpful or meaningful is conditioned by his or her own cultural upbringing.

The Challenges

This brings us back to the question: *How do we balance the need for biblical fidelity with the need for cultural sensitivity and relevance in our worship?* There are two primary challenges that make navigating this issue particularly difficult.

The Silence of the New Testament

As we saw in chapter 18, we search the pages of the New Testament in vain for guidelines for worship (except for some general elements, as discussed in chapter 27). Therefore we have considerable freedom to make choices (about buildings, dress, times, music, etc.)—choices which will inevitably be shaped by our cultural preconditioning.

We might ask, though: Why is the New Testament not more specific about what we are to do in worship? If Jesus or Paul had just laid out the plan, then we could follow it and avoid so many of our discussions, debates, and dissensions about worship practices!

John Piper[4] suggests this reason: In the Old Testament, we had a "Come and See" system:

---

1. Adapted from "culture" at www.dictionary.com.

2. *From the Field:* I was once teaching in Vietnam. When the driver picked me up at the hotel in the morning, he had to go left onto the main street. He proceeded to head directly into the oncoming traffic, then slowly worked his way over to the right side of the road! And amazingly, none of the other drivers blew their horns: this was normal, expected behavior. This is the way they turn left around there! This was an aspect of their driving culture that was not out of place in its own context—though it was terrifying to me as an outsider!

3. Kavanagh, *On Liturgical Theology*, 4.

4. Piper, "Our High Priest."

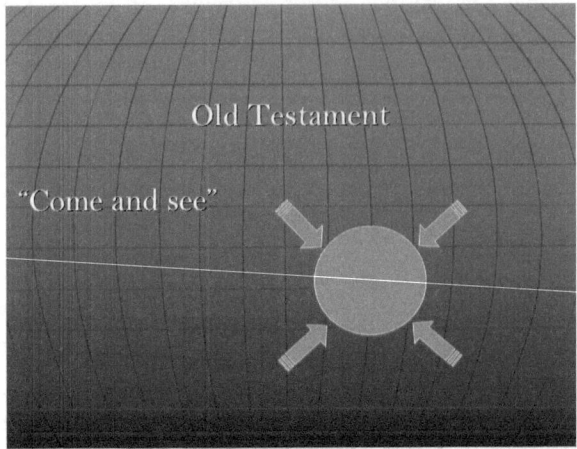

Worship was centralized in a particular time and place. To worship, you had to come to Jerusalem, come to the temple (or before that the tabernacle). And in fact, other people from other nations could worship God, but they had to come to Jerusalem, had to become Jews.

And because it was in a particular time and place, the instructions for worship could be *very* detailed. So in Exodus and Leviticus, we find chapter after chapter of instructions for worship: how to prepare, when to come, what to bring, what to do. It was very specific because it was to be in a specific time and place.

But, as Piper points out, the New Testament is exactly the opposite situation. It is *not* a "Come and See" system. It is a "Go and Tell" system:

There is no geographical center to Christianity, but rather the gospel is to go out into every nation, to every people. And so perhaps for this reason, Piper suggests, the New Testament leaves things so open regarding worship: so that as the gospel goes out, and the church is planted in different cultures, worship can "breathe the air" of, and find expression in, the various cultures in which the church is planted.

The New Testament leaves room for us to make choices about our worship practices. But that brings us face-to-face with the second challenge.

Human Diversity

Cultural preconditioning by no means leads to uniformity of opinion or preferences. People are different. Personality, temperament, and past experiences all play into a wide range of attitudes, perceptions, and responses.

Freedom Within Bounds

The virtual silence of the New Testament writers on matters of form and style for worship seems to indicate that the Lord intends for us to have considerable latitude and flexibility in these areas. But of course this leads to the worship debates that are so common in our day. At the root of these debates is the nature of the interface of worship and culture in the context in which a local church finds itself. The church cannot buy into the surrounding culture without discernment; but it cannot ignore its cultural environment either.

So how shall we then worship? How do we bridge the historical and practical gap between the scriptural mandates and our cultural context? How can our worship be "in" the world but not "of" the world? How do worship and culture intersect?

There is *freedom*, but *within bounds*.

The Bridge[5]

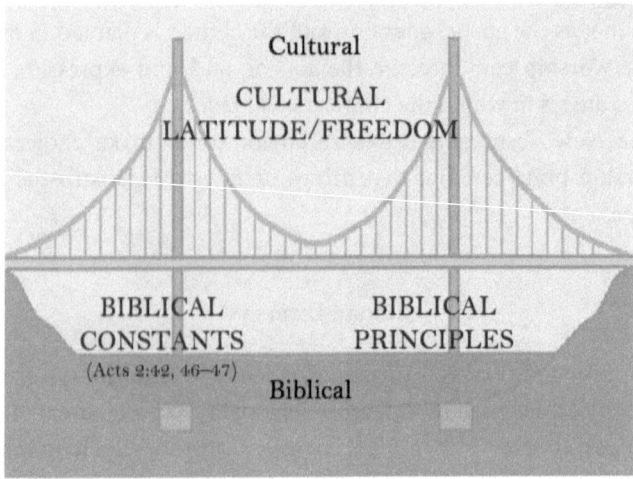

By way of illustration, this model is based on certain characteristics of a *suspension bridge* (familiar examples of suspension bridges are the Brooklyn Bridge in New York City and the Golden Gate Bridge in San Francisco).

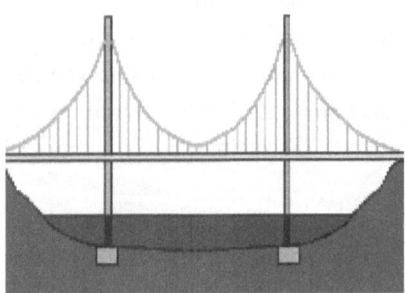

In a suspension bridge, the weight is supported by both the towers and the suspension cable. *The towers* are sunk deep in the earth and are meant to be stable and immovable, being essential to the bridge's integrity and durability.

---

5. See also Man, "Bridge" and chapter 4 in Krabill et al., eds., *Worship and Mission for the Global Church*, 17–25.

The *suspension cable* or *span*, on the other hand, while sharing a significant portion of the load-bearing, nevertheless has by design a great deal of flexibility to expand and contract, thus allowing the bridge to withstand variances in temperature, wind, weight load, etc.

What can we learn about our worship from this illustration? Our worship needs to be supported by firmly rooted biblical foundations, which are illustrated by the two towers. The flexible cable span suggests the liberty that the New Testament seems to allow for individual congregations to constitute their corporate worship. Like any art form, Christian worship allows for much creative expression, but within defined parameters.[6] The Bible gives those parameters as well as that freedom.

The First Tower: *Biblical Constants*

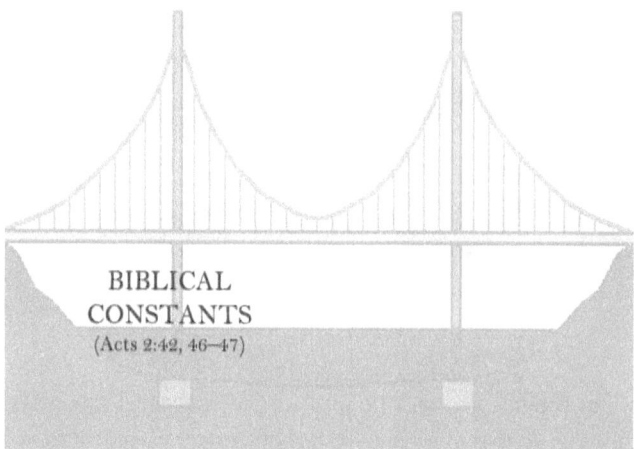

The first tower suggests an immovable aspect of Christian worship that we could term "Biblical Constants." These are nonnegotiables, elements that simply *must* be present for our worship to be considered Christian.

What are these elements? In chapters 25 and 27 we saw that Acts 2 gives us a good starting point, as Luke seems to be describing normative activities for the people of God when they congregate together (Acts 2:42, 46–47):

---

6. For example, a painter has freedom to paint what he or she desires, but *within the constraints* of the frame and the palette of colors.

- The word of God
- Fellowship
- The Lord's Supper
- Prayer
- Praise

These biblical constants serve as one foundational pillar for our worship.[7]

The Span: *Flexibility and Freedom*

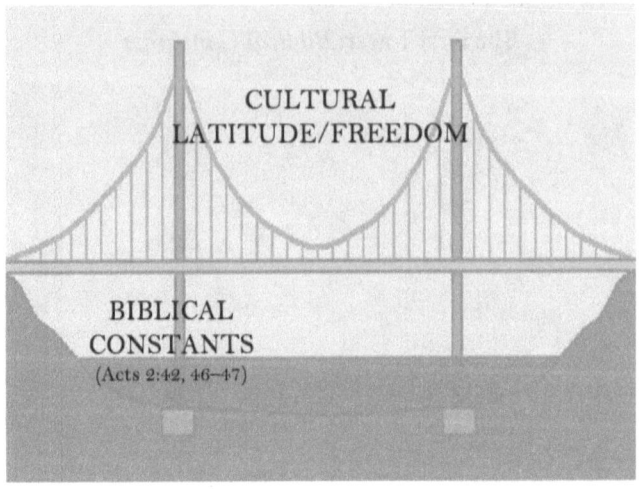

The span of the bridge, with its built-in elasticity and flexibility, represents the *latitude* that the New Testament seems to allow by its virtual silence regarding the specifics of worship: freedom for wise and prudent application of culturally meaningful expressions.

> [We are] free to find place and time and dress and size and music and elements and objects that help us orient radically toward the supremacy of God in Christ.[8]

---

7. It should be noted, however, that there are differences of opinion about what belongs in this realm of nonnegotiables. Some see more biblical guidance from the Old Testament for our New Testament worship forms, for instance. For much more on this, see Farley, "What Is 'Biblical' Worship?"; Meyers, *Lord's Service*; and Chapell, *Christ-Centered Worship*.

8. Piper, "Our High Priest."

We have *a biblical framework* (represented by the two towers), and we dare not go outside it and be truly honoring to God. But within that framework there is a lot of *freedom and latitude* in how we can honor God in our worship.

Freedom of Form Applied Globally

We certainly can see the application of this principle in the vast array of worship expressions seen down through the history of the Christian church and in churches around the world today. There has been, and is, an enormous variety in terms of architecture, atmosphere, form, structure, style, dress, music, liturgy, etc. And God, who has created the world and humanity with such incredible diversity, must certainly rejoice in such variety from his people.[9]

Piper insists that

> the New Testament is not a manual for worship services. Rather, it is a vision for missions in thousands of diverse people groups around the world. In such groups, outward forms of worship will vary drastically, but the inner reality of treasuring Christ in spirit and truth is common ground.[10]

And Tim Keller makes a fascinating point along these lines:

> Why has Christianity, more than any other major religion of the world, been able to infiltrate so many different radically different cultures? There is of course a core of teachings . . . to which all forms of Christianity are committed [=the two towers, the biblical framework].
>
> Nevertheless, there is a great deal of freedom in how these absolutes are expressed and take form within a particular culture [=the span, cultural freedom]. Contrary to popular opinion, then, Christianity is not a Western religion that destroys local cultures. Rather Christianity has taken more culturally diverse forms than other faiths.[11]

---

9. Reggie Kidd in his book *With One Voice* explores the various legitimate expressions of worship found today in the West using categories he calls art music, folk music, and popular music.

10. Piper, *Let the Nations Be Glad*, 247; Piper, "Pursuit of God."

11. Keller, *Reason for God*, 45.

Challenges and Conflict Resulting from Freedom of Form

As already noted, the New Testament's virtual silence on the details of worship and the resultant cultural freedom has led to all kinds of discussions, debates, and disagreements about what is acceptable and what is unacceptable.

The "Worship Wars"

One familiar example is the so-called worship wars in North American churches during the late twentieth century. Most of the controversy revolved around worship atmosphere (formal vs. casual) and music (traditional vs. contemporary, organ vs. band).

The music missionary and ethnomusicologist Tom Avery (1950–2008) once gave a seminar where he drew on his training and field experience to helpfully analyze the issues in these worship wars. Some of his insights were:

1. It is common for people to feel very strongly about the music with which they identify, and to find the music with which they don't identify to be extremely distasteful.
2. We live in a society where different generations may and often do have different musical cultures. (This is caused by the rapid rate of culture change experienced by society, probably unprecedented in the history of the world.)
3. We have people in the same churches who partake of radically different musical cultures.
4. Music is *not* a universal language. It can speak very differently to different groups of people, even within the same church.[12]

To illustrate this last point, Avery humorously but incisively reflected on the polar opposite reactions of an elderly "Joe Traditional" and a young "Johnny NewSong" as they both experience a contemporary and then a traditional worship service.[13]

---

12. Avery, "Worship Wars and Ethnomusicology."
13. Illustrations used with permission.

Completely opposite reactions to the same worship services!

Disputes about instrumentation, music styles, and texts in worship are nothing new. In the thirteenth century, a controversy raged whether it was appropriate to bring an organ into the church; some considered it "the devil's instrument"! "Mindless words, bad theology, emotional tunes": this was an assessment, not about a recent contemporary worship song, but about Isaac Watts's hymn "O God, Our Help in Ages Past" in the eighteenth century!

Contemporary worship music has of course been a flash point in recent decades. One cartoon has an elderly grandfather showing his grandson his upper arm and explaining: "... and I got that scar from the chairman of the board during the second battle of 'Guitars in the Sanctuary' back in '71." Of course, the controversy did not really devolve into violence, but many ministries were hurt by the divisiveness of the debates, and some churches even split over the issue.

Rays of Hope

John Frame provided a valuable service by providing a sound, balanced treatment in *Contemporary Worship Music: A Biblical Defense*.[14] His main point is that each song deserves to be judged on its own merits, rather than people automatically making assumptions about the entire genre (such as: all contemporary worship songs are "shallow," "me-centered," etc.).

In fact, there has been a real maturing in the contemporary worship movement over the years. I was shocked when in the 1980s I went through the first edition of the Maranatha! Music "Praise Chorus Book," searching for songs for a Communion service, and found exactly *one* reference to the death of Christ in the entire collection![15] At that point the emphasis was on Scripture songs (especially setting psalm texts) and songs focusing on the attributes of God; the imbalance may have been an overreaction to so much of nineteenth-century gospel hymnody, which focused almost entirely on the death of Christ to the exclusion of other themes. But, thankfully, recent years have seen a wider and deeper repertoire of songs being written, with works from (for example) Matt Redman, Chris Tomlin, the Gettys, and Sovereign Grace Music (among many others) dealing with profound biblical truths, including the redeeming work of Christ.

Consider a beautiful story from the "trenches" of the worship wars: I once heard Joe Stowell, who was at the time president of Moody Bible Institute, tell about the time the Moody radio network decided to change its standard programming from old-style gospel music to a more contemporary music format. The station received a letter from an older woman who had long been a financial supporter of Moody Radio. Her letter went

---

14. Frame, *Contemporary Worship Music*.

15. A Maranatha! Music board member, however, balances this point with the observation that the services where these songs were used commonly included preaching that was very cross-centered.

something like this: "For many years I have supported your programming, and I so enjoyed the music that was broadcast. But now I learn you have decided to change the format to one with more modern music. However, I want you to know that if that is what you think is necessary to reach the younger generation, I am behind you one hundred percent. Enclosed is my donation." What a mature response from a believer who understood that it was not all about her!

Implications of Freedom of Form

1. There is no one "right" way to do worship.

This is an absolutely crucial point that addresses the core of many if not most conflicts about worship. The fact of the matter is that, in the absence of New Testament specificity about forms, *no* church or denomination can claim to have discovered the one proper way to do worship (with the implication that other groups that do things differently are wrong). *It is arrogant to assume to have an inside track to the mind of God in areas where he has chosen to remain silent!*

In fact, severe disagreements about songs and instruments usually reveal a deeper problem than simply a musical one: they speak more often to *maturity* issues, to people wanting to have things their own way and to sing only the songs *they* like. They are forgetting what it means to be part of the body of Christ.

2. God's taste is broader than any of ours!

We all have preferences when it comes to music, style, etc. But again, we tend to conclude that what *I* think is most honoring to God just happens to coincide with what he himself thinks! When we look worldwide, it seems obvious that God is pleased to accept a huge breadth of different worship expressions.

3. God's priority is the heart of the worshiper.

God does *not* have favorite styles, or favorite instruments, or favorite songs! He is looking for hearts that are devoted to him, regardless of the outward form or expression that may take.

4. The Promised Presence of Christ Is Key.

As we saw in chapter 24, what makes our worship acceptable and pleasing to God is (along with our hearts) the promised presence of Christ leading us perfectly into the Father's presence.

Key Factors to Take Into Account

1. A Church's or Denomination's History and Traditions

While these should not be the final determinants, neither should they be ignored. It always proves to be a disastrous move to make radical changes in a church's worship practices overnight.

Protestants depart from Catholics in denying that church traditions have equal authority with Scripture. But tradition is *not* the enemy or without value; much can be learned from the way that past generations came to God in worship. The proper perspective is reflected in the statement (author unknown), "Tradition is a wonderful servant, but a terrible master." We can learn a lot from tradition, but it should never have the final say—only Scripture does.

2. The Local Cultural Context

The people in our churches are to a large extent a product of their culture in terms of how they look at things, how they respond to different artistic expressions and forms, and what tastes and preferences they come with. They "breathe the air" of the culture in which they have grown up, which then shapes what they consider as "normal" or "beautiful" or "moving."[16] Everyone has what is called a "heart language." And that heart language is be considered when making decisions about forms, styles, music, and other artistic expressions of faith—though not as the final determining factor. Culture is not the enemy—at least, once it is filtered through the lens of Scripture.

---

16. *From the Field:* The Canela, a tribal people group in Brazil, came to Christ in large numbers. They produced a Christian song that is characterized by tone clusters and sounds extremely harsh to Western ears. From that standpoint, one might conclude that it is a dirge or lament. Yet the text of the song is: "God's word makes me happy"! To the Canela, this is happy music! This is a vivid illustration that music is not a universal language.

Biblical? or Cultural?

The Critical Need

Recognizing that the New Testament has left so much (though not everything) open, and recalling Piper's observation that "almost every worship tradition we have is culturally shaped rather than biblically commanded,"[17] it is *absolutely critical* that we learn to carefully examine our worship practices and distinguish what is *biblical* from what is a *cultural* application or decision.

This is vital because most worship conflicts arise from people confusing these two categories: they take an accustomed practice and regard it as normative, the "right way," or even "biblical"—even when it is an aspect that is not directly addressed in the Bible itself! "The way we've always done it" is seen to carry an authority on that basis alone.[18]

A Case in Point

A helpful example is the frequency of Communion in different churches and denominations. Some celebrate the Supper weekly, some monthly, others quarterly or less often. Which is correct? Which groups have it wrong?

The point is that the New Testament does *not* specify *how often* we are to observe the Lord's Supper. It is *not* a right or wrong issue. There is freedom for a congregation and its leadership to decide what is best for that church.

On the other hand, what the Bible (in fact Jesus himself) commands is *that we practice Communion* "in remembrance of me." For a church to decide to no longer practice the Lord's Supper at all (as something outmoded, or for whatever reason) would be *wrong*, would be *sin*, because of refusing to obey *the explicit command of Scripture*.

The Bible is clear as to the necessity of the practice (it's *biblical*) but does not specify the frequency (that's a *cultural* decision).

---

17. Piper, "Our High Priest."

18. David Peterson incisively writes: "We all know that music is a great encouragement to snobbery.... We become so familiar with and comfortable with our particular styles of music that we end up saying, maybe overtly sometimes, 'I am not willing to listen to your kind of music. I am not willing to sing one of your silly songs.' We get even more intense than that. We say, 'Your music is not true worship. Your music is not honoring to God'" ("Psalms, Hymns").

A Helpful Exercise in Discernment

Consider the following list of worship practices to determine whether each to be either *biblical* or *cultural*. (In a few cases it may be possible to argue either way, but for the most part the distinction should be clear.)

Praise	Come up to take communion/giving	Sixty-minute sermon
Singing	Pass offering plates/bags	Fifteen-minute sermon
Choruses	Use offering chests at exits	Prayer
Guitars	Dark room	Prayer seated
Organ	Sunny room	Prayer standing
Loud music	Scripture reading	Prayer with eyes closed
Soft music	Responsive readings	Sit on floor
Hymns	Candles	Sit on chair
Communion	Sermon	When to stand
Pass communion trays	Thirty-minute sermon	Applause

The Bottom Line

To summarize, many of our worship conflicts would simply go away if we could learn to differentiate what is explicitly *biblical* in our practices (and therefore nonnegotiable), and what is a *cultural* decision (and hence negotiable). And we would look at the differing practices of other churches in a different, more accepting light (where negotiable areas are concerned).

Navigating the treacherous waters

The virtual silence of the New Testament as to the specifics of congregation worship practice seems to allow for local churches, as the fundamental unit of the body of Christ on earth, to have considerable autonomy and freedom as individual congregations in working out the issues involving the balance of biblical constants and cultural flexibility in the worship of that church.

That does not mean that it is an easy task, however—as the worship wars have amply demonstrated. John Piper has counseled:

> There is very little in the New Testament about the forms and style and content of corporate worship.... God must mean to leave the matter of form and style and content to the judgment of our spiritual wisdom—not to our whim or our tradition, but to prayerful, thoughtful, culturally alert, self-critical, Bible-saturated, God-centered, Christ-exalting reflection driven by a passion to be filled with all the fullness of God. I assume this will be an ongoing process, not a one-time effort.[19]

It will be up to the leadership of each congregation to make wise, prayerful, principle-based decisions about that church's worship practices. And then the leaders should be diligent to communicate to the church the *why* and not just the *what* of what is done. Crucially, the people must be constantly reminded that being part of the body of Christ means to not insist on one's own preferences, but rather to obey the biblical injunctions to "regard one another as more important than yourselves" (Phil 2:3) and to "give preference to one another in honor" (Rom 12:10), always striving to "maintain the unity of the Spirit in the bond of peace" (Eph 4:3).

The *Nairobi Statement on Worship and Culture*

In 1996 the Lutheran World Federation released a statement that is so rich in its insights and implications that it has been used widely to inform the discussion of the relationship between worship and culture.[20]

The statement in summary states that:

> Christian worship relates dynamically to culture in at least four ways.
> - First, it is *transcultural*, the same substance for everyone everywhere, beyond culture.
> - Second, it is *contextual*, varying according to the local situation (both nature and culture).
> - Third, it is *countercultural*, challenging what is contrary to the gospel in a given culture.
> - Fourth, it is *cross-cultural*, making possible sharing between different local cultures.

---

19. Piper, "Thoughts on Worship and Culture."

20. Lutheran World Federation's Study Team on Worship and Culture, "Nairobi Statement."

The trick is that all four of these aspects are operating at the same time! That of course adds a lot of complexity and challenge to the whole endeavor. And, needless to say, different churches will be stronger in certain of these areas than others. Overemphasis on one will lead to imbalance. For instance, being so culturally contextual that harmful elements are not sifted out (i.e., not being appropriately countercultural); or being so rigidly transcultural that there is not enough sensitivity to the local context and the heart language of the people; or being contextually so monocultural that due is not given to the rich possibilities of drawing on cross-cultural influences.

The Bottom Line in Worship and Culture

In applying the freedom, flexibility, and latitude in worship (represented by the span in our bridge illustration), we must insist on *an unchanging message* (biblical), while acknowledging the huge *variety of possible expressions* of this message (cultural). The key is to rigorously distinguish between what is *biblical* and what is *cultural*.

The Second Tower: Biblical Principles

These principles will be enumerated and unpacked in chapter 29.

> There is a biblical framework for our worship, but also much cultural flexibility.

For Reflection and/or Discussion

What is the worship service you have visited
that was most outside your normal experience?
Was your reaction positive, negative, or mixed?
How might this chapter shape your memory of it?

Part 7

Conclusion

29. Biblical Principles of Worship
30. Summary and Benediction

29

BIBLICAL PRINCIPLES OF WORSHIP[1]

The Second Tower: Biblical *Principles*

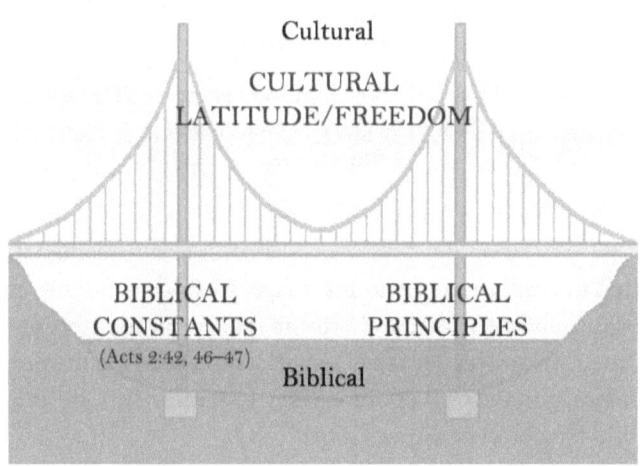

As we have already stressed, the freedom that the New Testament allows in worship practices does not mean "anything goes"! There are a host of principles that can be drawn from the pages of Scripture to guide the leadership of local churches in fashioning biblically appropriate yet culturally meaningful expressions of worship. As the second tower does

1. See also Man, "Biblical Principles of Worship."

in a physical suspension bridge, these principles give further stability and strength to the (worship) structure as a whole. The first tower (Biblical Constants) deals with more specific *practices*; Biblical principles are, by definition, more general and must be *applied* (and may legitimately be variously applied) in different church contexts and cultures.

This chapter develops and unpacks twelve biblical principles—general, transcultural, unifying principles—that grow out of our study of the biblical texts throughout this book. We want to stand firmly on biblical ground in the ordering of our worship life as local congregations, while allowing for the variety and freedom that the New Testament permits.

(Note: This chapter could also serve as a stand-alone study for individual or group use.)

> *Principle #1*: God's glory, and our joyful celebration of it in worship, should be the focus and goal of all life and ministry.

Doxological Worship

> For from him and through him and to him are all things.
> To him be glory forever. Amen.
> (Rom 11:36)

As children of God and citizens of heaven (Phil 3:20), our primary focus in all of life is to be on the God who created us and redeemed us and is committed to conforming us to his image. God has a unique claim on our allegiance and attention; his Lordship is to permeate, more and more, every corner of our lives. He is the center of our existence, the purpose of our existence, and the goal of our existence (Rom 11:36). He is both the subject and the object of our worship.

When we speak of his "glory" we are speaking of the sum total of all his perfections, the uniqueness of his being, the totality of what distinguishes him as Creator from his creation and his creatures. The Scriptures maintain that the created order (Ps 19:1; 72:19), the course of history (Isa 66:18), and above all the church of Jesus Christ (Eph 3:21) are all intended to reflect, manifest, and display his glory.

For us as believers, God's glory should be the ultimate motivation in all our endeavors ("Whatever you do, do all to the glory of God" [1

Cor 10:31].) We must consciously keep this goal before us and seek to submit all our activities (personal, family, vocational, spiritual) to that overarching design, in order to bring our lives value, meaning, and a divine orientation and significance.

It is also crucial to have this perspective as we undertake the work of the church. Human theories, techniques, ideas, systems, tastes, and structures must all be submitted to a compelling and overriding passion for the glory of God. How quickly we forget whose work, whose church, whose worship service we are involved in! How quickly we seek to supplement the revelation of Scripture with human ingenuity, demographic studies, and how-to seminars.

Our single-minded focus, in worship and in all our activities, must be on recognizing, reflecting, declaring, and celebrating the glory of God.

> Let them praise the name of the LORD,
> for his name alone is exalted;
> his glory is above earth and heaven.
> (Ps 148:13)

> To him be glory in the church and in Christ Jesus
> throughout all generations, forever and ever. Amen! (Eph 3:21)

Principle #2: Worship is first and foremost for God.

GOD-CENTERED WORSHIP

"Worship God."
(Rev 19:10; 22:9)

A Tapescrew Letter[2]

C. S. Lewis's *Screwtape Letters* consists of an imagined correspondence between the senior demon Screwtape and his young nephew Wormwood. Screwtape gives advice on tempting and leading humans astray. Lewis uses this correspondence to make some insightful and often biting

---

2. Man, "Letter from Tapescrew (with Apologies to C. S. Lewis)."

observations about the human condition, and how easily we are deceived by the forces of evil.

I am happy to report that a new letter has just been discovered, this time from Screwtape's relative Tapescrew, writing to his nephew Woodworm. This letter may shed some light on the state of worship in our churches today.

My dear Woodworm,

In today's world there are some delicious tendencies that make it particularly easy to confuse, distract, and divert the Enemy's people from the things on which they should be focused. Some of our unwitting agents among the philosophers and academics have paved the way for the current wonderful situation, whereby the pathetic creatures seem to each go around in their own little bubble, unaware of forces and values that extend beyond the boundaries of their own consciousness and concern.

While there are some isolated voices crying out things like "It's all about him!" these cries are, as it were, cries in the wilderness, and largely fall on deaf ears, thank Badness. There are blissfully few who can crack the barrier of their own self-absorption and truly focus even on other humans, much less on divine priorities and demands. That makes our work so much easier! The worms bounce around inside the shell of self-centeredness that is about all they know; and then they wonder why they feel that they are without a meaning or a purpose that extends beyond themselves! They do the work for us, in many respects, as they so successfully fill their lives with a multitude of sweetly irrelevant pursuits, leaving little time or energy for the Enemy's worrisome projects and plans.

In their churches, this kind of rampant individualism gets carried to hilarious extremes. In a delightfully blind way, these beings can recite creeds and sing songs and pray prayers that speak of the Enemy's sovereign (and, we would say, dictatorial) rule over all things, and then they turn around and act as though they themselves are the center of the universe! It is in their churches, those annoying places intended by the Enemy for corporate brainwashing and mutual encouragement in the perverse ways of holiness and godliness, that we find the most exciting displays of selfishness and narrow-mindedness. The smaller the issue, it seems, the more overwrought their emotions become in their stubborn campaign to get their own way! I tell you, we hardly need to whisper a corrupting suggestion into their ears before they are off fighting over the color of the carpet, the brand of coffee served, or even—most thrilling of all—over their worship! And each one with a self-righteous conviction that his or her own convictions or preferences on the matter just happen to exactly coincide with the Enemy's point of view!

I tell you, it warms our devilish hearts when we are able to use worship, of all things, as a way to divide the Enemy's people! The one activity that should unite them the most has become a wonderful seedbed for strife and disagreement. And it's all made possible when they begin to look out for themselves and their interests rather than the Enemy's. And that perspective, I'm happy to report, is everywhere. It's embarrassingly easy to promote among those creatures, and truly is one of our greatest successes!

Affectionately yours,
Your uncle Tapescrew

Principle #3: Worship is a dialogue between God and his people, a rhythm of revelation and response.

Dialogical Worship

> For all the promises of God find their Yes
> in him [Christ].
> That is why it is through him
> that we utter our Amen to God for his glory.
> (2 Cor 1:20)

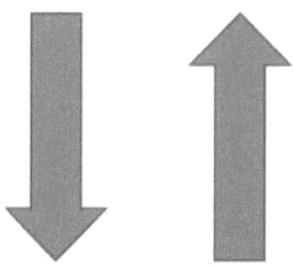

The rhythm of *revelation* and *response* is characteristic of all God's dealings with humans. And this ordering of these two elements is tremendously significant, for it speaks of the *initiative* that God takes, and the lengths to which he goes, to ensure a relationship with those whom he chooses. Throughout Scripture we see God's revelatory initiative with his people, with the result that all worship, obedience, and service should be seen as a *response* to God's prior activity in revelation and redemption. This is true because, as Eric Alexander has stated, "God needs to be known before He can be worshiped."[3] Nicholls expands on this idea: "Our worship is our answer to God who has first addressed us. Man worships the God who has made Himself known. We 'praise His holy Name'—that is, we worship Him in His self-revelation."[4]

Accordingly, worship is a *dialogue* between God and his people: that means that our services should alternate and balance elements of revelation and response: *hearing from God* (through his word, read and sung and prayed and preached) and *replying to him* (with our songs and prayers and confessions and the Lord's Supper).

But revelation should *precede* response: we should let God have the first word and be careful to listen before we speak. Too many services launch right into singing, but that means we are responding before we have heard anything to respond to! This does violence to the biblical pattern, and to God's preeminence. Until we have heard from God, we have nothing to say to him—we must worship him as he really is, not as we (or the songwriters) imagine or hope him to be. In this light, a "Call to Worship" is anything but outdated. Indeed, whether read or sung or prayed, it is an acknowledgment that we have come to worship God at his invitation and by and through his word.

> ## Principle #4: The word must be central in our worship.

Word-Saturated Worship

Let the word of Christ dwell in you richly.
(Col 3:16)

---

3. Alexander, "Worship: The Old Testament Pattern."
4. Nicholls, *Jacob's Ladder*, 37.

This principle grows directly out of the previous one, because of the primacy of God's revelation.

The word of God is of supreme importance in the life of the Christian, containing as it does God's revelation of his Person, his will, and his ways. The word needs to be pored over, ingested into one's mind and heart, meditated on, and acted upon. It is a unique and precious repository of spiritual truth and guidance and encouragement. There is no aspect of the life of the church or of the individual believer that should not be tied to a scriptural mooring and infused with biblical substance (2 Tim 3:16–17). The Bible is indeed "a lamp unto my feet, and a light unto my path" (Ps 119:105).

When Christians gather for corporate worship, it is logical that the word of God should play a central and dominant role. For since worship involves focusing our thoughts and hearts and voices on the praise of God, in response to his self-revelation and his gracious saving initiative, we of course need that view of God that the word gives us if our worship is to be "in truth" (John 4:23–24). Our worship can only duly honor God if it accurately reflects what he reveals about himself in his word.

James White insists: "The first step toward making our worship more biblical is in giving the reading of God's Word a central role in Christian worship on any occasion."[5] We simply cannot overstate the importance of Scripture for our worship. By all means, let us be as creative as possible in building in Scripture (verses on banners or projected onto a screen as people enter, verses on the bulletin cover, readers' theater, children reciting verses, original Scripture songs, etc.), as we make sure that the *primacy of the word in worship* is obvious throughout the entire service—not just during the sermon.[6] As White adds:

> Scripture is read, not just for a sermon text, but to hear what word God addresses to the gathered congregation. Preaching usually builds on that but Scripture is read for its own sake as God's Word . . . . It needs to be communicated to all that the centrality of Scripture stems from its functions as proclamation of God's Word to the gathered people.[7]

N. T. Wright concurs:

---

5. White, "Making Our Worship More Biblical," 38.
6. See footnote 13 in chapter 3.
7. White, "Making Our Worship More Biblical," 38.

The Bible is not simply read aloud in order to convey information, to teach doctrine or ethics or whatever, though of course it does that too. It is read aloud as the effective sign that all that we do is done as a response to God's living and active word, the word that, as Isaiah says, accomplishes God's purpose in the world, abiding forever while all flesh withers like the grass. The place of Scripture in Christian worship means that both in structure and content God's initiative remains primary and all that we do remains a matter of response.[8]

In Scripture we find the prerequisites for worship, the invitation to worship, the authority for worship, the material for worship, the regulation of our worship, the message of worship, and the end to which worship should lead.

> **Principle #5: Worship is the responsibility of all God's people.**

Participatory Worship

> Oh, magnify the LORD with me,
> and let us exalt his name together!
> (Ps 34:3)

Worship is something done *by* God's people, not *for* God's people. It is not a spectator sport; hence the title of Robert Webber's book *Worship Is a Verb*.[9] "The relevant question is not 'Do you have a *voice*?' but 'Do you have a *song*?'"[10] All believers in Christ have a song to sing in gratitude to their Redeemer.

Congregational participation in corporate worship is in fact a direct application of the biblical doctrine of (and the Reformation re-emphasis on) the priesthood of all believers, and thus is in itself a powerful testimony to the nature of the new covenant and the free access of every believer into the presence of God through Jesus our great high priest.

---

8. Wright, "Freedom and Framework" (unpaginated).
9. Webber, *Worship Is a Verb*.
10. Hustad, *Jubilate II*, 120.

The Singing Congregation

Music is a gift of God ideally suited for the praise of the Creator—in heaven and in the church on earth. And *the congregation is the most important singing group in the church* (the wonderful ministry of gifted musical leaders notwithstanding). Those leading should do everything they can to facilitate the active participation of the congregation in worship through song. This includes:

1. Modeling worship for the congregation
   It is critical that the pastor also be visibly engaged in worship, in order to set an example for the people.

2. Using hymns and songs creatively
   Well-known texts sung in unfamiliar ways can make those texts come alive to our people, being savored and reflected on, not just sung in a lifeless, rote manner. Try changing the tempo and/or dynamic range of hymns or songs (either slower or faster, or louder or softer). Doing a normally lively or majestic setting in a more contemplative way can bring new attention to, and appreciation for, the words being sung. Use contemporary harmonizations of classic hymns, and draw upon the movement that has set rich old texts to new contemporary tunes.[11]

3. Avoiding vocal strain
   It has often been pointed out that many contemporary songs, as well as quite a few settings in hymnbooks, are pitched too high for comfortable singing by untrained voices. People will simply stop singing if the range of the songs makes it uncomfortable to sing for any length of time. It is worth the trouble to transpose music into lower keys.

4. Not blowing the people away
   When sound systems are in use, it is important to use them judiciously so that the congregation is not overwhelmed by the flood of sound from the speakers. When the music from the front is too loud, people will just stop singing, and what results is a concert rather than a worship service. The primary function of those up

---

11. Some excellent examples may be found in the online RUF Hymnbook, https://www.igracemusic.com/hymnbook/home.html.

front is to support and facilitate the singing of the whole body—to help them sing better, not to drown them out.

5. Considering a thematic approach
Long strings of contextually unrelated songs or choruses are not conducive to reflective worship, for there is no time to linger on a single aspect of God's nature or work. There is a power to developing a single thematic focus throughout the time of corporate praise (perhaps, though not necessarily, related to the topic of the sermon), for it gives the people time to meditate on and respond to truth.[12]

6. Making creative use of the instruments and voices
Don't have all the instruments play full out all the time; vary the textures by leaving out one instrument or the other on occasion. And a cappella singing can be used in both traditional and contemporary contexts: there is no instrument like the human voice, and no better way to foster a sense of community in our singing.

The Speaking Congregation

Remember that worship is more than music. As emphasized repeatedly in this book, the word of God needs to have a prominent (and therefore, in most churches, a much greater) role in our worship.

Churches with pew Bibles or with a single-translation tradition can read Scripture passages aloud together, as can churches with projection capabilities.

Responsive readings should not be confined to those found in the back of most hymnals. It is well worth the effort to put together original responsive readings that incorporate a variety of Scripture texts (and then print or project them for the congregation). This is a wonderful way to help develop a theme in worship by pulling together related texts to instruct and encourage God's people. Such readings are not too difficult to develop with the use of a Bible concordance (especially a computer concordance).

The Praying Congregation

All the praying in church should not be left to the pastor. Some churches have small-group prayer during a worship service, or use a greeting time

---

12. See Man, "Power of Thematic Worship."

for sharing prayer needs. In smaller churches it is possible to have seasons of corporate prayer where different individuals may pray aloud. In larger churches where this is not feasible, the practice of "bidded prayer" can allow for greater participation in prayer; in this practice, borrowed from the Anglican church, the pastor or other leader will successively mention specific areas for prayer, then leave about thirty seconds after each for the people to pray silently about that area. In this way the members of the congregation are truly praying, rather than just listening to one person pray.

Conclusion

It is imperative that the members of our congregations leave, not just having attended a worship service, but *having worshiped*. It is worth all the creativity and effort we can muster to lovingly draw the people of God into meaningful participation in expressing praise to the God of their salvation.

Principle #6: Our worship is acceptable in and through Christ our high priest.

Christ-Led Worship

> Through him [Christ] then let us continually offer up a sacrifice of praise to God,
> that is, the fruit of lips that acknowledge his name.
> (Heb 13:15)

(See also the extensive treatment of this theme in chapter 24, and in Man, *Proclamation and Praise*.)

Christ's Role in Our Worship

1. The living Christ is present in our midst when we gather for worship.

    In the midst of the congregation I will sing your praise. (Heb 2:12b)

2. Only in and through Christ can we enter God's presence in worship. And because he leads the way, we can come confidently and boldly to the Father.

> There is one mediator between God and men, the man Christ Jesus. (1 Tim 2:5)

> Since we have confidence to enter the holy places by the blood of Jesus ... let us draw near with a true heart in full assurance of faith. (Heb 10:19, 22)

3. Our worship is pleasing and acceptable to God not because of its own excellence, but because of (and only because of) the excellence of his Son. *Worship is not a work!* It is a free gift of God's grace to us in Christ; we come with confidence (Heb 10:19) and gratitude (Heb 12:28) into God's presence when we come through Christ our Redeemer.

4. The word of God, by which Christ proclaims his Father's name to his brethren, deserves priority and centrality in our worship. When we preach or teach the word, we do so representing Christ whose ministry it is.

> I will tell of your name to my brethren. (Heb 2:12a)

> How are they to believe in him whom they have never heard? ... Faith comes from hearing, and hearing through the word of Christ. (Rom 10:14, 17)

5. The corporate praises of God's people, led by Christ himself, is an integral and crucial part of the gathering of the church. When we lead worship, we do so representing Christ whose ministry it also is.

> Let the word of Christ dwell in you richly, with all wisdom teaching and admonishing one another with psalms, hymns and spiritual songs; with grace singing to God in your heart. (Col 3:16)

> In the midst of the congregation I will sing your praise. (Heb 2:12b)

6. Jesus Christ is himself the ultimate fulfillment of the biblical pattern of revelation and response.

I will tell of your name to my brethren;
in the midst of the congregation I will sing your praise. (Heb 2:12)

7. No matter how they may differ in the externals, all true expressions of worship have in common that they are led and mediated by Christ in the power of the Holy Spirit.

8. Our singing Savior shows us the appropriateness and necessity of our own songs of praise. If Christ our Mediator deems it fitting to sing the Father's praises in the midst of the congregation (Heb 2:12) and among the nations (Rom 15:9), how can we do less?

    In the midst of the congregation I will sing your praise. (Heb 2:12b)

    I will praise you among the Gentiles, and sing to your name. (Rom 15:9)

9. We need to repent of trying to do worship in our own strength.

Conclusion

All true worship is in and through and by Jesus Christ. This is a supremely unifying understanding of Christian worship in all times and places and styles and forms.

> **Principle #7: Our response of worship is enabled, motivated, and empowered by the Holy Spirit.**

Spirit-Enabled Worship

> We are the true circumcision, who worship in the Spirit of God and glory in Christ Jesus and put no confidence in the flesh.
> (Phil 3:3)

(See also the extensive treatment of this theme in chapter 23.)

The Holy Spirit is committed to actualizing our worship in and through Jesus Christ in the body of Christ and in our personal lives.

Enabled by the Spirit

As we saw in chapter 25, the Holy Spirit's ministry may be seen as an extension of what Christ has done and is doing. The same holds true for worship. "Worship, through the presence and action of the Holy Spirit, is a meeting . . . between Jesus Christ and his people."[13]

Motivated by the Spirit

The role of the Spirit in worship is to open our hearts to Christ—to take what we know in our heads and drive it into our hearts; to engender thankfulness and praise for his grace, his love, and his presence; and then through and in Christ to draw forth our praises to the Father.

In other words, we *can* come into God's presence in worship because of the (objective) work of Christ (Heb 10:19–22); but we *want to* come into God's presence because of the (subjective) work of the Holy Spirit in our hearts. The Spirit completes in us the biblical cycle of *revelation and response*, taking the revelation of God and driving it home to our hearts, thus drawing forth our response of worship.

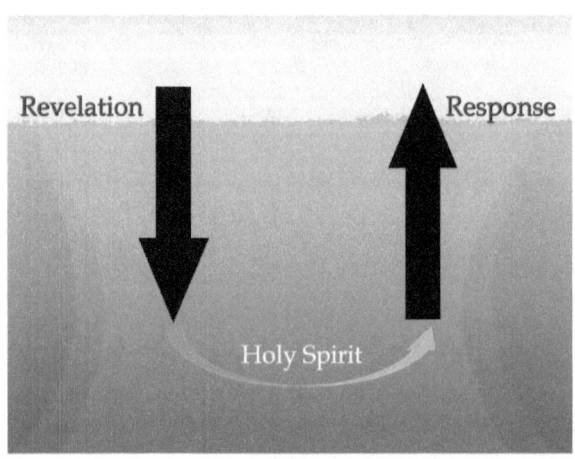

---

13. Allmen, "Worship and the Holy Spirit," 130.

Empowered by the Spirit

The true power of new covenant worship rests not in our own efforts to lift to God an appropriate and worthy response of praise, but rather in the continuing mediating ministry of Christ, who offers to the Father, as our representative and high priest, a perfect response of praise. And the Holy Spirit empowers our worship thus as he connects us to that perfect offering: by identifying us with Christ (Rom 8:9–11); by assuring us that we are children of God (Rom 8:14–17) and brothers and sisters of Christ (Rom 8:17; Heb 2:11); by encouraging us to therefore come boldly into the Father's presence (Heb 10:19–22); and by filling us that we might sing to, praise, and thank the Father through Christ from our hearts (Eph 5:18–20).

Here again we see *the Christ-centeredness of all the Spirit's doings.*

Principle #8: Worship is the response of our entire lives to God.

Whole-Life Worship

> Therefore I urge you, brethren, by the mercies of God,
> to present your bodies a living and holy sacrifice,
> acceptable to God, which is your spiritual service of worship.
> (Rom 12:1)

Jesus on Lifestyle Worship

As we saw in chapter 9, in John 4 Jesus makes a significant statement about the nature of worship under his Lordship. He tells the Samaritan woman that "an hour is coming when neither *in* this mountain nor *in* Jerusalem will you worship the Father" (v. 21), but rather "an hour is coming, and now is, when the true worshipers will worship the Father *in* spirit and truth" (v. 23). Jesus' redirection of the preposition "in" from speaking of external location to internal focus is a grammatical shift of enormous spiritual significance. He is saying that he is changing the rules: no longer is it a matter of *where* or *when* you worship, but *how* you worship.

Paul on Lifestyle Worship

Paul develops this thought further in Romans 12:1. As an appropriate response ("Therefore") to all the wonderful "mercies of God" he has been explicating in chapters 1–11 of his epistle, he enjoins believers to present their "bodies," that is their entire lives, to God as living sacrificial gifts of thanksgiving. There is to be no sacred/secular compartmentalization in the lives of Christians. Paul reminds us elsewhere that we have been "bought with a price," and again the fitting response is to "glorify God in your bodies" (1 Cor 6:20). As "temples of the Holy Spirit," both individually (1 Cor 6:19) and corporately as the church (1 Cor 3:16), the place of worship is always present *with us and within us*, and the time for worship is always *now*: "Whether you eat or drink, or whatever you do, do all to the glory of God" (1 Cor 10:31). This is not a devaluing of times and places for corporate worship, but rather a hallowing of *every* time and *every* place as suitable for worshiping God.

Implications for Us

Each believer has a responsibility to cultivate his or her own life of worship (cf. Gal 5:25; Heb 12:14).This crucial perspective has huge implications for what we do when we gather for corporate worship. It is *not* the responsibility of the pastor or the worship leader to supply or actuate worship for the people of God (only Christ in the power of the Spirit can do that anyway, as we have seen), but merely to facilitate its corporate expression. We should not be in the habit of coming to the service with an empty spiritual "tank," hoping to get it filled in order to be able to face the week ahead. The ideal for Christian living is rather to come to church out of a week of *daily* worship throughout all of life, and then to join our hearts and voices together in a corporate expression borne out of the fullness of our spirits. Sunday should be not only a preparation for our week, but also our week a preparation for Sunday! It is true that sometimes we may indeed come spiritually empty and dry, and God in his grace will meet us in our need. But our goal should be to come to church with a heart full of love and devotion to God from walking with him throughout the week.

A Parable

In the children's story *Stone Soup*, three soldiers are returning home from the war. They approach a village, but the villagers, seeing them coming, scurry to hide all their food, because there is a shortage and they do not want to have to share with outsiders. They tell the soldiers that they have no food to give them.

The soldiers, being rather shrewd fellows, tell the villagers that they will make some "stone soup," and ask simply for a large kettle filled with water. They choose several large, round stones and add them to the kettle, with the curious villagers looking on. Then the soldiers remark, "This soup should be excellent; but if we only had a couple of potatoes, it would be even better." One of the villagers sheepishly says, "Uh, I think I might just have a few potatoes," and goes off to retrieve some from her stash. The soldiers add these to the pot, taste the soup, and say, "Wonderful! Now if we just had a few carrots . . ." and someone runs off and gets some. The same happens with onions, and cabbage, and so forth, until a hearty soup has been prepared. The soldiers invite the villagers to join with them in their feast, and the villagers are amazed that such a marvelous soup could be made with *just stones!*[14]

In our corporate worship, our rituals, hymns, anthems, even our sermons are like those stones—they are nothing that particularly impresses God: they're just a framework, a skeleton. What makes the service special and makes it *worship* is when our members come and add to the pot from what's been stored up in their hearts during a week of worshiping and walking with God, a week of loving God and cherishing and savoring his glory—*then* we are ready to worship God *together*. When our corporate adoration is the overflow of many hearts rejoicing in the goodness and greatness of God, which the Spirit can then energize and transform into something far more than the sum of the parts—*then* our congregational worship will truly be a nourishing and invigorating feast for the people of God, and—more importantly—a fragrant aroma to the God of glory, who delights in the worship of his people.

> Principle #9: God is much more concerned with our *heart* than with the *form* of our worship.

---

14. Brown, *Stone Soup*.

PART 7 | CONCLUSION

Heart Worship

> Man looks on the outward appearance,
> but God looks on the heart.
> (1 Sam 16:7)

A Surprising Truth

In chapter 12, we looked at many Old Testament texts and saw resounding testimony to the priority God placed, even in the old covenant economy with its complex system of ritual and ceremony, on the worship of the *heart*. The Old Testament writers, and especially the prophets, made it abundantly clear that mere outward conformity to the requirements without an engaged heart meant nothing to God; in fact such offerings and rituals were detestable to him. C. S. Lewis warns us that it would be wrong to think that God "really needed the blood of bulls and goats." What he values rather is "the intention."[15]

Internal over External Worship

Jesus continues the prophets' criticism of the Jewish leaders for their external conformity to the law without an inward heart motivation. He calls the scribes and Pharisees "whitewashed tombs" (Matt 23:27), "blind guides" (Matt 23:16), and "hypocrites" (Matt 23:13, 23); who "tithe mint and rue and every herb, and neglect justice and the love of God" (Luke 11:42); and who "clean the outside of the cup and the plate, but inside they are full of greed and self-indulgence" (Matt 23:25).

Jesus, like his Father, has no tolerance for worship that is external only, no matter how carefully and painstakingly performed. Let us take heed!

A Lifestyle of Heart Worship

As we saw in chapter 9, the New Testament emphasis is on worship as a lifestyle. This worship in every time and place is in fact possible because it consists fundamentally of the *heart*'s response to God, rather than a set of prescribed rituals, practices, or forms.

---

15. Lewis, "On Church Music," 123.

The heart is also the wellspring of our *corporate* worship; Paul exhorts the church: "Be filled with the Spirit... singing and making melody to the Lord *with your heart*" (Eph 5:19; see also Col 3:16).

The Bottom Line

"Man looks on the outward appearance, but God looks on the heart" (1 Sam 16:7). This familiar passage is not often applied to the area of worship, yet it is resoundingly applicable. Most of what we think and talk about when it comes to worship are outward forms and styles, and usually with a very narrow perception of what is "appropriate" or "acceptable" to God. Yet when we look at the scope of various worship expressions down through the centuries, and across the world (or even across the street!) today, it is quite evident that God has a much, much broader spectrum of taste than any of us can claim to have! And it is the height of arrogance for us to presume (as most of us have, at one time or another) that our own particular set of preferences just happens to coincide with what the Almighty himself favors!

Lewis reminds us that "all our offerings, whether of music or martyrdom, are like the intrinsically worthless present of a child, which a father values indeed, but values only for the intention."[16] God does not have a set of favorite songs or a preferred style. He is looking for *hearts* of worship.

Principle #10: Worship should promote the unity and edification of the body.

Edifying Worship

Do nothing from selfish ambition or conceit,
but in humility count others
more significant than yourselves.
(Phil 2:3)

So then let us pursue what makes for peace
and for mutual upbuilding.
(Rom 14:19)

---

16. Lewis, "On Church Music," 99.

PART 7 | CONCLUSION

Another Tapescrew Letter

My dear Woodworm,

It's truly delightful to see what havoc we have caused around the world by perverting, of all things, the worship of the Enemy. In insisting that all honor and praise be directed to himself, he is certainly setting the creatures up for failure—just because so much of their existence is wrapped up in themselves and their individual wants and desires.

So stay the course! We are seeing marvelous results. Above all, promote the idea that the purpose of worship is each individual's enjoyment, satisfaction, and sense of well-being. This will result in a delightful clash of personalities and temperaments, since of course no two people will agree on what will bring the desired results. The more you can get people to focus on their own needs and preferences (which, after all, should not be too difficult, people being the selfish beings that they are!), the further they will stray from their apostle's admonition to "consider one another more important than yourselves" and to "prefer one another in love."

Delightfully, it never even occurs to them that the Enemy might want them to apply these principles to their practice of worship! How successful we have been to keep such dangerous ideas out of their minds! Most of them haven't any clue that worship is for anything other than their personal fulfillment. This is wonderful, because with such a self-focused attitude (which has been easy to exploit, from the garden until now) they will never realize that worship was intended by the Enemy to focus on himself and to bring him glory (horrors!) and satisfaction. As long as we can keep the Christians looking to themselves and their own personal agendas, rather than to the Enemy and his priorities, they will continue to be pathetic, narcissistic beings with little impact in the world.

Needless to say, our efforts to put a wedge between their generations (which has always been relatively easy) has succeeded more wildly than ever in the arena of worship. Each side is utterly convinced that their way is right, that they presume to know exactly what is and what is not acceptable to the Enemy, and that there is nothing at all to learn from the other side. And all the while they hide behind a smokescreen of supposed "biblical warrant" or "cultural necessity," when in reality all their studies of the subject inevitably end up where they started, with their foregone conclusions firmly and immovably in place. What they *like* always turns out to be identical with want they think is appropriate and correct! This is now so widespread that it is seldom questioned, and our work is that much easier for it.

And how delicious it is that it is music, like so many of the Enemy's supposedly "good" gifts, we have been able to twist to our purposes. Music now separates rather than unites the Enemy's people. They can indeed be a powerful and unified force when they sing together, but we have managed to shift their focus so that even if corporate singing does happen, half of the people are stewing over the song selection, the absence of their favorites, the volume, the types of instruments used, etc. And the other half seem to just be reveling in their preferences being as least temporarily satisfied. Hardly anyone focuses on the Enemy as the subject and object of the songs! We owe all of this to our incredibly fruitful efforts to promote radical individualism as the prevailing philosophy of the day. Such chilling concepts as "the good of the whole" and the "health of the body" fortunately never occur to them as they go about their selfish ways.

Our "divide and conquer" strategy seems to be progressing on schedule!

Affectionately yours,
Your uncle Tapescrew[17]

Principle #11: Young and old need each other in the body of Christ.

Trans-generational Worship

> Young men and maidens, old men and children:
> Let them praise the name of the LORD,
> for his name alone is exalted.
> (Ps 148:12–13; cf. Titus 2:2–8)

God has called us in Christ into one body (Eph 4:4), and the Spirit is the one who must make us one in all our diversity (4:3). The fellowship of the church is intended to be a laboratory where, guided by divine love, we learn to break down barriers (Eph 2:14) and recognize and enjoy the fact that in Christ what bonds us is far deeper and more significant than the trappings of generation, background, culture, and personal preference.

---

17. Man, "Tapescrew Letter 4." There are two more "Tapescrew Letters": see Man, "More from Tapescrew" and "Tapescrew Letter 3."

Yet in many churches, different segments of the body gather at different times, and perhaps even in different places, to pursue musical worship according to their own preferred style. The congregation is divided into musical affinity groups with the admitted purpose of giving people what they want, what they are comfortable with, and what is most meaningful to them. The melting pot nature of the church gives way to homogeneous groupings that value choice over unity.[18]

Unity in Diversity

Can you imagine the early church structuring itself in that way? Surely there wouldn't have been separate services for Jews and for Greeks, for slaves and for free, though their backgrounds and hence their tastes would have undoubtedly shown much variety! Paul taught against the institutional recognition of factions within the church at Corinth; far from advocating separate services for those of Paul, of Apollos, of Cephas, of Christ (1 Cor 1:12–13), he decried gathering under any banner but that of Christ alone.

Surely the unity of the body should be demonstrated and lived out in a congregation's corporate worship life. We should be under no illusion that such a pursuit will be easy. It will take much work and prayer on the part of the church leaders and those responsible for worship; most importantly, it will demand a mature response on the part of the people. Rather than vying for what they like or want, their goal must be the good of the whole body. The people must continually be taught about the gravity and importance of what they're doing when they gather for worship, and the significance of moving forward in unity of heart and expression.

A Parable

> And he also told this parable to certain ones who trusted in themselves that their worship style was the only acceptable form:

---

18. *From the Field*: It should also be pointed out that in areas of the world today where the church is persecuted, there are rarely any debates about worship styles; rather, God's people are deeply grateful simply for the opportunity to worship with other believers. May we learn from them! Our worship wars grow out of a complacency and arrogance to which we are susceptible because of our spiritual affluence.

"Four men went up into the temple to pray, two traditional music directors and two contemporary worship leaders. One of the music directors stood and was praying thus to himself, 'God, I thank thee that I am not like many other church musicians: untrained, unrefined, undignified, or even like these contemporary worship leaders. I program only the finest art music; I present only those works truly worthy of Thee.'

"One of the contemporary worship leaders was standing off to the other side, praying like this: 'O Lord, I thank you that I am not like many other church musicians: stuffy, inhibited, stuck in a rut of boring and irrelevant music of the past. I present only the very latest songs and reach people where they're at.'

"In another corner the other music director and the other contemporary worship leader were kneeling and praying together. The music director prayed: 'Lord God, you know how easily the striving for artistic excellence can become idolatrous. When I use my gifts, may I always remember that they come from your hand, and that you delight in all the genuine gifts of worship that your children bring, in all their variety.' The worship leader prayed: 'God, I only know four chords on the guitar, and I am not a polished performer; but I thank you for your grace in allowing me to come near in worship, and for the privilege in leading of inviting others in their worship. Thank you for all the different ways that your people can praise you.'

"I tell you, these last two went away with their offerings of worship received by the Lord, rather than the others; for God is not so much concerned with the style of the musical gifts you bring, as he is with the humility of heart and genuineness of love with which you bring them."[19]

> The one who eats is not to regard with contempt the one who does not eat,
> and the one who does not eat is not to judge the one who eats,
> for God has accepted him. (Rom 14:3)

Principle #12: These truths must be taught and retaught.

---

19. Man, "Parable."

Taught Worship

> Finally then, brethren, we request and exhort you in the Lord
> Jesus, that as you received from us instruction
> as to how you ought to walk and please God
> (just as you actually do walk), that you excel still more.
> (1 Thess 4:1)

There is a critical need for preaching and teaching on worship in the church. And the above principles need to be *repeatedly* taught, as we all have the tendency to return to our default mode of what we want and what we like when it comes to worship. We need to be constantly reminded of what worship is, how it happens, and whom it is for!

BIBLICAL PRINCIPLES OF WORSHIP
(short summary)[1]

1. *Doxological Worship*: God's glory, and our joyful celebration of it in worship, should be the focus and goal of all life and ministry.

    > For from him and through him and to him are all things. To him be glory forever. Amen. (Rom 11:36)

2. *Theocentric Worship*: Worship is first and foremost for God.

    > "Worship God."(Rev 19:10; 22:9)

3. *Dialogical Worship*: Worship is a dialogue between God and his people, a rhythm of revelation and response.

    > For all the promises of God find their Yes in him [Christ]. That is why it is through him that we utter our Amen to God for his glory. (2 Cor 1:20)

4. *Word-Saturated Worship*: The word must be central in our worship.

    > Let the word of Christ dwell in you richly. (Col 3:16)

5. *Participatory Worship*: Worship is the responsibility of all of God's people.

    > Oh, magnify the Lord with me,
    > and let us exalt his name together!
    > (Psalm 34:3)

---

1. Also downloadable at https://worship-resources.org/2023/02/21/biblical-principles-of-worship/.

6. *Christ-Led Worship*: Our worship is acceptable in and through Christ our high priest.

> Through him [Christ] then let us continually offer up a sacrifice of praise to God,
> that is, the fruit of lips that acknowledge his name. (Heb 13:15)

7. *Spirit-Enabled Worship*: Our response of worship is enabled, motivated, and empowered by the Holy Spirit.

> We are the true circumcision, who worship in the Spirit of God and glory in Christ Jesus and put no confidence in the flesh. (Phil 3:3)

8. *Whole-Life Worship*: Worship is the response of our entire lives to God.

> Therefore I urge you, brethren, by the mercies of God, to present your bodies a living and holy sacrifice, acceptable to God, which is your spiritual service of worship. (Rom 12:1)

9. *Heart Worship*: God is much more concerned with our heart than with the form of our worship.

> "Man looks on the outward appearance, but the LORD looks on the heart." (1 Sam 16:7)

10. *Edifying Worship*: Worship should promote the unity and edification of the body.

> So then let us pursue what makes for peace and for mutual upbuilding. (Rom 14:19)

11. *Trans-Generational Worship*: Young and old need each other in the body of Christ.

> Young men and maidens, old men and children: Let them praise the name of the LORD, for his name alone is exalted. (Ps 148:12–13; cf. Titus 2:2–8)

12. *Taught Worship*: These things must be taught and retaught.

> Finally then, brethren, we request and exhort you in the Lord Jesus, that as you received from us instruction as to how you ought to walk and please God (just as you actually do walk), that you excel still more. (1 Thess 4:1)

30

SUMMARY AND BENEDICTION

Our Gift to God

Recommended is an insightful little children's book *Worship: Our Gift to God* (out of print, but used copies are available). The author reflects and summarizes simply and effectively many of the perspectives on worship that we have considered in this book (and in chapter 29).[1]

The title itself is instructive, and reflective of Principle #2 in chapter 29: "Worship is first and foremost for God." It cannot be repeated too often that most of our worship debates and arguments would fade away if we could truly take this principle to heart: worship is primarily *for God*, not for me!

Worship is always a *response* to God's *revelation*, a grateful reply to his gracious initiative in our lives. We praise and thank him for who he is, and for all that he has done for us and given to us in the Lord Jesus. It is *our gift to him* for all his good gifts to us!

---

1. The book emphasizes the centrality of worship as "one of the most important things mothers, fathers, boys, and girls can do," and that "worship can happen anywhere [Principle #8] . . . because worship happens in your heart" [Principle #9] (Trzeciak, *Worship*, 21, 2, respectively).

Benediction

Paul's words in Romans 15:5–6 express beautifully my prayer for all of you who have made it through this study, as you go forth as students and teachers and leaders of worship, and as worshipers:

> May the God of endurance and encouragement
> grant you to live in such harmony with one another,
> in accord with Christ Jesus,
> that *together* you may *with one voice*
> *glorify the God and Father of our Lord Jesus Christ.*

BIBLIOGRAPHY

Alexander, Eric. "Acceptable Worship: Sermons on Worship from John Chapter 4." https://www.ericalexander.co.uk/sermons/acceptableworship.php.
———. *Our Great God and Saviour*. Carlisle, PA: Banner of Truth Trust, 2010.
———. "Thirsting for God." iHeart, November 14, 2016. https://www.iheart.com/podcast/256-more-of-god-please-31024294/episode/eric-alexander-thirsting-for-god-38066971/.
———. "Worship: The Chief End of Man." Presentation at Philadelphia Conference on Reformed Theology, April 26, 1998.
———. "Worship: The Old Testament Pattern." Presentation at Philadelphia Conference on Reformed Theology, April 25, 1998.
———. "Worship God!" Sermon at First Evangelical Church, Memphis, TN, July 31, 2023. https://worship-resources.org/2023/07/31/worship-god-revelation-1910-sermon-eric-alexander/.
Allmen, Jean-Jacques von. "Worship and the Holy Spirit." *Studia Liturgica* 2 (1963) 124–35.
———. *Worship: Its Theology and Practice*. London: Lutterworth, 1968.
Anderson, Bernhard W. *Out of the Depths: The Psalms Speak for Us Today*. Philadelphia: Westminster, 1974.
Atkins, Peter. *Ascension Now: Implications of Christ's Ascension for Today's Church*. Collegeville, MN: Liturgical, 2001.
Augustine. *Confessions*. Translated by Albert C. Outler. New York: Barnes and Noble, 2007.
Avery, Tom. "Worship Wars and Ethnomusicology." Presentation at the Global Consultation on Music in Missions, St. Paul, MN, July 11–15, 2006.
Bailey, Mark. "Dispensational Expressions of Worship." Chapel message at Dallas Theological Seminary, January 12, 2010. https://tinyurl.com/BaileyDisp. https://voice.dts.edu/chapel/dispensational-expressions-of-worship-mark-l-bailey/.
Block, Daniel Isaac. *For the Glory of God: Recovering a Biblical Theology of Worship*. Grand Rapids: Baker Academic, 2016.
Brink, Emily, and John D. Witvliet. *The Worship Sourcebook*. 2nd ed. Grand Rapids: Faith Alive Christian Resources, 2013.
Brown, Marcia. *Stone Soup: An Old Tale*. New York: Aladdin, 1986.
Calvin Institute of Christian Worship. "Ascension Resource Guide." 2011. https://worship.calvin.edu/resources/resource-library/Ascension-Resource-Guide.

Calvin, John. *Institutes of the Christian Religion*. Edited by John T. McNeill. Louisville: Presbyterian, 1960.

Carson, D. A., ed. *Worship by the Book*. Grand Rapids: Zondervan, 2002.

Castleman, Robbie F. *Story-Shaped Worship: Following Patterns from the Bible and History*. Downers Grove, IL: IVP Academic, 2013.

Chapell, Bryan. *Christ-Centered Worship: Letting the Gospel Shape Our Practice*. Grand Rapids: Baker, 2017.

Cherry, Constance M. *The Worship Architect: A Blueprint for Designing Culturally Relevant and Biblically Faithful Services*. 2nd ed. Grand Rapids: Baker Academic, 2021.

Clowney, Edmund P. *The Church*. Contours of Christian Theology. Downers Grove, IL: IVP Academic, 1995.

Cocksworth, Christopher. *Holy, Holy, Holy: Worshipping the Trinitarian God*. London: Darton, Longman and Todd, 2004.

Crider, Joseph R. *Scripture-Guided Worship: A Call to Pastors & Worship Leaders*. Fort Worth, TX: Seminary Hill, 2021.

Dawn, Marva J. *Reaching Out without Dumbing Down: A Theology of Worship for the Turn-of-the-Century Culture*. Grand Rapids: Eerdmans, 1995.

———. *A Royal Waste of Time: The Splendor of Worshiping God and Being Church for the World*. Grand Rapids: Eerdmans, 1999.

Dawson, Gerrit Scott. *Jesus Ascended: The Meaning of Christ's Continuing Incarnation*. Phillipsburg, NJ: P&R, 2004.

Detwiler, David F. "Church Music and Colossians 3:16." *Bibliotheca Sacra* 158 (September 2001) 347–69.

Dillenberger, John, ed. *Martin Luther: Selections from His Writings*. New York: Anchor, 1961.

Due, Noel. *Created for Worship: From Genesis to Revelation to You*. Fearn, Scotland: Mentor, 2005.

Duncan, J. Ligon. "Foundations for Biblically Directed Worship." In *Give Praise to God: A Vision for Reforming Worship: Celebrating the Legacy of James Montgomery Boice*, edited by Philip Graham Ryken et al., 51–73. Phillipsburg, NJ: P&R, 2003.

Farley, Michael A. "Jesus' Ascension and Christian Worship." Central Presbyterian Worship, May 15, 2012. https://centralpresworship.files.wordpress.com/2020/05/ascension-jesus-ascension-and-christian-worship-farley.pdf.

———. "What is 'Biblical' Worship? Biblical Hermeneutics and Evangelical Theologies of Worship." *JETS* 51 (September 2008) 591–613.

Frame, John M. *Contemporary Worship Music: A Biblical Defense*. Phillipsburg, NJ: P&R, 1997.

Fromm, Chuck. "New Song: The Sound of Spiritual Awakening (A Study of Music in Revival)." Paper presented to Oxford Reading & Research Conference, July 1983. https://buddysheets.tripod.com/newsongthesoundofspiritualawakening.htm.

Gloer, W. Hulitt. "Worship God! Liturgical Elements in the Apocalypse." *Review and Expositor* 98 (Winter 2001) 35–57.

Grudem, Wayne A. *Systematic Theology: An Introduction to Biblical Doctrine*. 2nd ed. Grand Rapids: Zondervan Academic, 2020.

Hawthorne, Steve. "The Story of His Glory." *Mission Frontiers*, May 1, 1993. https://www.missionfrontiers.org/issue/article/the-story-of-his-glory.

Horton, Michael Scott. "Worship: The New Testament Pattern." Presentation at Philadelphia Conference on Reformed Theology, April 25, 1998.

Hustad, Donald P. *Jubilate II: Church Music in Worship and Renewal*. Carol Stream, IL: Hope, 1993.

Justin Martyr. "The First Apology of Justin." In *The Apostolic Fathers with Justin Martyr and Irenaeus*, edited by Alexander Roberts et al., 159–87. Ante-Nicene Fathers 1. New York: Scribner's Sons, 1903.

Kauflin, Bob. "Praise Choruses: Mainly Man-centered?" *Worship Matters*, December 30, 2003. https://www.scribd.com/document/262238024/Hymns-vs-Praise-Choruses.

———. *Worship Matters: Leading Others to Encounter the Greatness of God*. Wheaton, IL: Crossway, 2008.

Kavanagh, Aidan. *On Liturgical Theology*. Reprint of The Hale Memorial Lectures of Seabury-Western Theological Seminary 1981. New York: Pueblo, 1992.

Keller, Timothy. *The Reason for God: Belief in an Age of Skepticism*. New York: Penguin, 2009.

Kidd, Reggie. *With One Voice: Discovering Christ's Song in Our Worship*. Grand Rapids: Baker, 2005.

Krabill, James R., et al., eds. *Worship and Mission for the Global Church: An Ethnodoxology Handbook*. Pasadena, CA: William Carey, 2013.

Lathrop, Gordon. *Holy Things: A Liturgical Theology*. Minneapolis: Fortress, 1999.

Leafblad, Bruce. "Leading in Worship." Presentation at worship conference, Southwestern Baptist Theological Seminary, Fort Worth, TX, 1995.

Leithart, Peter J. *From Silence to Song: The Davidic Liturgical Revolution*. Moscow, ID: Canon, 2003.

Lewis, C. S. "On Church Music." In *Christian Reflections*, 117–23. Grand Rapids: Eerdmans, 2014.

———. *The Problem of Pain*. New York: MacMillan, 1944.

———. *Reflections on the Psalms*. San Francisco: HarperCollins, 2017.

Lucado, Max. *Traveling Light: Releasing the Burdens You Were Never Intended to Bear*. Nashville: Thomas Nelson, 2013.

Luther, Martin. "1528 Preface to the Psalms." In *Martin Luther: Selections from His Writings*, edited by John Dillenberger, 37–41. New York: Anchor, 1961.

———. *Lectures on Titus, Philemon, and Hebrews*. Luther's Works 29. Edited by Jaroslav Pelikan. St Louis: Concordia, 1968.

———. *What Luther Says: A Practical In-Home Anthology for the Active Christian*. Edited by Ewald M. Plass. St. Louis: Concordia, 2006.

Lutheran World Federation's Study Team on Worship and Culture. "Nairobi Statement on Worship and Culture Full Text." January 1996. https://worship.calvin.edu/resources/resource-library/nairobi-statement-on-worship-and-culture-full-text/.

Man, Ron. "Biblical Principles of Worship and Their Application to Local Church Ministry." Worship Resources International, February 18, 2023. https://worship-resources.org/2023/02/18/biblical-principles-of-worship-and-their-application-to-local-church-ministry/.

———. "The Bridge: Worship and Culture." Worship Resources International, June 25, 2023. https://worship-resources.org/2023/06/25/the-bridge-worship-and-culture.

———. "False and True Worship in Romans 1." Worship Resources International, June 8, 2023. https://worship-resources.org/2023/06/08/false-and-true-worship-in-romans-1 18-25/.

———. *Let Us Draw Near: Biblical Foundations of Worship*. Eugene, OR: Cascade, 2023.

———. "A Letter from Tapescrew (with Apologies to C. S. Lewis)." *Reformed Worship*, September 2009. https://www.reformedworship.org/article/september-2009/letter-tapescrew. (Also at https://worship-resources.org/2023/06/09/a-letter-from-tapescrew-with-apologies-to-c-s-lewis/.)

———. "More from Tapescrew." *Reformed Worship*, September 2010. https://www.reformedworship.org/article/september-2010/more-tapescrew.

———. "Music for Worship: Excellence as a Means Rather Than an End." *Church Musician Today*, March 1999. https://worship-resources.org/2023/06/09/music-for-worship-excellence-as-a-means-rather-than-an-end/.

———. "A Parable." Experiencing Worship, September 16, 2025. https://www.experiencingworship.com/articles/general/2001-8-a-parable.html.

———. "Paul as Theologian and Worshiper." *Worship Notes* 8.10 (October 2013). https://worship-resources.org/2013/10/31/important-new-testament-worship-passages-part-6/.

———. "The Power of Thematic Worship." https://worship-resources.org/2023/06/09/the-power-of-thematic-worship/.

———. *Proclamation and Praise: Hebrews 2:12 and the Christology of Worship*. Eugene, OR: Wipf & Stock, 2007.

———. "Rejoice with Trembling." *Church Musician Today*, September 1998. https://worship-resources.org/2023/05/16/rejoice-with-trembling-psalm-211/.

———. "Tapescrew Letter 3." Worship Resources International, June 9, 2023. https://worship-resources.org/2023/06/09/tapescrew-letter-3/.

———. "Tapescrew Letter 4." Worship Resources International, June 9, 2023. https://worship-resources.org/2023/06/09/tapescrew-letter-4/.

———. "Worship and the Word." Presentation at Calvin Symposium on Worship, Grand Rapids, 2009. https://worship.calvin.edu/resources/resource-library/symposium-2009-worship-and-the-word/.

———. *A Worship Reader: Short Studies and Reflections on Biblical Worship*. Eugene, OR: Wipf & Stock, 2025.

Markey, Dell. "What Effects Did the Babylonian Exile Have on the Jewish Religion?" Classroom, June 25, 2018. https://classroom.synonym.com/effects-did-babylonian-exile-jewish-religion-7222.html.

Merker, Matt. *Corporate Worship: How the Church Gathers as God's People*. Kindle ed. Edited by J. Ligon Duncan. Building Healthy Churches. Wheaton, IL: Crossway, 2021.

Meyers, Jeffrey J. *The Lord's Service: The Grace of Covenant Renewal Worship*. Moscow, ID: Canon, 2003.

Milligan, William. *The Ascension and Heavenly Priesthood of Our Lord*. Eugene, OR: Wipf & Stock, 2006.

Morgan, G. Campbell. *The Gospel According to Mark*. New York: Revell, 1927.

———. "Psalm 96:9: Worship, Beauty, Holiness." https://biblejesus.com/worship-beauty-holiness-george-campbell-morgan/.

Nicholls, William. *Jacob's Ladder: The Meaning of Worship*. Louisville: John Knox, 1955.

Packer, J. I. "The Greatness of God." In *New Geneva Study Bible, New King James Version*, edited by R. C. Sproul, 599. Nashville: Thomas Nelson, 1995.

———. *Keep in Step with the Spirit: Finding Fullness in Our Walk with God*. Rev. and enlarged ed. Grand Rapids: Baker, 2005.

Perowne, J. J. S. *The Book of Psalms: A New Translation with Introductions and Notes Explanatory and Critical.* Vol. 1. London: Bell and Sons, 1885.

Peterson, David. *Engaging with God: A Biblical Theology of Worship.* Downers Grove, IL: IVP Academic, 2002.

———. "Psalms, Hymns, and Spiritual Songs: Does the Bible Direct Us in the Choice of Musical Styles?" Presentation at the Institute for Christian Worship, Southern Baptist Theological Seminary, Louisville, KY, April 14, 2005.

———. "Worship and Evangelism." https://davidgpeterson.wordpress.com/worship/worship-and-evangelism/.

Piper, John. *The Dangerous Duty of Delight: Daring to Make God Your Greatest Desire.* Colorado Springs: Multnomah, 2011.

———. "Gospel Worship: Holy Ambition for All the Peoples to Praise Christ." Desiring God, January 31, 2017. https://www.desiringgod.org/messages/gospel-worship.

———. *Let the Nations Be Glad! The Supremacy of God in Missions.* 30th anniversary ed. Grand Rapids: Baker Academic, 2023.

———. "Our High Priest Is the Son of God Perfect Forever." Desiring God, December 8, 1996. https://www.desiringgod.org/messages/our-high-priest-is-the-son-of-god-perfect-forever.

———. "The Pride of Babel and the Praise of Christ." Desiring God, September 2, 2007. https://www.desiringgod.org/messages/the-pride-of-babel-and-the-praise-of-christ.

———. *Providence.* Wheaton, IL: Crossway, 2020.

———. "The Pursuit of God in Corporate Worship." Desiring God, November 11, 2011. Session 1 of Gravity and Gladness Seminar. https://www.desiringgod.org/messages/gravity-and-gladness-session-1.

———. "Thoughts on Worship and Culture." Desiring God, 1990. https://www.desiringgod.org/articles/thoughts-on-worship-and-culture.

———. "Worship Is an End in Itself." Desiring God, September 13, 1981. https://www.desiringgod.org/messages/worship-is-an-end-in-itself.

Plantinga, Cornelius, and Sue A. Rozeboom, eds. *Discerning the Spirits: A Guide to Thinking about Christian Worship Today.* Calvin Institute of Christian Worship Liturgical Studies Series. Grand Rapids: Eerdmans, 2003.

Ralston, Tim. "The Ambiguity of 'in Spirit': Addressing Disparate Approaches." Evangelical Theological Society Annual Meeting, Colorado Springs, October 2011. https://etsworship.files.wordpress.com/2011/10/in-spirit-article.pdf.

Ross, Allen P. *Recalling the Hope of Glory: Biblical Worship from the Garden to the New Creation.* Grand Rapids: Kregel, 2006.

Sjogren, Bob. *One Degree Off Theology.* Mechanicsville, VA: MMPublishers, 2018.

Smith, Gordon T. *A Holy Meal: The Lord's Supper in the Life of the Church.* Grand Rapids: Baker Academic, 2005.

Sproul, R. C., ed. *New Geneva Study Bible, New King James Version.* Nashville: Thomas Nelson, 1995.

Spurgeon, C. H. *The Treasury of David: Containing an Original Exposition of the Book of Psalms; A Collection of Illustrative Extracts from the Whole Range of Literature; A Series of Homiletical Hints upon Almost Every Verse; and Lists of Writers upon Each Psalm.* Peabody, MA: Hendrickson, 2011.

Stott, John R. W. *Romans: God's Good News for the World.* Bible Speaks Today. Downers Grove, IL: InterVarsity, 1994.

Tait, William. *Meditationes Hebraicae, or, a Doctrinal and Practical Exposition of the Epistle of St. Paul to the Hebrews*. London: Seeley, Burnside and Seeley, 1845.

Torrance, James B. "Christ in Our Place: The Joy of Worship." In *A Passion for Christ: The Vision That Ignites Ministry* by Thomas F. Torrance et al., 35–52. Eugene, OR: Wipf & Stock, 2010.

———. "The Doctrine of the Trinity in Our Contemporary Situation." In *The Forgotten Trinity*, edited by Alisdair I. C. Heron, 3:3–17. London: Inter-Church, 1991.

———. "The Place of Jesus Christ in Worship." In *Theological Foundations for Ministry: Selected Readings for a Theology of the Church in Ministry*, edited by Ray S. Anderson, 348–69. Grand Rapids: Eerdmans, 1979.

———. *Worship, Community and the Triune God of Grace*. Downers Grove, IL: IVP Academic, 1997.

Torrance, Thomas F. *The Christian Doctrine of God, One Being Three Persons*. 2nd ed. T&T Clark Cornerstones. London: T&T Clark, 2016.

Torrance, Thomas F., et al. *A Passion for Christ: The Vision That Ignites Ministry*. Eugene, OR: Wipf & Stock, 2010.

Tozer, A. W. *Whatever Happened to Worship?* Camp Hill, PA: Christian, 1985.

———. *Worship: The Missing Jewel*. Camp Hill, PA: Christian, 1992.

Trzeciak, Cathy. *Worship: Our Gift to God*. St. Louis: Concordia, 1986.

Webber, Robert E. "Blended Worship Response." In *Exploring the Worship Spectrum: 6 Views*, by Paul F. M. Zahl et al., 129–30. Grand Rapids: Zondervan, 2004.

———. *Worship Is a Verb: Eight Principles Transforming Worship*. 2nd ed. Peabody, MA: Hendrickson, 1996.

White, James F. "Making Our Worship More Biblical." *Perkins Journal* (Fall 1980) 38–40.

Witvliet, John D. "Isaiah in Christian Liturgy: Recovering Textual Contrasts and Correcting Theological Astigmatism." *Calvin Theological Journal* 39 (2004) 135–56.

———. "Prism of Glory: Trinitarian Worship and Liturgical Piety in the Reformed Tradition." In *The Place of Christ in Liturgical Prayer: Trinity, Christology, and Liturgical Theology*, edited by Bryan D. Spinks, 268–99. Collegeville, MN: Liturgical, 2008.

———. "Singing Our Prayers, Praying Our Songs: Historical and Cross-Cultural Music in the Context of Worship." Unpublished manuscript.

———. "Trinity Sunday and the Call to Worship." *Reformed Worship* 83 (March 2007). https://www.reformedworship.org/article/march-2007/trinity-sunday-and-call-to-worship?utm_source=chatgpt.com.

Wright, Christopher J. H. *The Mission of God: Unlocking the Bible's Grand Narrative*. Downers Grove, IL: IVP Academic, 2006.

Wright, N. T. "Freedom and Framework, Spirit and Truth: Recovering Biblical Worship." 2002. https://ntwrightpage.com/2016/04/05/freedom-and-framework-spirit-and-truth-recovering-biblical-worship-2/.

———. "Worship and the Spirit in the New Testament." February 21–23, 2008. https://ntwrightpage.com/2016/04/25/worship-and-the-spirit-in-the-new-testament/.

Zahl, Paul F. M., et al. *Exploring the Worship Spectrum: 6 Views*. Counterpoints. Grand Rapids: Zondervan, 2004.

SUBJECT INDEX

Aaron, mediator between people and God, 13
Abram/Abraham, 13, 16–17, 81–83
    call of, 81–82
acceptable worship, ix, 6, 17, 62, 62n, 73, 80, 106n, 116, 121, 138, 161, 170, 172, 173, 204, 208, 225, 226, 229, 233, 234, 236, 240
access to God through Christ, *See* drawing near to God
Alexander, Eric, 34, 40, 52, 53, 62, 220
all of life, worship as. *See* whole-life worship.
Allmen, Jean-Jacques von, 140, 183n, 228
altars, 15–1680, 82, 83, 84
Apostles' Creed, 62, 193
assurance, 153, 158, 171, 226
Augustine, 161

Babel, 80–81
balance between biblical fidelity and cultural relevance, 197
Bangladesh, 169n
Bible
    the story of God's glory, 28–33
    worship as unifying theme of, 46, 69
biblical constants, 177–78, 201–2, 216
biblical or cultural?, 209–10
biblical understanding of worship, why important, 5–7, 27
Block, Daniel I., 71n
blood of Christ, v, 3, 50–51, 118, 142, 148, 150, 151–52, 166, 171, 190, 191n, 193–94, 226

Book of Common Prayer, 194–95
Brazil, 208n
Bridge, The, 200–216, 200n

Call to Worship
    in worship service, 20, 220
    missions as a, 52
    the gospel as a, 49–51, 53
Calvin, John, 40
Castleman, Robbie, 12, 15–16
catechisms, 193
centrality of worship, 37–68, 242n
change
    attitudinal, 6, 63, 170n
    cultural, 6, 204
    worship in the church, 7n, 173n, 208
Christ-centeredness
    of the Holy Spirit's ministry,
    of Hebrews, 147, 153
Christian life, God's glory and the, 31–32
church, the, 165, 184–85, 250–51
    congregational song in, 133–38
    doxological purpose for, 217
    God-centered view of, 56
    God's glory in, 32
    preferring one another in, 211
    worship in, 177–212
church planting, 199
communion with Father and the Son, 52
competing worships, 39–40
completing the cycle of revelation and response, 21, 22–26
confession, 191

confidence, 153, 171, 226
conflict over worship, 205–6
conquest of the Promised Land, 92–93
contemporary worship, 205, 206
corporate worship, 130–31, 152–53, 183–86
    builds community, 185–86
    challenge to the world, 185, 185n
    gives identity to the church, 184–85
    invitation to the world, 185
    mediated by Christ, 170
    nurtures the believer, 185
creation
    for God's glory, 29, 216
    of humanity for worship, 79
creeds, 62, 193, 218
cultural context, 208
cultural diversity in worship, 203
culture
    and worship, 7n, 41, 196–212
    definitions of, 196–97
cycles in Israel's history, 100

David, King
    composer of songs for worship, 97
    development and expansion of public worship, 95–96
    example of true worshiper, 96–97
    incorporation of music in worship, 95–96
Day of Atonement, 91
definition of worship, 33
dialogue, worship as, 20–21, 26, 219–20
discernment, need for (biblical commands, cultural applications), 209–10, 212
discipleship as building better worshipers of God, 59\
disobedience, Israel's 90
doxology, 127–29
    theology and, 22–25, 28
drawing near to God, v, 3–4, 51–52, 117–18, 127–29, 136, 136n, 147, 151–53, 166–69, 172–73, 226, 228
dual mediation of Christ. *See* two-way mediation of Christ.

early church, worship in the, 161, 178–79, 196, 233–35, 236
edification, 233–35
evangelism as winning more worshipers for God, 59
everybody worship, 39–40, 46
excellence in music, a means not an end, 192, 192n
exilic worship, 101
exodus, the, 86
external worship, 62, 75, 77–78, 80, 121

fall, the, 15
    Christ reverses effects of, 49–50
    God's glory and, 30
    worship the central issue in, 44–45, 46, 52, 79
false gods, 15, 41, 86
false worship, 39–40, 45–46, 50–51, 79, 86, 92–94, 98, 186
fellowship in the church, 25, 177, 178, 202, 235
fellowship within the Trinity, 29
fellowship with God
    goal of the gospel, 50
    humanity created for, 131
    with Christ, 184, 190
    with God, 51, 184
flesh, weakness of the, 89
flexibility of form. *See* freedom of form
freedom of form, 117, 202–12, 216
    within bounds, 199
From the Field, xiv, xivn, 7n, 23n, 27n, 37n, 63n, 106n, 108n, 136n, 166n, 169n, 170n, 173n, 178n, 185n, 188n, 197n, 208n, 236n

gift, salvation as a, 127–28
gift to God, worship as our, 242
glorification of Christ. *See* exaltation of Christ.
glorifying God, xivn, 14, 33, 35, 45, 79, 129–30, 132–33, 140–46, 162, 243, 129–30, 129–30, 132–33, 140–46, 162, 243
    believers' goal, x, 31–32, 34, 76, 230
    church's purpose, the, 182, 243
    denied in the fall, 30, 44

SUBJECT INDEX

in worship, 180–82
Israel's purpose, 30
worship as, 33
glory of God, the, 28–35, 45–46, 67, 87, 129–30, 139, 145, 183, 216–17, 243, 254
    centrality of, 32–33, 216–17
    departing the temple, 101
    filling the tabernacle, 101, 102, 164
    filling the temple, 87, 97–98, 102
    God's purpose, 34, 132–33
    God's purpose in redemption, 132–33
    humanity's purpose, 34
    in creation, 42–43, 45
    in heaven, 145
    in Jesus Christ, 102
    no return to the rebuilt temple, 102
    revelation of, 79
    robbed in the fall, 53
    story of the Bible, 29–33
    worship about and for, 33
goal of missions, worship as the, 180
goal of the church, worship as the, 180–82
God
    alone worthy of worship, 43, 46, 49, 51, 52, 79
    beauty of, 89
    blessing Israel, 94
    Creator, the, 52, 73, 79, 141–42
    disciplining Israel, 94
    glorified for his grace, 162
    glory of God. *See* glory of God.
    grace of, 18, 89, 127–28, 132, 133, 144
    greatness of his name, 86
    heart for the nations, his, 56
    holiness of, 88
    immanence of, 110
    majesty of, 89
    mercy of, 129–30
    names of, 17, 83
    presence of. *See* presence of God.
    revealing initiative of, 73, 81, 86
    seeks worshipers, 64–65
    sovereignty of, 13, 29, 81, 109, 128, 132
    uniqueness of, 43, 44
    worship for and about, 5
God-centered worship, 217–19, 242
gospel, the, 127–33, 144
    as a call to worship, 50–52
    God-centered view of, 56
    preached in many cultures, 199
grace, God's. *See also* God, grace of.
    as ultimate expression of God's glory, 133
    for our salvation, 162
    for our sanctification, 162
    for our worship, 162–73
grace, throne of, 4, 110, 151, 152, 202, 281n, 283, 285
gratitude. *See* thanksgiving.
Great Commandment, 57–59, 121
    priority of, 57–59
    relationship to Great Commission, 57–50, 181

ḥesed, 74–75, 97, 101, 104
hallelujah!, 106, 144–45
heart worship, priority of, v, 3, 24, 33, 33, 45, 51, 55, 57–58, 60–61, 62–63, 75–78, 80, 96–97, 100, 104, 106n, 115–16, 118, 121–22, 124–25, 130, 135, 137, 138–39, 158–60, 170, 171, 180, 181–82, 187, 193, 207–8, 226, 229, 231–33, 240, 242n, 251n
heaven
    centrality of worship in, 66–67
    God's glory in, 32
heavenly worship, 66–67, 184
    present participation in, 67
Heidelberg Catechism, 194
history, revolving around the question of worship, 46
"Holy, Holy, Holy," 25, 141
Holy Spirit, the, 140, 184, 227–29, 251
    and salvation, 158
    and worship, 155–60
    building up the church, 159–60
    Christ-centeredness of all his work, 157–60, 229
    connecting revelation and response, 158–59

Holy Spirit, the (*cont.*)
  continuing Christ's earthly ministry, 158
  empowering Christ's earthly ministry, 157
  giving enablement for Christian living, 159–60
  glorifies Christ, 155–60
  motivating and empowering worship, 158–59
  prompting our worship, 168
  worship of, 156
humility, need for, 23n, 132, 137, 160, 172, 185, 206–7, 233, 237

idolatry, 39, 43, 92–93, 94, 98, 100
individualism, 218, 235
inward worship. *See* heart worship.
Isaac, 83–84
Israel
  bad kings of, 98
  destiny follows its worship, 94, 98, 98
  disobedience of, 90
  exile of, 99
  good kings of, 98
  idolatry in, 94, 98, 189
  obedience of, 90
  return from exile, 190–93
  special relationship with God, 87
  testimony to the nations, 90, 189
  theocratic nation, 87–88
  to reflect God's glory, 30
  unique worship people, 82, 86, 139

Jacob, 84–86
Jacob's Ladder, 84–85
  Jesus Christ as fulfillment of, 85, 16364
Jerusalem
  destruction of, 100
  established as capital, 95
Jesus Christ
  and our teaching and preaching ministry, 165
  ascension of, 125–26, 126n
  birth of, 48, 157n
  continuing ministry, of, 165
  continuing priesthood of, 166–67
  continuing revelatory ministry of, 165
  death of, xi, 4, 89, 118, 142, 147, 157, 184, 190, 206,
  deity and humanity of, 163
  deity of, 149
  devotion to, 123
  dual mediation of. *See* Jesus Christ, two-way mediation of.
  earthly ministry of, 165
  exaltation of, 110, 125, 126, 140, 165
  fulfills revelation and response pattern, 149, 164
  glory of God seen in, 30–31
  high priest, 149
  humanity of, 149
  incarnation of, 85, 142, 163, 167
  intercession of, 151–52, 168, 171
  King, 114, 126
  Leader of our worship, ix, x111, 132–33, 166–68, 225–27
  makes worshipers out of rebels, 49
  Mediator, v, 113n, 126n, 148–51, 162–69, 173, 184, 226, 227
  past work of, 152, 166
  perfecter of our worship, 168, 172
  permanent priesthood, 150–51
  present in our services, 164, 166–69, 172, 173n, 208, 225–27
  present ministry of, 152, 164, 166, 168
  priesthood of, 149z–51
  Redeemer, 142–43
  restores true worship, 49–50, 52
  resurrection of, xi, 56, 126, 151, 157, 190
  revealer of the Father, 149, 165
  reverses effects of the fall, 49–50, 52
  sacrifice of, 113n, 118, 177
  Second Adam, 48–49
  speaking through the word, 138
  takes us into the Father's presence, 4, 118, 126, 136, 184, 208, 222, 226, 228
  teaching about worship, 59–64
  temptations of, 48–49
  two-way mediation of, 85, 149, 163, 164, 167

SUBJECT INDEX

worshiped, 149
worshiped and worshiper, 166–67
worshiper of the Father, 149, 166
Jewish influence on Christian worship, 177
John the Baptist, 103
Jordan, xivn, 166, 173n
judgment, 81, 86, 90, 99, 144
justification, 127

Kauflin, Bob, ix–xi, 24, 169
kings of Israel
    false worship of, 98
    true worship of, 98

Lamb of God, 32, 65–66, 81, 142–45
languages, 81
latitude in form. *See* freedom of form.
lavish worship, 122–25
law of Moses, 13–14, 86–91, 104
legalism, 102–3, 120
Leithart, Peter, 95–96, 95n
"let us draw near" (Heb 10:22), v, 3, 4, 51, 118, 151, 152–53, 226
Let Us Draw Near: Biblical Foundations of Worship (Ron Man), x, xiii, xivn, 58n
Levitical priesthood, 149–50
Lewis, C. S., 35, 108
lifestyle worship. *See* whole-life worship.
local context, 208
Lord's Supper, 177–78, 189–91, 202
    freedom in frequency of, 209
lovingkindness. *See* ḥesed
Lucifer, 44
Luther, Martin, 25–26, 105, 192

Man, Ron, 110, 127, 164n, 192n, 200n, 215, 215n, 217–19, 224n, 225, 23435, 235n, 237
mediation in Israel, 162–64
Mediator, Christ as. *See* Jesus, Christ, Mediator.
Melchizedek like Christ, 149–50
mercy, God's, 129–30. *See also* h[set dot under h]*esed*
ministry, its ultimate vertical purpose, 181–82

ministry of the word, the entire service as a, 25, 25n
missions
    as a call to worship, 53
    as God's work, 57
    God-centered view of, 56
    worship as goal of, 54–55, 59
    worship as fuel of, 55–56
Moldova, 185n
Mosaic covenant, 86–91
Moses as mediator between God and the people, 163–64
music
    David develops for public worship, 95–96
    not a universal language, 204 208n
    See also singing

Nairobi Statement on Worship and Culture, 211–12
nations, the, 86, 90, 142–43
    God's goal for, 57
    God's heart for, 82
    worship of, 129–30
Nepal, 106n
"new and living way, the," v, 3–4, 50–51, 118, 136, 147, 151, 161, 167, 172
new covenant, 14–15, 90, 104
    superiority of, 147–54
new covenant worship
    access to God in, 169
    decentralization of, 198–99
    through Christ, 167
Nicean Creed, 194
Nicholls, William, 182, 220
Nigeria, 136n
Noah and the flood, 80
non-negotiable elements of worship, 175, 177–78
normative elements of worship, 177–778

old and new covenants, contrasts between, 149–50
Old and New Testament worship
    differences, 113n
    similarities, 113n

old covenant, 13–14, 74, 76, 91
  centralization of worship under, 197–98
  duty of worship under, 86–91
  inadequacy of, 89–90
  key worship take-aways, 104
  priests mediating between the people and God, 163–64
  typological nature of worship under, 90–91

Packer, J. I., 23, 156
participation, congregational, 222–25
pastor and worship, the, x, xi, xiii, xiv, 19, 23n, 27, 63, 64, 108n, 116, 116, 169, 170, 173n, 191, 223, 224, 225, 230
Peterson, David, 37, 51, 209n
Philippines, 173n
Piper, John, 35, 40, 54, 55, 57, 59, 92, 115, 117, 128n, 129–30, 133, 162, 180, 197–99, 202, 209, 211
post-exilic worship, 102–3
praise, 106, 133, 153, 177–78, 202, 227, 242
  prayers of, 191
prayer, 82, 177–78, 202
  bidded, 192, 225
  corporate, 191–92, 224–25
  in Jesus' name, 136n
preaching, 170, 101, 165, 101, 129, 138, 165, 166, 170, 181, 186, 188, 206n, 220–22, 226, 238
  mediated by Christ, 165, 170
  synagogue's influence on, 101
preferences, differing personal, 6, 196, 199, 207, 208, 211, 219, 233–35
presence of God, the, 226, 228
  with believers, 68, 89, 97, 108, 116, 194
  with Israel, 89, 98, 100, 101, 118
  Christ seated in the, 170, 208
  entering into in worship, 20, 40, 116, 147, 152, 153, 167, 168, 169, 188, 229
  entering into with Christ, 4, 118, 126, 136, 184, 208, 222, 226, 228

presence of Christ in worship, 170, 208, 228
presence of Holy Spirit in believers, 228
pride
  human, 43–44, 80–81, 234, 237
  Israel's, 82
  Satan's, 43, 47
priesthood, royal, 34, 138–89
principles of worship, biblical, x, xiv, 7, 7n, 11, 117, 215–41, 215n
  summary of, 239–41
proclamation. *See* preaching.
Proclamation and Praise: Hebrews 2:12 and the Christology of Worship (Ron Man), ix, xiii, 164n, 166n, 173n, 225
promises of God, 81–82, 83, 131
prophets of Israel, 99
  mediating between the people and God, 163
Psalms, book of, 17, 105–10
  authors of, 106–7
  balanced perspective of, 109–10
  Davidic, 106–7
  poetry in the, 108–9
  tone of, 108
  types of, 107–8
  uniqueness of, 105–6
"psalms, hymns, and spiritual songs," 133–38, 192, 226

readings besides Scripture in corporate worship, 193–94
reading of Scripture in corporate worship, 19–21, 177, 179, 186, 188–89, 210, 221, 224
rebellion against God, 45
redemption, 74, 142–43, 184
  God's glory seen in, 31
  God's purpose in, 132–33
  revelation and response pattern of, 13–15
  worship as central to, 48–50
Reformation, Protestant, 26, 172, 222
"rejoice with trembling" (Ps 2:11), 110, 110n, 141
remembrance, in Lord's Supper, 100

SUBJECT INDEX

response, worship as, 33–34, 64, 73–74, 79, 80, 82, 86, 87–91, 116, 128, 132, 141
responsive readings, 193, 210, 224
rest of worship, the, 120–21
revelation and response, xiii, 11–27, 33, 45, 73, 81–83, 87, 131–32, 139, 141, 158–59, 189, 219–20, 242
  alternate in worship service, 21, 25, 220
  complete cycle of, 22–26
  fulfilled by Jesus Christ, 149, 164, 226–27
Revelation, worship in, 66–67, 81, 140–46
ritual worship
  developed by David, 95–96
  developed by Solomon, 98
  established by Moses, 88–904
Ross, Allen, 71n

Sabbath, 120
  legalistic view of, 102–3
sacrificial system, 13, 88–90, 138, 162
salvation, 143–44
  eternal, 151
  gift of, 127–28
Samaria, Samaritans, 60–61, 60n
Scripture in worship
  as ultimate authority, 208
  importance of, 18–20, 27
  neglect of, 19, 188
  reading of, 19–21, 177, 179, 186, 188–89, 210, 221, 224
  ways to use, 19–20
selfishness, 216–18, 233–35
service, worship precedes, 56
silence of New Testament on worship forms, 197–99
sincere worship. *See* heart worship.
Singapore, 27n, 63n, 170n
singing, 178, 191, 192, 220, 222–24, 227, 235
Solomon, King, 97–87
sovereignty of God, 13, 29, 81, 109, 128, 132
spirit and truth, worship in, 61–63
spirit, worship in, 61–62

spiritual maturity, 206–7
spiritual sacrifices. *See* heart worship.
steadfast love. *See* h[set dot under h]*esed*
Stott, John R. W., 18, 22, 23, 128, 129
synagogue, influence on Christian worship, 177, 189–90

tabernacle, heavenly, 86, 88, 114, 126, 150–52
tabernacle, Israel's, 75, 87, 97, 102, 198
  access limited at, 118
  influence on Christian worship, 177
  ritual worship at, 88
Tabernacle of David, 95
Tapescrew Letters, 217–19, 234–35, 235n
Te Deum, 194
teaching on worship, x, xiv, 7n, 23, 23n, 27n, 57, 62, 110, 147, 238, 241, 243, 106n, 109n, 169n, 173n, 178n, 185n, 198n, 237–38
  Jesus', 59–64
temple, Jerusalem, 75, 198
  access limited at, 103, 118
  building of, 97–98
  curtain torn at Christ's death, 3
  destruction of, 100
  influence on Christian worship, 177
  magnificence of, 98
  rebuilding of, 102
  ritual worship at, 88
Ten Commandments, 13–14
testimony of corporate worship, 185
thanksgiving, 15, 30, 31, 44, 45, 48, 52, 76, 79, 83, 95, 107, 120, 133, 135, 136, 143, 146, 159, 171, 179, 180, 190, 191, 230
theology and doxology, 127–29
theology of worship, 5n
Torrance, James, 91, 167, 169, 189
Torrance, Thomas, 157
Tozer, A. W., 48, 49, 182
tradition, 102–3, 108
traditional worship, 205
transcultural principles of worship, xiv, 7n, 211, 212, 216
trans-generational worship, 235–37, 240
trinitarian worship, 136, 168

Trinity, 136, 155
  different roles, 155
true worship, turn from false worship to, 49–51
truth, worship in, 62–63
two-way mediation of Christ, 85, 149, 163, 164, 167
typological worship, 91

unity in Christ, 131, 136, 137, 138, 184, 196, 211, 233–35, 236, 240, 243
  forged by Holy Spirit, 196, 211
  in worship service, 7
unity in diversity, 131, 136, 138, 196, 236
universal language, music not a, 204, 208n
unselfishness, 207

Valley of Vision, 104
Vietnam, 197n

Webber, Robert E., 171, 222
White, James F., 221
whole-life worship, 6, 60–65, 87–88, 116–17, 132, 229–31, 242n
Witvliet, John, 27, 157n, 168
"word of Christ" (Col 3:16), 19, 137–38, 185, 188, 220, 226, 239
word of God, 177–78, 202
  central in worship, 187–89, 195, 220–22, 226

entire service as ministry of, 25, 25n, 221
ultimate foundation for worship, 27, 87
work, worship not a, 121, 173, 174, 225
worship, centrality of, 37–68, 140, 146
worship leader, xiii, xiv, 23, 27, 63, 116, 161, 169, 169n, 170, 230, 237
Worship Leader, Jesus our, ix, 166–67, 169, 225–27, 240
worship service,
  balance of revelation and response, 21, 35–39, 45, 170
  centrality of the word of God in, 187–89, 195, 220–22, 226
  entire service as ministry of the word, 25, 25n, 221
  entire service as worship, 25
  reading of Scripture in, 19–21, 177, 179, 186, 188–89, 210, 221, 224
  readings besides Scripture in, 193–94
  styles, 7, 202–11
worship wars, xiii, 204–7, 210, 236n
worshipers
  Jesus came to make, 49
  the Father is seeking, 50, 64–65
Wright. Christopher, 93, 106
Wright, N. T., 130–31, 135, 221–22

"Yes and Amen," 131–32, 219, 239

SCRIPTURE INDEX

Genesis

1–2	79
1:1	42
1:16	40
1:26–28	28
1:28	80
3	15, 79
3:5	44
3:6	44
3:8–10	13
4:1–17	80
6–8	80
8:20	16, 80
9:1	80
11	80
11:4	80
11:9	81
12:1–3	13, 16, 81–83
12:4	82
12:7–8	16, 82, 83
13:3–4	16, 83
13:18	16, 83
14:18–19	83
14:20	83
15:5–6	83
15:5	13
15:6	13, 167
15:7	13
15:18–21	13
17:1–8	13
17:1–2	83
17:5	82n
18:22–23	83
21:33	83
22:7	83
22:9	16, 83
22:14	83
22:15–18	13
24:12	83
25:29–34	84
26:23–24	83
26:25	16, 84
27:1–40	84
27:41–45	84
28	164
28:10–22	84
28:12	85, 170
28:13–15	85
28:16–17	86
28:18	16
32:28	84
33:20	16
35	84
35:7	16

Exodus

1–19	86
3	13
3:12	74
3:13–14	73
6:6–7	87
6:7	74
7:5	86
7:16	86
7:17	86
8:1	86
8:9–10	86
8:10	43

Exodus (cont.)

8:20	86
8:22	86
9:1	86
9:11	86
9:13	86
9:14	86
9:16	86
9:29	86
10:1–2	86
10:3	86
12:12	86
14:4	86
14:17–18	86
14:31	86
15:11–13	86
15:13–16	86
19:6	88
20:1–3	13–14
20:3	87
24:3	89, 104
32	89
39:7	90
40:34	87, 97, 101

Leviticus

11:45	87
16	118
25:38	87
26:11	87
26:12	87

Numbers

15:41	87
33:3–4	86

Deuteronomy

6:3	101
9:4–7	92
29:13	87

Joshua

	92–93
2:8–11	86
4:23–24	86

1 Samuel

12:22	94
13:14	96
16:7	76, 78, 136, 231, 232, 239, 231
16:12–13	13

1 Kings

8:27–29	98

2 Kings

18–19	98
18:1–3	98
22–23	98
22:8–13	89

1 Chronicles

15	95
15:1	95
16	95
16:4–7	95
16:39–43	95
17:20	43
23	95
25	95

2 Chronicles

7:1–3	101
7:1	87, 97–98
29:2	76
29:25	96
30	89
30:18–20	76–77
33:1–2	98
36:15–16	99
36:17–20	100

Ezra

	102

Psalms

1:5	109
1:6	109
2:11	110, 142

8:1	110	148:13	217
16:11	40	150	106
19:1	216	150:2	17, 23
19:1	29		
22:22	165	**Isaiah**	
23	96, 107	5:16	90
27:4	108	6:3	25
32	107	14:14	44
34:3	222, 238	42:8	43
34:11	185	43:6–7	29
42	108	43:20–21	82
48:10	17	43:21	86, 140
50:13–14	76	46:9	43
50:23	76	49:5	30
51	107	66:18	216
51:16–17	76		
63	96–97	**Jeremiah**	
63:1	108	9:24	75
63:3	75	22:8–9	90, 100
65:4	108	31:31–33	90
67:1–4	56	31:33	104
67:1–2	82, 90		
67:3–4	54	**Ezekiel**	
69:30–31	76	10:15–19	101
71:19	43	11:22–25	101
72:11	54	26:27	104
72:19	216	36:26–27	90
84:11–12	108	45	114
89:6	33		
95:6	43	**Amos**	
96:1–5	57	5:21–24	62n
96:4	17, 55		
96:7	54	**Zechariah**	
96:8	183	6	114
100:1–2	108		
103:13	109	**Matthew**	
106:34–36	92	3:17	171
114:1–2	86	4:8–9	48
115:1	33	4:10	48, 126
115:4–8	185	5:17	102
117:1	57	6:1–6	121
119:89	6	6:5	77
119:105	6, 220	6:16	77
136	74	6:33	56, 64
146–50	106	11:27	166
148:12–23	234		
148:11–13	56		
148:12–13	239		

Matthew (cont.)

11:28–30	103, 120–21
12:28	158
13:52	194
15:7–9	77
15:8–9	62
17:5	171
22:37–38	58
22:39	59
23	121
23:1–3	62
23:2–4	120
23:4	103
23:5	62, 77
23:13	231
23:16	231
23:23	231
23:25–28	62
23:25	231
23:27–28	121
26:8	123
27:46	165n
27:51	3, 116

Mark

2:27–28	103
7:5–7	77
7:7–9	102
12:13	121
12:28–34	121–22
12:33	133
12:38–40	121
14:1	123
14:3–9	122–25
14:10	123
15:34	165n
15:38	3, 116

Luke

1	103
1:15	158n
1:35	158
1:41	158n
1:67	158n
2:19	189
2:25–27	158n
3:21–22	158
4:1–2	158n
4:16–21	101
4:18	158
6:1–2	103
7:37	123n
10:21	158
10:29–37	60n
11:42	231
21:1–3	77
22:16, 18	190
22:20	90
22:30	184
22:42	156
23:45	3, 116

John

1:14	30, 102
1:18	166
1:32–33	158
1:47–51	85
1:51	164, 170, 174
3:5	159
3:16	125, 156
4:4	60n
4:10–15	60
4:16–21	60
4:20–24	60–63
4:21	116, 229
4:22	62
4:23–24	220
4:23	50, 64, 116, 133, 229
4:24	60n
4:34	156
5:24	156
5:36–38	156
6:29	156
7:16	156
12:3	123n
12:4–5	123
14:2–3	126
14:6	63
14:16	158
14:26	158
15:8	32
15:26	158
16:7	126
16:8	159

16:12–15	166	5:1	128
16:13–14	157, 158	5:2	129 153
16:14	156	5:11	129
16:25	166	5:15	129
17:6	166	5:17	48, 129
17:14–16	184	5:18	129
17:24	29	5:19	128
17:26	166	5:21	129
19:30	190	6:4	129
		6:5	129
		6:23	129
		8:1–11	129

Acts

1:1	158, 166
1:9–11	125–26
2:41	177
2:42, 47	177–78, 187–92, 201
2:42	101
3:15	174
9	13
10:38	158
13:16–41	101
14:1	101
14:7	51
14:14–15	51
17:2–3	101
17:17	101
17:22–31	51
17:24–25	29
18:4	101
18:19	101
19:8	101

8:2–4	89, 160
8:2	190
8:3–4	90
8:9–11	228
8:9	160
8:14–17	228
8:15	129, 159
8:26	163
8:34	152
9–11	129
11:30	129
11:36	32, 140, 216, 238
12:1	6, 17, 63, 116, 133, 228, 229, 239
12:10	211
14:3	236
14:19	233, 239
15:9	226

1 Corinthians

1:12–13	235
1:20	140
2:12	160
3:16	229
6:19–20	116
6:19	229
6:20	14, 190, 229
10:31	31, 64, 116, 216, 229
11:26	190
12:4–6	137
14	131–32
14:24–25	184
14:26	134, 178
15:10	163
15:45	48

Romans

1:4	190
1:16	128
1:20–21	15
1:21	31, 53, 79
1:25	15
3:9–18	128
3:22	128
3:23	30, 128
3:24–25	117
3:24	128
3:25	128
3:26	128
4:1–5	13
4:5	128

2 Corinthians

1:20	18, 132–34, 219, 238
3:18	160

Galatians

3:28	184
4:6	159
5:25	160, 229

Ephesians

1:7–8	125
1:20–21	126
2:6	67
2:8–10	14
2:8–9	163
2:14	235
2:18	153
2:22	160
3:11–12	153
3:11	154
3:21	32, 216, 217
4:3	196, 211, 235
4:4	235
4:13–16	185
5:18–20	134–37, 178, 228
5:19	192, 232

Philippians

2:3	211, 233
2:9	82n
2:12–13	163
3:3	135, 159, 160, 227, 239
3:20	67, 216

Colossians

1:27	174n
1:29	163
3:1–10	138
3:1	126
3:11	138
3:12–15	185
3:13–15	138
3:15	178

3:16	19, 134, 138–39, 185, 188, 192, 220, 226, 232, 238

1 Thessalonians

1:9	50
4:1	237, 239
5:21–24	163

1 Timothy

2:1–2	191
2:5	v, 126, 170, 174, 225
3:16	126
4:13	19, 188

2 Timothy

2:21	184
3:16–17	220
4:2	101

Titus

2:2–8	234, 239
2:11–12	163
3:4–5	159

Hebrews

1–2	150
1:1–2	11–12
1:1–3	31
1:2–14	149
1:4	80
1:6	167
2:2–3	149
2:11	153, 228
2:12	126, 165–68, 174, 174n, 184, 192, 225, 226
2:13	153
2:17	153
2:18	169
3:1	149, 150. 153, 169
3:12	153
4:14–16	169
4:14–15	126

4:14	174	9:23–24	150–51
4:15	149	9:23	149, 150–51
4:16	4, 110, 151, 153, 154	9:24	149, 169
		9:25	89, 150–51
5–10	150–52	9:26	149
5:1	150–51	10:1, 3, 11	150–51
5:2	150–51	10:1–3	89
5:3	150–51	10:1	89, 104, 150–51
5:6	126, 167	10:4	150–51
5:9	150–51	10:10, 12, 14	150–51
6:20	126, 167	10:10	150–51
7:5	150–51	10:11–14	152
7:7, 15–17	149	10:11	89, 150–51
7:11	150–51	10:12, 14	149
7:14	150–51	10:16	149
7:17	126, 167	10:19–22	v, 3, 51–52, 116, 126, 148, 149, 152–54, 170n, 171, 184, 227
7:18	150–51		
7:19	149		
7:21	126, 149		
7:22	149, 150–51	10:19–20	169
7:23–25	152	10:19	153, 167, 225
7:25	126, 150–51, 153, 169	10:20	162
		10:21	126, 153, 167, 169
7:26	150–51	10:22	149, 154, 167, 225
7:27	149, 150–51	10:24–25	154
7:28	149, 150–51	10:24	185
8:1–2	126, 151, 167, 169	11:13	67
8:1	126	11:21	84
8:2	149, 150–51	12:2	174
8:5	150–51	12:14	229
8:6	149, 150–51, 169	12:18	154
8:7	150–51	12:22–23	154
8:10	149	12:22	149
8:11	149	12:28	149, 154, 225
8:19	149	13:9	149
9:7	150–51	13:10	149
9:9	150–51	13:15	154, 168, 169, 173, 225, 239
9:11, 23–24	150–51		
9:11–12	151	13:20–21	163
9:11	149	13:21	169
9:12, 25–26	150–51	13:22	153
9:12, 26, 28	150–51		
9:12	149, 150–51	**James**	
9:14–15	149	2:23	83
9:14	149, 150–51, 158	5:13	134
9:15	150–51		
9:18–22	150–51		

1 Peter

1:11	160
1:15–16	163
2:5	139–40
2:9	34, 139–40
3:18	116
4:10–11	163

2 Peter

1:17	171

1 John

2:1	126
3:2	184
4:19	12

Revelation

1	141–42
1:6	146–47
4–5	184
4	114, 142–43
4:9	146–47
4:11	146–47
5	114, 143–44
5:11–14	66
5:12–13	146–47
6	114
7:9–12	144–45
7:9–10	81
7:12	146–47
14:6–7	51, 145
14:7	146
19:1–7	145–46
19:1	146–47
19:7	147
19:10	217, 238
21–22	146
21:23	32
22:8–9	43
22:9	69, 217, 238

www.ingramcontent.com/pod-product-compliance
Lightning Source LLC
Chambersburg PA
CBHW022002220426
43663CB00007B/931